CW01646203

Reiki Evolution

Reiki First Degree
Course manual (Shoden)

Taggart King

www.reiki-evolution.co.uk
Email: taggart@reiki-evolution.co.uk

Introduction

Hi,

My name is Taggart King and I would like to welcome you to Reiki.

You may be reading this before attending one of our live courses and in that case I would like to congratulate you for deciding to take some steps that are going to lead to many positive changes in your life. I hope you enjoy reading about the history and background of Reiki, and the practical aspects of treating people. I have tried to make this manual a complete guide to basic Reiki, so there is no need to take notes on the day of your course: everything that we will cover, and everything that you need to know at this level, is in this manual and on the Audio CD which accompanies it. The manual will also act as a useful permanent reference for you once you have completed the course.

Congratulations, too, if you are reading this manual as part of your Reiki First Degree home study course. This manual, together with the audio CD, the detailed course instructions and the e-mail support that you will receive, are all you need to get to grips with Reiki at First Degree level. Your home study course is equivalent to the live course in every way and by the end of your course you will have carried out a great deal of practical energy work.

You may be reading this manual as someone who has already trained in Reiki in another lineage. In that case I hope that you find many things of use to you in this manual, which is based largely on the system that Mikao Usui was teaching in the early part of the 20th century. What Reiki's founder was teaching is very different from the Reiki system that is taught in most Western lineages, and there may be some surprises in store for you. I ask you to keep an open mind.

Finally, you may be reading this manual in order to find out about Reiki for the first time. In that case I hope you find clear and easy to understand explanations, and end up with a fair idea of what Reiki is all about and what it can do for you and the people who are close to you. I hope you decide to make Reiki part of your life.

About This Manual

I have written the vast majority of this manual. Where information has come from other sources, I have stated this clearly. I am particularly grateful for the generosity of Reiki Master Rick Rivard from Canada, who has made various translations of documents from Japan freely available to the Reiki community worldwide and which you can find in the appendix.

Reiki is a tradition that is passed on from master to student; the student becomes a master and passes it on to others and so on. Below you can find your Reiki lineage as far back as Mikao Usui, the originator of Reiki, and this lineage applies to people who have trained with me or with one of my team of teachers.

Acknowledgements

I would like to thank Diane Whittle, a lovely lady, for taking the time, trouble and care to introduce me to Reiki at all levels. Diane taught myself and my fellow students with gentle humour, wisdom and compassion and provided me with a solid foundation to build on. My Reiki Master attunements in the woods and on the beach in Suffolk were something very special!

During my travels throughout the UK and Europe, teaching the methods of Mikao Usui's original system, I had the honour to meet and share knowledge and experiences with many talented and experienced Reiki teachers. It would be difficult to list them all, but in particular I am grateful to Carly Horbowiec from Holland and Chris Deefholts from Oxfordshire for giving me the benefit of their wisdom and experience. I am also indebted to Frank Arjava Petter, Chetna Koyabashi, and Fiona McCallion for introducing me to Japanese-style Reiki.

In particular I need to single out Chris Marsh for thanks: the person who finally led me to real Usui Reiki by providing me with patient training over several years and offering me insights into Mikao Usui's original system, sharing things that I could not have obtained anywhere else in the world.

I would like to thank the hundreds of students who have been through my Reiki courses, who have taught me so much, and I would like to thank Margaret Craig for her help in reading through the text of this new manual and providing me with invaluable feedback.

With best wishes,

Taggart King
Reiki Master/Teacher

ReikiEvolution
5 Rose Lane, Pinchbeck, Spalding, Lincs PE11 3RN
Tel/Fax: 0845 458 3004 (Local Rates Apply) and +44 (0)1775 722082

E-Mail: taggart@reiki-evolution.co.uk
Web Sites: www.reiki-evolution.co.uk

Using the Course Audio CDs

This course is accompanied by two Audio CDs which focus you on the main points of the course and provide guided meditations for you to use. The commentary should be listened to in conjunction with the corresponding sections of the course manual, rather than just being listened to in their entirety. You will learn more effectively if you use audio and visual learning together, focusing on one section of the manual at a time.

The course instructions for your home study course, or the instructions you received with your live course study pack, let you know which tracks to listen to in conjunction with which sections of the course manual.

Please note that the "Reiki Meditations" audio CD also contains two tracks that relate to the Reiki Second Degree course, so do take good care of this audio CD: you will need it when taking your Second Degree course.

Students' Experiences

In various parts of the manual, you can read the experiences of some of our students who have been working with the Reiki First Degree course through home study, and who have been giving detailed written feedback by e-mail. We hope that doing this will enhance your experience of the course, whether working at a distance or on a 'live' course.

It is useful to be able to see how other people have been doing with a particular exercise, what they have noticed, what they have discovered, what they were surprised about. By including such feedback in the manual you can benefit from the experiences of many people who have been working through the same exercises that you will be following.

Whenever a new student gives their feedback, the section will begin with this icon:

Lineage

All Reiki practitioners can trace their 'spiritual lineage', following a trail of Reiki teachers back to the originator of Reiki, Mikao Usui. Apparently the Reiki etiquette is to quote the lineage of the first person that attuned you to Master level as your Reiki lineage, so if someone asks you what your lineage is, then you should quote the list shown below:

If you followed a home study course with Taggart, here is your lineage:	If you attended a Reiki Evolution Live Course, here is your lineage:
Mikao Usui Chujiro Hayashi Hawayo Takata Phyllis LeiFurumoto Florence O'Neal Jerry Farley June Woods Simon Treselyan Marcus Hayward Diane Whittle Taggart King ... your name goes here ...	Mikao Usui Chujiro Hayashi Hawayo Takata Phyllis LeiFurumoto Florence O'Neal Jerry Farley June Woods Simon Treselyan Marcus Hayward Diane Whittle Taggart King ... your teacher's name goes here ... ... your name goes here ...

I have various other Reiki lineages, where I have received attunements and informal training from several Reiki teachers in Europe, all variations on Mrs Takata's "Western" style of Reiki. I have also trained in more Japanese-style Reiki with Frank Arjava Petter and I have been taught various techniques that Reiki Master Hiroshi Doi has presented in the West.

One lineage of special note involves my having received empowerments and instruction from Chris Marsh; these empowerments pass on the energy of Usui Sensei through the intermediary of a Tendai Buddhist nun – Suzuki San - who trained with Usui and is now over 100 years old; I received ongoing training from Chris for several years. This would be the most direct transmission:

Mikao Usui
Suzuki San
Chris Marsh
Taggart King

BACKGROUND

What is Reiki?

Reiki is a complementary therapy. Reiki is faith healing. Reiki is a form of spiritual healing. Reiki comes from Atlantis. Reiki comes from ancient Tibet. These are some of the ways that Reiki is presented to the world via hundreds of thousands of web sites, and books and leaflets. Reiki is practised and taught in many different ways: some simple, some complex, some dogmatic, some free. Some teachings are more faithful to the system that was first taught in the West in the 1970s; some diverge wildly from these teachings, to include such New Age preoccupations as crystals, chakras, spirit guides and Angels; some teachings are based on what was taught by Reiki's founder, in Japan, in the 1920s.

In the West, Reiki is practised very much as a form of complementary medicine, where practitioners give Reiki 'treatments', though with Reiki it is also possible to treat yourself, which cannot be done easily or comfortably by people who practise, for example, Indian Head Massage or Reflexology! Reiki is largely seen as an oriental version of spiritual healing, based on the laying on of hands and the channelling of a form of energy, or a "spiritual" energy, and this energy can also be used for the benefit of the practitioner.

When Reiki was taught by its founder in the 1920s in Japan, what was being taught was a spiritual path, a self-healing method, a path to enlightenment, so Reiki has certainly gone through an interesting journey during the last century, to end up now being presented to the world as a treatment technique, and we will find out how this happened later.

So most Reiki practitioners will treat other people, they will treat themselves, and they will also follow a simple set of 'rules to live by' that were set down by Reiki's founder, Mikao Usui. The system was made available to people from different religious backgrounds, so you do not need to be a Buddhist, or a Christian, or follow Shinto, or have any religious beliefs, in order to benefit from the teachings and the practices. Reiki is 'neutral'.

Reiki is all about moving more into a state of balance on all levels, achieving more balance in your life. Moving into a state of balance may involve the resolution of some health problems, it may involve a change in beliefs and attitudes, it may involve making decisions that have been put off or ignored for a long time, and a realisation of one's true values and priorities in life. Reiki is all about change: change for the better, finding out what is right for you in your life and making decisions to move you closer to what is right for you.

The successful practice of Reiki involves committing some time, regularly, to invest in yourself through working with energy to achieve more of a state of balance. The beneficial effects of working with Reiki develop over time, they build cumulatively, and the positive changes that you can experience through working with Reiki are governed by your commitment to working with the system. You invest in yourself and you reap the benefits.

Learning Reiki does not mean that you are committing yourself to becoming a Reiki practitioner, and many people who learn Reiki do so because they are looking for some benefits for themselves, and they are looking to be able to do something to help their friends and family members. Some people take Reiki First Degree and stop there, though most people seem to go on to Second Degree level. How far you progress with the system is up to you, and how much time you invest in working with Reiki is up to you.

What Energy?

The energy that Reiki practitioners work with – when they treat other people and when they treat themselves - can be referred to as 'chi', which you may have heard of. When you visit an acupuncturist they use needles to encourage energy to flow through a series of meridians or energy channels that run the length of your body; that energy is called 'chi'. You may have heard of a Japanese massage technique called Shiatsu, which uses finger pressure on acupuncture points to achieve a similar effect; the Japanese adopted the Chinese view of the body's energy system. You will probably have heard of Tai Chi (or maybe Chi Kung or QiGong), a graceful system of exercises that are designed to build up, or cultivate, your personal reserves of this energy, and the graceful movements that you make serve to circulate this energy smoothly throughout your body, breaking down any blockages and bringing things into balance on all levels. The energy is seen as animating all living things.

If we move from China to India, the same energy is referred to as 'prana', and breathing exercises and yoga techniques have been developed to again bring your energy system into balance. In India they do not think in terms of meridians, but of chakras: energy centres running the length of your body from the crown of your head to the base of your spine, seven main ones and further subsidiary ones in other locations.

The intention with all these energy techniques is that if you can harmonise your energy system, you are putting your body in the best possible position to heal itself on all levels: physical, mental, emotional and spiritual. In fact, the Chinese view is that chi not only flows through your body, but surrounds and engulfs you. For example, feng shui has been developed as a way of arranging your living environment to allow for the smooth flow of chi around you, eliminating areas where stagnant chi might accumulate, for example.

Reiki seems to deal with this same energy, to an extent.

However, when you practice Reiki you are not just dealing with a 'cold' 'clinical' energy, the same energy that is manipulated by acupuncturists or controlled by practitioners of yoga or tai chi. There is more to Reiki than that. When you channel Reiki, it does not feel like a neutral energy that you are dealing with: it feels beautiful, loving, nourishing, and the more you practice Reiki the more beautiful it becomes!

Reiki has important similarities to conventional spiritual healing, particularly in terms of the things that people feel when they are having a Reiki treatment, and many people see the Reiki energy as having divine origins, interpreting the energy as divine love or divine light. Reiki opens you up to the divine, however you wish to interpret that; Reiki reinforces your individual connection to your deity, and it feels beautiful.

Reiki is not attached to any religion or belief system, so it does not conflict with an individual's beliefs, or lack of beliefs. So Reiki is acceptable to atheists and believers alike; agnostics, Anglicans and Catholics; Moslems and Pagans. There are some more fundamentalist Christians who will denounce Reiki, along with Yoga, Reflexology, and other 'healing' practices, as the work of the Devil, but we have taught many Christians, including a Roman Catholic priest.

The Reiki Symbol

The Japanese characters making up the word 'Reiki' are usually translated in the West as meaning 'Universal Life Energy' , but the characters can be translated as meaning 'soul energy', or 'aura' or 'mysterious spirit', or even 'spiritually guided life force energy'.

So we're not just thinking of a cold, clinical energy that you can move round the body by sticking needles into a person. We are thinking also of an energy that has a definite connection to or resonance with a person's soul or spiritual side.

Interestingly, the latest interpretation of the word 'Reiki' is that it can mean 'a system that has been arrived at through a moment of enlightenment', or "a gift given through satori', and we will talk more about the history and development of Reiki shortly.

To summarise, Reiki is a versatile healing system based on the channelling of energy at various frequencies, sometimes akin to dealing with the fundamental energy of oriental medicine, but sometimes more akin to channelling energy of divine origin for the benefit of a person's spirit or soul. It is both at the same time.

Reiki and Chi Kung

In fact, the thing that approximates most closely to the Reiki treatment ability is the practice of advanced Chi Kung (also known as qi gong or chi gong). Chi Kung is an energy cultivation technique similar to, but not the same as, Tai Chi. If you were to practice Chi Kung diligently for 20-30 years, you might be able to reach the level of Chi Kung Master. Chi Kung Masters are able to cultivate their personal levels of chi to such an extent that they are able to direct this externally to treat others. Such treatments are called 'projection healings'. There is at least one hospital in China that prescribes Chi Kung exercises to treat a variety of ailments. It has a team of Chi Kung Masters who treat people by directing chi externally, by aiming the energy at and channelling it into various acupuncture points on the patient's body. This ability is way beyond the reach of most individuals, and the Chi Kung practitioner has to practice the technique continually to build up energy reserves that are depleted in treating others. The Chi Kung Master's personal energy is given out in treating others.

The Reiki attunements seem to give an individual this same 'Chi Kung' ability but with two important differences. You do not have to stand there for 20 years doing the exercises, and when you treat someone it is not your personal energy that you giving out. Reiki attunements 'connect' you to an unlimited external source of healing energy that benefits you as you channel it into others. In fact, the connection is already there, and the attunements allow you to recognise or notice something that is already within you.

The origins of Reiki have until quite recently been quite obscure, and plagued with misinformation, but ongoing research is giving us a better picture of how it was discovered and developed. That is what you can read about next.

Incidentally, there is no evidence that Reiki has anything to do with Atlantis (is there strong evidence for the existence of Atlantis in any case?), it has nothing to do with ancient Tibet, and there is no 'faith' required to either practise Reiki or receive benefits from Reiki treatments. Reiki works just as well for sceptics as for believers!

Suggested Reading

There are many, many books about Reiki on the market today and I have to say that most of them are not worth reading. Most have very little content, what content they do have is inaccurate or misleading or unnecessarily dogmatic; they tell you very little that is useful.

Here are a couple of books and a few web sites that are worth reading and visiting. Don't believe everything that you read, though!

Books

The Reiki Sourcebook
Frans & Bronwen Steine
O Books 2003

The Japanese Art of Reiki
Frans & Bronwen Steine
O Books 2005

Web sites

International Center for Reiki Training
www.reiki.org

Reiki and All Energy-Therapies Web Site
www.aetw.org

The Reiki Threshold
www.threshold.ca/reiki/

Reiki Evolution
www.reiki-evolution.co.uk

Where did Reiki come from?

The History of Reiki

This section could almost be given the subtitle of "how a simple self-healing and spiritual development system ended up being presented to the world as a hands-on treatment technique". You can read below about the background to the development of the system, about what we know of Mikao Usui's life, what he taught, how he taught, who he associated with, and how the system ended up being taught in the West.

Japan in Usui's time

Mikao Usui
1865 - 1926

Mikao Usui grew up at a time when Japanese society and culture was going through a period of rapid change. It was not until the 1850s that Japan opened itself up to the Western world; for two centuries starting in 1641, all Europeans except the Dutch had been expelled from Japan. Those Chinese and Dutch that remained were confined in special trading centres in Nagasaki, and no Japanese were allowed to leave the country. Christianity was declared illegal and all Japanese were forced to register at Shinto temples. Those Japanese who refused to renounce Christianity were executed, and so were a few Christian missionaries who refused to leave the country. This ban on Christianity was not lifted until 1873. It was the United States that finally forced Japan to open its borders, and open its economy, to the outside world, and this event led to a great flood of new ideas and esoteric systems coming into Japan from all over the world.

Not only that, but Japan underwent a period of rapid industrialisation, transforming itself from a feudal society into an industrialised nation - able to compete with the West on an equal footing - within a period of only 30-40 years. Such a period of rapid change created a real climate of 'wanting to keep hold of traditional culture'. Japan was looking for a spiritual direction and people wanted to rekindle and maintain ancient traditions, while embracing the new. This is what Usui did when he developed Reiki. In the time when Usui was growing up, Japan was a melting pot of new ideas, with many new spiritual systems and healing techniques being developed. Reiki was one of these systems.

Usui's Life

Mikao Usui was born on August 15, 1865 in the village of 'Taniai-mura' (now called Miyama-cho) in the Yamagata district of Gifu prefecture, and he died on March 9, 1926 in Fukuyama. He had an interesting life. He grew up in a Tendai Buddhist family and had a sister and two brothers, one of whom studied medicine. As a child he entered a Tendai Buddhist monastery near Mt. Kurama ("Horse Saddle Mountain"). He would have studied 'kiko' (the Japanese version of Chi Kung) to an advanced level - and maybe practised projection healings - and he was exposed to martial arts too. From the age of 12 he trained in a martial art called Yagyu Ryu - Samurai swordsmanship - in which he attained the level of Menkyo Kaiden in his 20s, this being the highest licence of proficiency in weaponry and grappling. He continued training in the Arts and reached high levels in several other of the most ancient Japanese methods. He was renowned for his expertise and highly respected by other well-known martial artists of his time.

In his younger life he experienced much adversity, lack of money, no security or regular employment. He seemed not to attach importance to material things and was regarded as something of an eccentric. He married, his wife's name was Sadako, and they had a son (born 1907) and daughter. Usui followed a number of professions: public servant, office worker, industrialist, reporter, politician's secretary, missionary, and supervisor of convicts. Usui was private secretary to Shimpei Goto, who was Secretary of the Railroad, Postmaster General, and Secretary of the Interior and State. The phrase 'politician's secretary' can be taken as a euphemism for 'bodyguard'! It is during his time in diplomatic service that he may have had the opportunity to travel to other countries. In 1868 (when Usui was 3) there was restoration of rule by Emperor, the Meiji Restoration. Mutsuhito reigned until 1912 and selected a new reign title - Meiji, which means enlightened rule - to mark a new beginning in Japanese history. It is known that Usui travelled to China, America and Europe several times to learn and study Western ways, and this practice was encouraged in the Meiji era. At some point Usui became for a while a Tendai Buddhist Monk, or Priest, (maybe what we in the west call a lay priest) but still having his own home, not living in the temple. This is called a 'Zaike' in Japanese: a priest possessing a home.

Usui Sensei was interested in a great many things and seems to have studied voraciously. His memorial states that he was a talented hard working student, he liked to read and his knowledge of medicine, psychology, fortune telling and theology of religions around the world, including the Kyoten (Buddhist Bible) was vast. There was a large University library in Kyoto, and Japanese sources believe that he would have done most of his research there, where sacred texts from all over the world would have been held. He studied traditional Chinese medicine and Western medicine, numerology and astrology, and psychic and clairvoyant development. Usui also took Zen Buddhist training in 1922 for about three years. Many different spiritualist/healing groups were in existence at the time, and one of these - attended by Usui - was 'Rei Jyutsu Kai'. Today this organisation consists of the most spiritual monks and nuns in Japan, psychics and clairvoyants.

The Roots of Reiki

Usui's system was rooted in Tendai Buddhism and Shintoism. Tendai Buddhism (a form of mystical Buddhism) provided spiritual teachings, and Shintoism contributed methods of controlling and working with the energies. The system was based on living and practising the Mikao Usui's spiritual principles; that was the hub of the whole thing. Usui had a strong background in both kiko (energy cultivation) and a martial art with a strong Zen flavour (Yagyu Shinkage Ryu).

Usui also took Soto Zen training with Kanazawa, mentioned in the book "Crooked Cucumber" (biography of Shunryu Suzuki, a Zen Buddhist monk partly responsible for introducing Zen Buddhism to America) – Kanazawa was a close friend. Japanese people followed several paths at a time, so Usui can have been a Tendai Buddhist but followed Soto Zen for a while.

These studies may have contributed in some way to the system that he developed, and there also seems to be a strong connection between Usui's system and Shugendo (mountain asceticism). Shugendo was a blend of pre-Buddhist folk traditions of Sangaku Shinko and Shinto, Tantric Buddhism, Chinese Yin-Yang magic and Taoism. Interestingly, Usui Sensei's precepts are his rewording of a set of precepts used in a Tendai sect of Shugendo and which can be traced back as far as the early 9th century.

Usui's Associates

During his life, Usui associated with many men and women of very high spiritual values. Some were famous people in Japan, for example Morihei Ueshiba (founder of Aikido), Onasiburo Deguchi (founder of Omoto religion) and Toshihiro Eguchi (founded his own religion and was a good friend of Usui). There are even connections between Usui and Mokichi Okada, the founder of Johrei, and there are also connections between Usui and Jigoro Kano (founder of Judo) though Kano was not a significant member of the group.

Morihei Ueshiba	Onisaburo Deguchi	Mokichi Okada

Usui the Man

Usui Sensei was a big man, physically big and extremely powerful, but quiet in manner. He had powerful personality and his presence would fill a room or a space. That got him respect. He was kind and compassionate, though he was also impatient with people who were abusing others or their beliefs or ideas. He could be very outspoken, apparently, and controversial: a bit of a “loose cannon”. He followed his own path regardless, and his friends would often be concerned about his welfare. His answer to them would be 'just for today do not worry'. Usui Sensei did not suffer fools gladly, and could be quite abrasive at times. He could become righteously angry and quite impatient, particularly with people who wanted results but were not prepared to work for them.

Usui's Motivation

But what prompted Usui to pursue all these studies? Well, according to Hiroshi Doi, a member of the Usui Reiki Ryoho Gakkai in Japan (see later), Mikao Usui was wondering what the ultimate purpose of life was, and set out to try to understand this. After some time he finally experienced an enlightenment: the ultimate life purpose was 'Anshin Rytsu Mei' - the state of your mind being totally in peace, knowing what to do with your life, being bothered by nothing. Doi says that with this revelation, Usui researched harder, for 3 years, trying to achieve this goal. Finally, he turned to a Zen master for advice on how to attain this life purpose. The master replied "If you want to know; die!" Usui-sensei lost hope at this and thought, "My life is over". He then went to Mt. Kurama and decided to fast until he died.

So it seems that - according to Hiroshi Doi anyway - Usui was looking for a way of knowing one's life's purpose and to be content, and despite all his exhaustive research, he could not find a way to achieve this state. The monk's advice prompted him to go to Mount Kurama and to carry out a 21-day meditation and fast. We now know that Usui Sensei carried out a meditation called 'The Lotus Repentance', which comes from Tendai Buddhism. Usui carried out the meditation and, according to his memorial stone, he experienced an enlightenment or 'satori' that led to the development of Reiki.

But this does not seem to have the ring of truth to it, because he performed this meditation five times during his lifetime, and Usui's system wasn't something new that came to him in a flash of inspiration, but a system that was rooted in many existing traditions. In fact, Usui was already teaching his system long before he carried out the meditation. Originally, Usui's system did not have a name, though he referred to it as a 'Method to Achieve Personal Perfection'. His students seem to have referred to the system as 'Usui Do' or 'Usui Teate' (Usui hand-application). The name 'Reiki' came later, perhaps first used by the founders of the 'Gakkai.

Mount Kurama, where Usui carried out one of his meditations, is a holy mountain. It is near Kyoto, the former capital of Japan, a place which I heard described on a recent television travel programme as being 'the spiritual heart of Japan' - a place with a thousand temples representing a whole range of deities. Mount Kurama is also important from a martial arts perspective, being the place where mountain spirits - Tengu - are said to have given the secrets of fighting to the Samurai. Morihei Usheiba, founder of Aikido, often took students to the mystical Shojobo Valley to train.

Usui Sensei Teaches his System

According to Usui's Memorial stone, Usui was a very well-known and popular healer, and he taught nearly 2,000 students all over Japan, but this should be taken as just meaning a large number, maybe 1,000 or more though. All of his students started out being treated by him. Usui would give them empowerments so that they were connected to Reiki permanently, so they could treat themselves in-between appointments with him, and if they wanted to take things further then they could begin an open-ended programme of training in his system. His teachings were very popular amongst the older generation, who saw them as a return to older spiritual practices; Usui was teaching at a time of great change for the Japanese people. In April 1922 Mikao Usui opened his first 'Seat of Learning' in Harajuku, Tokyo, and he used a small manual which had come into use about 1920. It did not contain any hand positions for healing others: it contained the Precepts, Meditations and Waka poetry.

Of the people that he taught, 50-70 went on to the first level of Second Degree, and maybe 30 went on to the second level of Second Degree. Usui trained 17 people to Shinpiden level. There were 5 Buddhist nuns, 3 Naval Officers, and nine other men, including Eguchi who was said to have been Usui's main friend/student. Eguchi later formed his own religion called Tenohira-Ryouchi-Kenyuka, which was Shinto revivalism, getting back to the early Shamanic roots. Even to this day in Japan there is a spiritual community on Hokkaido – called “ITTOE” - which carries on Eguchi's tradition, and where they carry out a simple hands-on treatment technique based on the use of intuition, and carry out simple initiations. Usui's teachings were what is called a 'Ronin' (leaderless) method. This was to make sure that no one person could lay claim to them and they would be freely available for all who wanted to learn them. So Usui Sensei left no heir in terms of his spiritual teachings; no provision was made for the continuation of this. It would have been more usual for Usui to have kept his system as an Usui family method, rather than passing it on to outsiders.

Usui Sensei did not only practise and teach his Spiritual Teachings in his school but he also gave healing. He became very well known for his healing skills and his fame spread very quickly throughout Japan. In 1923 the Kanto earthquake struck 50 miles from Tokyo, destroying Tokyo and Yokohama. An estimated 140,000 people died from the 'quake or the fires that followed it. This was the greatest natural disaster in Japanese history, and Usui gave many treatments to victims. The Usui Memorial says that Usui Sensei "reached out his hands of love to suffering people", and in recognition of his services to the people during this emergency he was awarded an honorary Doctorate. It is when he was giving healings at a Naval base that he met a group of Imperial Officers, who became students, including the man who would be responsible for allowing Reiki to come to the West.

Mikao Usui died from a stroke in a town called Fukuyama in Hiroshima in 1926. He had been a Tendai Buddhist all his life, and there has been some speculation as to why he was buried in a Pure Land Buddhist cemetery, but this is not significant: there was no Tendai Buddhist cemetery nearby and the Pure Land cemetery was the next best bet. There are a lot of Tendai teachings in Pure Land Buddhism.

How Usui Taught

The teachings were given one-to-one, and they varied according to the students' needs. There was no single system that was passed on in a standard way. There were various levels, which could be described as first, second and Master levels. The spiritual teachings were:

- Life teachings
- Mystery teachings
- Deep mystery teachings

Our First and Second Degree and Master courses are about half way into the Mystery teachings, apparently.

Students would go to Usui Sensei's home. He taught from home. They would spend 1-2 days with him and then went away to do the work. They would record their thoughts, feelings and insights in a notebook and then this was reviewed with him when they went to see him again, or when he was available. He would deal with their queries and their questions.

Some Unusual Students

It seems that Usui's fame as a healer had spread as far as the Japanese military – there were about 30 famous healers in Japan in Usui's time, and he was one of them. He had been approached by them to teach a simple hands-on healing system that could be used by Imperial Officers as a sort of 'energy paramedic' system. There was a dire shortage of medically trained personnel in the Military (one Doctor for 5,000 ratings), and they needed some system that could be used to tide people over while they awaited medical attention. This led Usui Sensei to teach the Imperial Officers a method that was focused on the treating of others rather than working on the self – meeting their specific needs – and the symbols were introduced jointly by Usui Sensei and Eguchi as a quick way of depicting the energies. In fact, Eguchi played a significant role in the development of this system. The Imperial Officers simply did not have the time to get to grips with the energies in the way that Usui had been using with his other students: using meditations or chanting sacred sounds over a long period of time.

So the "Reiki" treatment system was probably first taught in about 1923, though Usui's spiritual teachings were being passed on as early as 1915. The 'Navy' system that Usui put together was actually implemented, and there are 1930s Japanese Defence Manuals that detail the "Reiki" system depicted by the Usui Reiki Ryoho Gakkai. So we can see that the "Reiki" treatment system taught to the Imperial Officers did not represent an evolution of Usui Sensei's system in the last few years of his life: rather he put together an ad-hoc system to meet the needs of a group of people who approached him for a particular purpose.

The Imperial Naval Officers were Jusaburo Gyuda/Ushida, Ichi Taketomi and Chujiro Hayashi. It was certainly surprising to Usui's students that Usui would teach such people as Officers of the Imperial Navy. Indeed, it seems that there was some 'resistance' to this taking place, and Usui's friends were upset that he would teach his spiritual system to military men. But Usui had been doing some healing at a naval base, and it seems that there was some metaphorical 'arm twisting' that led to the officers being taught by Usui.

In terms of "treatment techniques" we do not know what Usui taught to the Imperial Officers. The various methods used in the 'Gakkai may have been taught to the Imperial Officers by Usui, they may have been hinted at, but what we can say is that symbols were introduced and taught to the Imperial Officers as a way of depicting a particular aspect of the energy, and the energies/symbols are likely to have been used in a simple way when treating others. The complicated system of mixing symbols and symbol 'sandwiches' that are used in the world of Western Reiki is a very un-Japanese approach.

Dr Hayashi, like the other Imperial Officers, does not seem to have been interested in the 'spiritual path' aspects of Usui's system. He was a Christian, apparently, and he was fascinated by the treatment possibilities of Usui's system. This led him to put together a healing guide containing various sequences of hand positions that could be used to treat a wide range of specific medical conditions. This guide was included in materials given to students of the Usui Reiki Ryoho Gakkai, and has been published as "Dr Usui's Handbook", though it was in fact the work of Dr Hayashi.

Dr Chujiro Hayashi

Chujiro Hayashi was born in 1878. He graduated from Naval School in 1902 and by the time he was doing his Master training with Usui Sensei in 1925 he was 47 years old, a former Captain in the Imperial Navy, and he was a Naval Doctor. He and the other Naval Officers Ushida and Taketomi were the last people to be taught by Usui. It seems that Hayashi was one of Usui's less experienced Master students since he may have trained with Usui for only 9 months. When you reached Master level with Usui, this represented the commencement of a long period of training which culminated in learning the connection rituals, and considering that other students of Usui spent 9 months meditating on only one energy at second-degree level, Dr Hayashi cannot have learned the inner teachings of Reiki in such a short space of time, nor reached the higher levels of Mastership. Together with the other naval officers, Dr Hayashi was a founder member of the Usui Reiki Ryoho Gakkai, a 'memorial society' set up after Usui's death. The 'Gakkai was described by Tatsumi (one of Hayashi's Master students), rather disparagingly, as an 'officer's club'.

Although he was one of the founding members of the 'Gakkai, he left, it seems, because the nationalism displayed by the other officers conflicted with his Christian beliefs and went against Usui's teachings, and because of the many changes that the other Imperial Officers were introducing into the system, for example the introduction of many kiko (Japanese QiGong) techniques. But Hayashi changed things too, as we'll discover shortly.

After he completed his training, Hayashi opened a clinic with eight beds and 16 healers working there, and clients were treated by two or more people. He kept detailed records of the treatments that were given, and used this information to create 'standard' hand positions for different ailments which ended up being published in the training manual given to the Gakkai's students (the Usui Reiki Hikkei). In fact this work had already been started when Usui was alive, and it seems that Dr Hayashi was carrying out the research with Usui's knowledge and approval. Usui was interested to see if his spiritual system would 'stand alone' as a healing system. This guide to 'hand positions for different ailments' is very much trying to mould Reiki into the 'medical model', where you diagnose a particular ailment and then 'prescribe' a particular set of hand positions to deal with it, very different from Usui's simple and intuitive approach. Despite this research, though, Hayashi still expected his students to be able to use scanning or intuitive techniques to work out their hand positions, with his 'standard' positions as a fallback position.

Dr Hayashi founded his own society in 1931, five years after Usui died. It was called Hayashi Reiki Kenyu-kai, which means Hayashi Reiki Research Centre. Since Dr Hayashi had made some changes to the system he had been taught by Usui, he was honour bound to change the name of the system, but the changes that he introduced were not popular: some of his senior students left the school, including Tatsumi, who believed that the teachings were no longer Usui's. Hayashi's focus was very much on hands-on healing. Dr Hayashi would teach First Degree over a five-day structured course, with each day's training taking 90 minutes, and students would receive his more complicated attunements on four occasions during this training, by way of echoing Usui's weekly empowerment sessions. Dr Hayashi trained 17 Reiki Masters and produced a 40 page manual which contained the hand positions for different ailments.

Since Dr Hayashi would not have been taught Reiju by Usui Sensei, it seems that attunements were developed by the Imperial Officers as a 'constructed' ritual that gave them the same sort of experience that they had when receiving empowerments from Usui Sensei. Certainly the ritual that was taught to Tatsumi by Dr Hayashi is not Usui's Reiju, and neither is the ritual being used by Mrs Yamaguchi, another of Dr Hayashi's Master students.

Chujiro Hayashi died on May 10th 1940. Sadly, he took his own life; it seems that he was very concerned at the build up of nationalism in his country, and it was the threat of war that led to his death. Dr Hayashi's wife Chie continued as President of his school, teaching in the 1940s, but their children did not continue the clinic.

Hawayo Takata

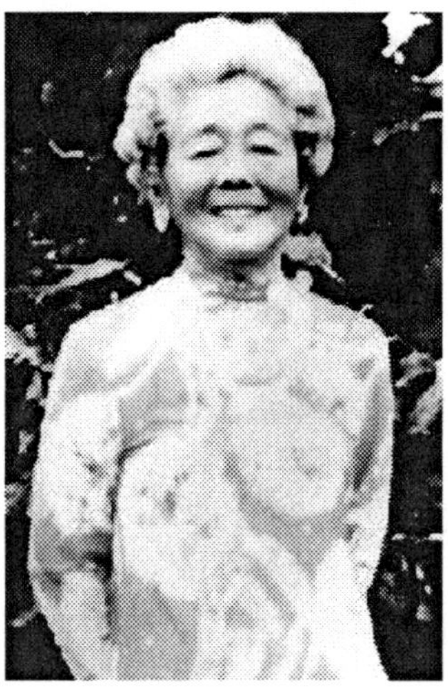

Hawayo Takata was born in 1900 on the island of Kauai, Hawaii. She came to Dr Hayashi's clinic suffering from a number of serious medical conditions that were resolved through Reiki, but she was originally intending to receive conventional Western medical treatments for her tumour, gallstones and appendicitis. The story goes, though, that on the operating table (just before the surgery was about to start) Mrs Takata heard a voice that said "The operation is not necessary". She is said to have refused the operation, and asked her Doctor if he knew of any other way to restore her health. The doctor referred her to Dr. Hayashi and she began receiving a course of treatments.

Mrs Takata was quite sceptical about Reiki. She felt so much heat from the practitioners' hands that she was sure they were using some sort of electrical equipment - maybe little electric heaters secreted in the palms of their hands! She looked in the large sleeves of their Japanese kimonos, under the treatment table, but of course there was nothing there. Her scepticism turned into belief as her health problems resolved themselves, and she decided that she wanted to learn Reiki for herself.

Dr Hayashi wanted to teach Reiki to another woman besides his wife (someone who would not have to be called up to fight in a war), and since Mrs. Takata was so persistent he decided to teach her to Master level, which happened in 1938. Dr Hayashi gave Mrs Takata permission to teach Reiki in the West, and she did so in the USA. She was the 13th and probably the last Reiki Master that Dr. Hayashi initiated, and between 1970 and her death in 1980 Mrs Takata taught 22 Reiki Masters. Until quite recently, all Reiki practitioners in the Western world derived their Reiki from this lady, and could trace their 'lineage' through her to Dr Hayashi and Mikao Usui.

The original twenty-two teachers have passed on the Reiki tradition, and Reiki has spread throughout North and South America, Europe, New Zealand and Australia to many parts of the world. It is almost impossible to estimate the number of Reiki Masters and practitioners in the world, but it must run into tens of thousands, and maybe millions, respectively.

But is cannot have been easy for Mrs Takata, teaching a Japanese healing technique in the United States, after the Second World War, with memories of Pearl Harbour still in everyone's minds. The American population was not particularly well disposed towards anything connected with Japan. Also, while nowadays people are exposed continually to magazine articles about feng shui, tai chi and other energy cultivation techniques, ideas of traditional Chinese medicine, meridians, chi and the like, and alternative medicine in general, at that time in the United States these ideas must have seemed to have come from another planet. Mrs Takata was trying to transmit her whole culture, and a totally alien one as far as her students were concerned.

For this reason, Hawayo Takata was obliged to modify, simplify and change the Reiki that she had been taught by Chujiro Hayashi, in order for it to be acceptable to the Westerners that she dealt with, and the Reiki that she had been taught by Dr Hayashi had already been modified by him after he had been taught by Mikao Usui. Not only did Mrs Takata modify the practices of Reiki, but she also felt obliged to put together a story about the history of Reiki to make it more acceptable to a hostile American public. Out went Mikao Usui, Tendai Buddhist, and in came Dr Mikao Usui, Christian theologian, who travelled the world on a great quest to discover a healing system that explained the healing miracles that Jesus performed. Mrs Takata's upbringing in Hawaii was one where it was traditional to tell stories or parables to convey important principles or truths, and she applied this tradition to Reiki; perhaps she should have realised that such stories would have been taken to be historically accurate by her Western students. Stories about Usui being a Christian Doctor, going on a world-wide quest, and studying theology at various Universities along they way, are not true. Despite this, they are repeated in Reiki books, even ones that have been published recently.

As well as putting together a Reiki 'history', Mrs Takata ended up being referred to as 'Grand Master' of Reiki, to make a distinction between herself and the Masters that she taught. This is an office, position or title that was not envisioned by Mikao Usui. Reiki is not based on the idea of gurus or great masters to whom one has to pay homage. Unfortunately, some people in the Reiki community are greatly wedded to the idea of 'The Office of Grand Master' and what I see as the narrow and dogmatic view of Reiki that is approved by the current incumbent, Mrs Takata's grand-daughter, Phyllis Lei Furumoto.

Reiki in Japan

Now the story turns full circle, and Western style Reiki has returned to its country of birth. At one stage people believed that Reiki had died out in Japan, and that the only Reiki that remained in the world was the Western version. But Reiki Masters travelling in or living in Japan in the 1980s and 1990s discovered that there were Reiki practitioners there who were doing things that were very different from the Reiki that we had become used to in the West. It was also discovered that there was an association called the Usui Reiki Ryoho Gakkai (Usui's Reiki Healing System Association) which to begin with seemed to have been established by Usui. Now we know that this is not the case. The Gakkai was set up as a sort of 'memorial' society by the three Naval Officers. Tatsumi described it as an 'officer's club' and now it has almost the sort of place in Japanese society that Freemasons occupy in the West: most people have heard of the 'Gakkai, but they are not quite sure what they do. It's all a bit mysterious but you need to be a member if you are going to get on in business in politics.

As well as the 'Gakkai', there are other Reiki practitioners in Japan whose Reiki to varying degrees follows some of Usui's original form of Reiki.

Now Japan is experiencing a big explosion of Reiki, but it is mostly Western-style Reiki.

Learning Reiki

In this section I would like to give you an idea of what sort of people learn Reiki and what effects Reiki is likely to produce within you when you start your training. I would also like to talk about the difference that Reiki can make in your life in the longer term, and give some examples of the sorts of experiences that people can have, by way of demonstrating to them that Reiki actually works. In doing this I draw heavily on feedback that has been given to me by some of my students, and I am indebted to them for allowing me to publish their comments.

Who learns Reiki?

As an ongoing project, I have been asking students at irregular intervals to let me know their job/occupation, so I can compile a list of their backgrounds. I display the list on my web site, and here is the list from October 2005. As you can see, there is no trend running through these occupations: Reiki seems to attract people from every different background, all learning Reiki for their own individual reasons:

Account Analyst
Accountant
Actress
Airline Pilot
Applied Scientist
Aromatherapist
Artist
Bank Clerk
Bathroom designer/installer
Bowen Technique Therapist
Builder
Business Manager
Butcher
Call Centre Training Coach
Career Adviser
Chemistry Teacher
Childminder
Chiropodist
Circus Performer
Civil Engineer
Civil Servant
Clairvoyant
Composer
Conductor
Counsellor
Credit Administrator
Croupier (Casino)
Database Administrator
Delivery Driver
Dentist
Disability Advisor
Doctor
Dog Trainer/Behaviour Consultant
Drama Teacher
Driving Instructor
Engineer
Farmer
Financial Controller
Florist
Hairdresser
Headmaster
Health Visitor
Healthcare Assistant
Herbarium technician
Holistic Therapist
Homoeopath
Housewife
Hypnotherapist
I.T. Manager
Inventory Controller
Insurance Consultant
Interior Designer
Iridoligist
Jewellery Quality Controller
Job Analyst
Journalist
Kinesiologist
Lawyer (USA)
Legal Secretary
Librarian
Life Coach
Lorry Driver
Magician
Manager/Teacher at Secondary School
Managing Director
Masseuse
Make-up Artist
Management Consultant
Market Research Executive
Martial Arts Instructor
Medical Rep
Meditation Instructor
Midwife
Molecular Geneticist

Musician
Network Engineer
Nurse
Nursing Manager
Nutritionist
NVQ Assessor
Occupational Therapist
Personal Assistant
Phlebotomist
Physiotherapist
Police Officer
Porter
Potter
Priest
Primary School Teacher
Principal Business Analyst
Production Manager
Program Manager
Professor
Psychologist
Publican
Receptionist
Reflexologist
Retired Teacher
Retired Lecturer
Revenue Controller
Salesman
Secondary School Teacher
Shop Owner
Social Worker
Software Tester
Speech and Language Therapist
Spiritual Healer
Student
Systems Analyst
Telephone Market Researcher
Translator
Travel Consultant
Tree Surgeon
University Lecturer
Veterinary Surgeon
Ward Manager
Web Site Producer
Writer

Short term effects of Reiki

For people undergoing a course of Reiki treatments, there is something that they experience that I like to call 'the Reiki effect': a set of effects that the energy tends to produce in most people, whether they came along with a pain in their big toe, or depression. The 'Reiki effect' is as follows, making people feel:

1. More laid back, calm and serene
2. Better able to cope
3. More positive
4. Less affected by stressful people and stressful situations

These effects are perhaps the first ones that you will notice once you have been attuned to Reiki, though they are not necessarily earth shattering in their intensity and will not usually arrive by way of a big overnight transformation. This sometimes happens, but a definite and noticeable difference in the way you feel about things is more likely to be noticed in hindsight.

You are connected permanently to a source of beautiful healing energy that works on you, in the background, all the time. This is very comforting. When you practice energy exercises, carry out self-treatments or treat someone else you intensify the beneficial effect that the energy has on you. You won't end up walking around with a big inane grin on your face all the time, but you should feel a definite difference that will be with you always, a background feeling that 'everything is going to be alright'.

'Clearing Out'

It is traditional within Reiki to think in terms of a 21-day period of clearing out or cleansing, as the energy starts to work on you as its first priority. Common reactions are to have a 'Reiki cold' or other respiratory infection, an occasional surprising migraine, or to feel quite tired and sleepy for some days during the 2-3 week period after attunement. Emotional ups and downs are quite common, and you may find that you are seeing things in 'Technicolor' for a while, with colours taking on an amazing intensity. For some, Reiki leads to a period of dissatisfaction, leading you to think carefully about your life and your priorities. For the most part Reiki works gently, and seems to have built-in mechanisms to prevent the 'clearing out' period from being particularly eventful.

The "21 Day" period is a bit of a Reiki myth, actually, because Reiki continues to work on you months and even years later, and it is possible that you will release things further down the line, too, not just in the first 21 days. Stronger reactions are more common in the first few weeks after going on a course, if you are going to have a strong reaction (such things are not compulsory!), though they can happen at any time, based on what is right for you. We receive what is right for us at any given time. We are all different.

Powerful Reactions on the day of the course

Once you have been attuned to Reiki, the first priority for the energy is YOU! Depending on what you bring along to the training day to be dealt with, Reiki will rush in to try and bring things into balance. If you are basically fine on the physical, mental and emotional level then the energy will not have a great deal to do, but if you have a lot to be sorted out, then the energy will rush in like a tidal wave and start to get things moving! This is the reason why a small number of people have strong reactions to the attunements. For most people they are a lovely experience on the day of the course, bringing feelings of great peace and tranquillity, but for a very small minority they can produce a bit of a healing crisis, as problems are brought to the surface so that they can be dissipated.

For example:

One lady spent the afternoon being sick, and spent the next day in bed with a migraine headache. Interestingly, her migraines usually went on for at least three days, yet she was able to get rid of this one in a few hours by doing Reiki self-treatments.

One lady was an 'emotional wreck' by lunchtime, beside herself and inconsolable, but by the end of the day she was fine, energised, and with the feeling that a great weight had been lifted from her.

One lady had been in a bad motor accident a few years ago, having broken her neck, dislocated her shoulders, stoved in her chest and shattered her pelvis. During the attunements some of the pain of her injuries started to come back to her, preventing her from moving her neck. The experience released itself by the end of the day.

However, these three examples are three cases out of hundreds and hundreds of attunements, so they are highly unlikely to happen to you. They are a really remote possibility. You are much more likely to experience an immediately positive reaction, like the people mentioned below...

Resolving Health Problems

On a number of occasions, people have experienced an immediate resolution of an ongoing health problem. Here are a few examples:

Scoliosis

Tracy was in her mid-20s and her back pain was no longer being controlled by the eight painkillers that she took each day. She was thinking of trying a T.E.N.S. machine which blocks pain impulses through a series of electrodes that you place on the skin in the affected area. Tracy didn't have any Reiki treatments, but the week after being attuned to Reiki First Degree she was able to cut her painkillers down to 2 per day, and that was enough to control the pain. Six months later she was pain free.

Back Pain

Anne came on the Reiki First Degree course having experienced long-term back pain which necessitated her having to take painkillers most days. The pain disappeared on the day of the course, and the following week she only needed to take painkillers a couple of times. This trend has continued for her.

Plantar Fasciitis

Plantar fasciitis is a painful condition in the foot. Sue had been in daily pain for 10 months before taking her First Degree course. The day after First Degree the pain disappeared and has not returned, much to the astonishment of the Consultant she visited!

It is not uncommon for people to come along to their Reiki Second Degree course a month after going through First Degree, to report a definite improvement in their conditions, and recent examples include depression and I.B.S. (Irritable Bowel Syndrome)

Longer term effects of Reiki

In this section you can read a series of quotes given to me by some of my students, where they respond to the question: "What has Reiki done for you?" I hope that these quotes will give you a better idea of what Reiki can do for you, and what you might look forward to:

> *"I would say that Reiki is inspirational, the feeling and experiences that I have had are amazing and mysterious. Having the ability to make someone feel better is one of the best feelings in the world and also knowing that I have that energy around to connect onto gives me strength to carry on especially in the last few months.*
> *Thanks for this gift ."*
> ***Maria, Essex***

> *"Reiki has changed my life around completely, from being a totally bored secretary to owning my own beauty and healing salon! How's that for a transformation in two years?"*
> ***Jean, Essex***

> *"In two sentences: In Reiki I have an instant form of stress relief like no other. It centres me straight away."*
> ***Espen, Essex***

> *"Reiki has turned my attitudes and my life around completely. A few years ago I was very intolerant, impatient, depressive and with a very short fuse. That has nearly all gone now and it has set me on a spiritual search and a real feeling that if my life can be turned around so completely, the more people Reiki can reach the better for all of us. It is a long time now since I was angry, worried, depressed and Reiki has obviously been working on all levels over the last year."*
> ***Joy, Gwynedd***

> *"I have found that Reiki has given me a much more positive outlook on life and I seem to be able to deal with problems and stress more effectively."*
> ***Gill, Suffolk***

> *"I find Reiki quite magical, giving me control over my bodies aches & pains and helping me progress spiritually. I am always very amazed how effective it is. Reiki's biggest benefit to me has been its ability to break my reliance on Osteopathy. Now I'm able to get my body back on track before it breaks. Thanks heaps Taggart."*
> ***Richard, Berkshire***

> *"Reiki has had profound effects on my life, I haven't set foot in a doctors surgery since I started and I am more happy and centred than I have ever been ! But in a sentence I would have to say ...... Reiki is the most amazing and beautiful thing I have ever encountered, I love it and am so happy to be sharing it with the world."*
> ***Jennifer, Surrey***

"Reiki has given me inner peace and serenity. It's the ultimate chill-out! My students at the chiropody school where I teach are always amazed at how I manage to help run a busy training clinic without getting stressed - I tell them that it's the Reiki... and that leads me on to explain to them how they can also acquire this beautiful gift. Any of my students who happen to be staying at the same B&B as I do when I am working at the college in Maidenhead also get a full treatment into the bargain!"
Karen, Hampshire

"If I were to sum it up in one sentence I think I would say: Reiki is an amazing adventure with many wonderful surprises along the way... or... Reiki offers hope, peace and a life time of support."
Tina, London

"The full impact of the changes and benefits did not happen overnight and at times it has been a rocky road, but as I look back over the past five years since I did my First Degree Reiki I can't imagine what life would be without Reiki. I have learnt to live and breathe Reiki, to trust in the Universe, to see love & beauty in everyone and everything, to tackle problems with a smile, to turn negativity into positivity & laugh to myself as lessons are learned. The world is a brighter place - even a dull day can feel bright. My senses are more acute, I observe & listen in a more compassionate way and I feel more in turn with nature. Reiki has brought a feeling of peace & calm and acceptance that life is unfolding as it should. What is the biggest benefit that Reiki has given me? Reiki has given me a purpose in life and the energy & enthusiasm to fulfll my dreams. I bless each day - it is a joy to be alive and if I can help to pass this on to others what more can I ask for?"
Jeannie, West Sussex

"For many years I have been searching for answers to issues that have kept cropping up in my life, the unusual things that seemed to happen to me (and at that time, I felt didn't seem to happen to anyone else!).
When I began my Reiki 1 course - I didn't have to look any further. Doors started opening up in all directions, I felt confident I could cope with what I would find (before this, I was terrified). So for me, on a personal level - its given me back my trust and faith in myself (also my guides and spirit friends). There is so much more I could write here, but the final thing for me, it gave me the tools to help me to help my husband heal."
Sue, Wales

"For me Reiki is coming home."
Ellen, Middlesex

"Reiki for me has changed me by:
Making me a calmer person, fewer things seem to worry me now.
Things and colours seem brighter and clearer.
I feel an uncontrollable love towards people.
I am more patient with my two teenage daughters.
I don't hoard so much junk in my house and I am a tidier person.
I seem to live each day as it comes - Just for today..."
Bev, Suffolk

Believing that Reiki actually works

In this section you can read some feedback given to me by some of my students, where they talk about the moment when they realised that Reiki did actually work! Reiki does seem rather a strange thing to do to begin with, and people naturally doubt whether they can 'do this thing'. Although on the day of a live course some quite weird and exciting things can happen, when you get home again those little doubts start to creep in and we start to think 'I know Reiki works for everyone... but maybe it just won't work for me'.

Alternatively, maybe we start to compare our experiences with the experiences of other people on our live course, for example, and perhaps the other students experienced stronger sensations than we did. Such comparisons are disempowering: each person grows and develops at their own rate.

It is perfectly natural to doubt and compare in the early stages, of course. But when we start to work with the energy regularly some surprising things can happen, and this is what happened to some of my students:

> *"The first time I thought there was definitely some sort of Reiki energy out there that people could channel was on the Reiki one course, whilst the lady treating me had her hands on the back of my head I felt such strong sensations coming from her hands I new it wasn't my imagination. The first time I felt that Reiki could actually do something as far as healing or spiritual growth was concerned was probably just before Reiki 2 when I woke up one morning and thought, Wow I had a really good night's sleep and felt all nice and cosy then I thought hang on a minute when did I last have a bad night's sleep, that is when I realised I had been sleeping so much better than before I did Reiki. I couldn't quite believe my luck and had no idea that Reiki would help me with my sleeping problems. Since then there has been so many occasions where Reiki has amazed me."*
> ***Tina, London***

> *"The first time I realised there was something to Reiki was during my First Degree course when I was doing my first full treatment. I felt extra heat and a sensation in my hand when I got to the person's lower left leg. Afterwards I asked if she had a problem in that area. Her immediate reaction was no and then she suddenly remembered she had knocked her leg a week ago and had a small bruise there. Well, it was as if I had won the lottery - I was so excited! Even after doing Reiki for four years the amazement and excitement hasn't diminished when my hands start vibrating over a particular area in need of healing. My only problem is having to control my inner excitement in front of clients!!"*
> ***Jeannie, West Sussex***

> *"I realised Reiki worked on the same day of the Reiki 1 course. Taggart had told us to get as much practice as possible, so that evening I was giving Suzanne a Reiki treatment. I wasn't really expecting very much to happen so I was very shocked & surprised when it did. Soon after I got to the heart position, my hands became extremely hot, & Suzanne's body began to shake*

all over. She says that she remembers her chest feeling so heavy that she could hardly breathe. I felt terribly sad & as though I was going to cry. I asked her if she thought she was going to cry & she said she wasn't but a few seconds later she did. I've never known anyone to cry like that! It was quite distressing, but I knew it was helping her so I just carried on until it stopped & then moved on to the next position. I did all of the hand positions I had learnt, including her knees & ankles & at each position the same thing happened: extreme heat in my hands, followed by her body shaking all over, hysterical crying, & then a pause as the heat subsided. So that proved it for me!"
Michelle, Spain

"I was working with a Reiki master in nursing and heard her speak of Reiki often; she always seemed so excited and worked differently during these times. I left that hospital and heard from her one evening at my new place of work. I had expressed an interest in Reiki, no more, to her. She told me a place for become available for a Reiki one residential weekend and asked if I would be interested. Funnily enough, I had the weekend off and no plans, synchronicity! So off I went with no real great expectations, though some excitement. Through the course of the weekend, I was opened up like a flower, I just couldn't believe the energy I was feeling and how unaware I'd been until that time. I used Reiki on myself and co-workers were amazed at my new found contentedness and open heart.

One night we had an admission to the ICU, transferred in from another hospital, a young man in his early thirties, he was dying. He looked well and fit and there was nothing we could do despite all our use of technology and drugs. When I went into the relatives' room with our doctor (Margaret) there was a large gathering of family, his wife, siblings, and children under the age of 10. I was very aware of the shock, anger, disbelief, and grief in the room. I sat on the floor while Margaret explained what was actually happening, the family's pain was audible at this stage and there were tears and cries. My hands just opened and I felt a calm, soothing energy crossing and filling the room. I felt their pain abate and I really felt connected to the family on a deep spiritual level. I already felt changes within myself and knew I would remain very connected to Reiki but that moment opened me up to the limitless love, unconditional love of the Divine. I later felt this with many of my patients and their families and continue to feel that connection of love through Reiki.

I was truly blessed through that weekend I was introduced to Reiki and am full of gratitude for my continued open heart through the use of Reiki in my own life on a daily basis. I will be ever grateful for that unexpected gift of Reiki. I later did my Reiki 2 with my nursing colleague; I then took Reiki 2 with Taggart and did my Mastership with Taggart. I am especially grateful to have had this opportunity as I love Taggart's gentle style of teaching and the original methods have been beautiful to have found. I have used various healing methods in my own life but Reiki has always been my foremost practice daily and the one I really want to practice and share as fully as I can."
Jean, Australia

FOLLOWING THE SYSTEM

What did Mikao Usui teach?

Since the 1990s Reiki has been going through some changes in many quarters. Until then everyone had assumed that the Reiki that Mikao Usui taught was the same as the Reiki that Mrs Takata had been teaching, in fact her teachings are usually referred to as "traditional" Usui Reiki. It was thought that Reiki had died out in Japan, and that the only Reiki that had survived was the system that Mrs Takata had been teaching. But the 1990s ushered in a new stage in Reiki's development, when information started to filter through from Japan, in dribs and drabs, from different sources. Some information made sense, some seemed confusing, a lot of the information contradicted what people had believed about Reiki, and some of the information was inconsistent or contradictory.

Over time, though, we have built up more of a consistent picture of what Usui Sensei's system was all about, what he taught and how he taught it, though you can find books that contain the earlier – now contradicted – view of what Usui's system was all about. The main confusion arose when the Usui Reiki Ryoho Gakkai (Usui Memorial Society) was discovered. Everyone thought that this society had been founded by Usui himself and that it had continued Usui Sensei's system in its original form, but now we know that the society was set up after his death by the Imperial Officers, who had been taught a system that was not representative of the system that Usui had been teaching to the majority of his students, and we know that the Imperial Officers changed and altered what they had been taught early on in the 'Gakkai's history. 'Gakkai Reiki proved to be very different from Usui Reiki.

We discovered that Usui's system was not called "Reiki". In fact the system had no real name. Usui seems to have referred to his system as a 'Method to Achieve Personal Perfection', and some of his students seem to have called the system 'Usui Teate' (teate means 'hand application' or 'hand healing') or 'Usui Do' (way of Usui). The word Reiki appeared in the Reiki precepts, but the word 'Reiki' seems there to mean 'a system that has been arrived at through a moment of enlightenment', or 'a gift of satori'. The name 'Reiki' as a description of system came later, and may have been used first when the naval officers set up the Usui Reiki Ryoho Gakkai.

We also discovered that the purpose of Usui's method was to achieve satori, to find one's spiritual path, to heal oneself. Usui's system was not really about treating others. Treating others was not emphasised; it was not focused upon; it was a side issue. This came as rather a shock to a Reiki world that saw Reiki as a hands-on treatment method first and foremost.

The Original System

The information that we have about the system that Mikao Usui taught has come mainly from a group of surviving students who are in contact with one or two people in the West. They were twelve in number when they were first discovered, though I understand that now – in 2005 – there are only a handful of them left. These are people who knew Usui, trained with him, and passed on his teachings to others in a quiet and limited fashion. Their information has helped to 'make sense' of the sometimes confusing and contradictory information from other sources in Japan, and they paint a picture of a simple spiritual system that is very different from the treatment-based Reiki that we see routinely in the West.

So the original Japanese form of Reiki is very different from the way that it has ended up being practised in the West. The thing that strikes me most about original Usui Reiki is the fact that it is so simple, so elegant, powerful and uncluttered. The system is not bogged down in endless mechanical techniques and complex rituals that now clutter up a lot of Western-style Reiki, with endless rules and regulations and restrictions.

The prime focus of Mikao Usui's Reiki was the personal benefits that would come through committing oneself to working with the system, in terms of self-healing and spiritual development. Reiki was a path to enlightenment. Healing others was a minor aspect of the system, not emphasised, not focused upon; it was simply something that you could do if you followed Usui's system.

Original Usui Reiki involved committing yourself to carrying out daily energy exercises, self-healings, and receiving spiritual empowerments on a regular basis. You would have received training in an open ended fashion, rather like the way that martial arts is taught in the West today: you kept turning up and slowly developing your skills, and when it was thought that you had progressed sufficiently, you were allowed to move on to the next level.

The system was rooted in Tendai Buddhism and Shintoism, with Tendai Buddhism providing spiritual teachings and Shintoism contributing methods of controlling and working with the energies. The system was based on living and practising the Reiki precepts. The vast majority of Usui's students started out as his clients – he was well known as a healer, though what he taught was not really a treatment method. He would routinely give people empowerments so that they could treat themselves in between appointments, and if they wanted to take things further then they could start formal training with him, to learn how to heal themselves.

First Degree (Shoden)

Mikao Usui's First Degree training ("Shoden", which means 'first teachings') was very simple, and it seems that Usui taught hundreds of people at this level. Shoden was all about opening to the energy through receiving many Reiju empowerments (simple connection rituals), it was about cleansing and self-healing.

The student would practice different forms of self-healing, including self-healing meditations, they would chant and live the Reiki affirmations, and they would practice a couple of energy exercises. The exercises taught at first-degree level were Kenyoku and Joshin Kokkyu Ho, which are taught in the Usui Reiki Ryoho Gakkai as part of a longer sequence of exercises, called 'Hatsurei Ho', which you will find described in this manual.

Students would study some specially selected 'Waka' poems, chosen by Usui because they contained various sacred sounds (kotodama), and they would be introduced to the concept of mindfulness. They would focus on developing their awareness of their Tanden (see later), and that would, for some, lead to second-degree level.

Students would not treat others at first-degree.

How can we follow the teachings?

We know that the system that Mikao Usui taught to the majority of his students was a spiritual development and self-healing practice, based on these five areas:

1. Focusing on and living Mikao Usui's precepts
2. Practising mindfulness
3. Receiving Reiju empowerments regularly
4. Carrying out energy exercises
5. Practising self-healing

These areas can form the basis of our Reiki practice too. Now obviously we are not going to learn and practise Reiki in exactly the same way as was done in 1920s Japan. This is simply not possible since we live in the 21st Century in the West. We do not have the same history or cultural and spiritual background as Usui Sensei's students, and we do not know the precise details of everything that Mikao Usui taught.

But what we can do is to make part of our routine the basic practices of Usui Sensei's system, which was designed by him to be accessible to people from different backgrounds. Below I have touched on the five areas, and in subsequent chapters I will go into more details about how we can follow Usui Sensei's simple system in the modern world.

Reiju empowerments

Mikao Usui's students received empowerments from him again and again throughout their training at all levels. The training was more like martial arts style training, with ongoing and sometimes sporadic contact between student and teacher – rather than the day-courses or two-day-courses that are usual in the West (and usual in Japan now, for that matter).

But we can echo the practice of giving and receiving empowerments over an extended period as follows:

Live Reiki Courses	Reiki Home Study Courses
By receiving several Reiju empowerments from your teacher on the day of your live course	By receiving distant empowerments sent to you specifically by your teacher, during the course of your home study programme
Subsequently, by receiving distant empowerments on a weekly basis	Subsequently, by receiving distant empowerments on a weekly basis

It is simply not practical, given the distances that many people travel to attend live Reiki courses, or given the distance between many home study course students and their teacher, for the teacher and student to get together every week so that the student can receive a 'live' Reiju empowerment from the teacher.

But, since there is no difference between a 'live' Reiju empowerment and one received at a distance, we can effectively echo this original practice of empowering on a regular basis, so long as the student is prepared to commit a few minutes each week tuning into the distant empowerments which we Taggart sends out, and which can be 'tuned into' any time on a Monday.

Mikao Usui's Precepts and Mindfulness

The foundation of Usui Sensei's system was to follow a simple set of rules to live by. These 'precepts' are Buddhist or Shugendo in origin, have a very long history, and it was said that by following the precepts the student would obtain more spiritual development than was possible by carrying out any of the energy work. So the precepts – and the idea of mindfulness which is strongly linked to or suggested by the precepts – are a very important part of Mikao Usui's spiritual system and should not be glossed over.

They are the very foundation of his system. You start with the precepts.

Daily energy exercises

Later on in this manual you will read about the simple energy exercises that Mikao Usui taught his students at First Degree level, and the slightly more elaborate sequence that this developed into in the Usui Memorial Society in Japan. You will find detailed instructions and images, and you will also have received an audio CD containing a guided meditation that you can use to help you get to grips with this exercise – called "Hatsurei ho" – which ideally should be carried out every day.

Self-healing practices

At First Degree Usui Sensei taught his students to practise self-healing in a variety of ways. Later on in this manual you can read about the various approaches that he taught, and the way that self-treatments are generally carried out in the West. We recommend a meditative approach to self-healing, something that should ideally be carried out daily, and you will find a guided meditation on your audio CD to help you with this.

Treating others

In a world where Reiki is presented to the world as a sort of complementary therapy, something that you do to other people, we need to continually remind ourselves that the treatment of other people was not what Usui's system was all about. Treating others was not focused upon or emphasised and, at First Degree level, Usui's students would probably have just worked on themselves. They might have treated others at Second Degree level.

But there is no reason why you should not treat others at First Degree level, and we positively encourage you to do so to help build your confidence and to give you practice in channelling energy. Reiki is presented to the world as a treatment technique and this course gives you what you need to treat others confidently and successfully.

Reiki Evolution courses and their content

The logo to the left says "Shin Reiki", which translates approximately as "Reiki Evolution". So I suppose you could refer to the form of Reiki that you learn on this course as "Shin Reiki" but the last thing I want to do is to promote yet another version of Reiki with a different name! What I have done with all my Reiki courses is to blend the Western approach to Reiki teaching (day-courses rather than martial-arts style teaching, with a system based on the treatment of others) with simple and powerful methods that were part of the system developed by the founder, Mikao Usui, but which were never taught in the West.

You will have read earlier in this manual that Reiki was modified and changed a great deal during its journey to the West, through Dr Chujiro Hayashi and Mrs Hawayo Takata, and then changed again as it passed through the New Age movement and from teacher to teacher in the West. What I have tried to do is to complete the circle by bringing my teaching more in line with what seems to have been intended by Mikao Usui. I have kept the Western teaching format (day courses) but I have added a home study element to the live courses so that the student has the opportunity for the information to sink in and to carry out some simple energy work over - usually - several weeks, depending on the interval between receiving their booking and the date of their live course. Home study students follow a course that is perhaps more in line with the teaching approach that Mikao Usui used, by following a course of study and energy work over at least a six week period. I have also made sure that the courses are in sympathy with the 'treatment' emphasis of most Reiki courses, so students will learn as much, and more, about treating others as is available on other First Degree courses.

I have adapted and changed my Reiki by, as far as I can, bringing it into line with the system that Usui set down in the early part of last century, but presenting it to you in the Western teaching format, and in a way that is compatible with other people's Reiki First Degree courses.

The information in this manual is partly based on the traditions of Western Reiki, as taught to me by a variety of Western Masters, partly based on some of the teachings of the Usui Reiki Ryoho Gakkai in Japan (Mikao Usui's Reiki Association) which have come to us through Frank Arjava Petter and Hiroshi Doi, but mainly based on information coming from a group of Usui's surviving students, through Chris Marsh. This last source takes us the closest to Usui Sensei's original form. Please see the appendix for more information about these sources.

MIKAO USUI'S PRECEPTS & MINDFULNESS

Precepts and Buddhism

Mikao Usui gave his students a series of 'precepts' to follow. The Concise Oxford Dictionary (9th Edition) defines a precept as (1) a command, a rule of conduct, and (2) a moral instruction, and they are an important part of Buddhist practice. We know that Mikao Usui was a Tendai Buddhist, and so precepts would have been an important part of his spiritual life. Lay followers of Buddhism generally undertake to follow (at least one of) five precepts, which are given in the form of promises to oneself: "I will (try) to...". Here are the five Buddhist precepts:

1. To refrain from harming living creatures (killing).
2. To refrain from taking that which is not freely given (stealing).
3. To refrain from sexual misconduct.
4. To refrain from incorrect speech (lying, harsh language, slander, idle chit-chat).
5. To refrain from intoxicants which lead to loss of mindfulness.

So precepts are a list of guidelines for living your life. They are not framed in terms of "thou shalt not..." as in the Judaeo-Christian tradition but rather are a set of ideals to work towards, recommendations about thought and behaviour that you should follow as much as you can.

The origin of Mikao Usui's precepts

Mikao Usui gave his students a special set of precepts to follow (now referred to as "the Reiki Precepts") and there has been a lot of speculation about where these precepts came from. It has been claimed that they originated in a book that was published in Usui's time, and it has been suggested that they are based on the edicts of Mutsuhito, the Meiji Emperor. Certainly it seems that many Tendai and Zen teachers were in Usui's time passing on principles similar to those of Mikao Usui.

But now we know that Usui's precepts were his wording of an earlier set of precepts that have been traced back to the early 9th century, precepts that were used in a Tendai sect of Shugendo with which Usui Sensei was in contact. These precepts were a way of addressing aspects of the Buddhist eight-fold path in a simplified form, and they are the very 'hub' of the whole system.

These are Mikao Usui's precepts

Here is the full wording of Mikao Usui's precepts. The actual precepts start at "just for today" and end with "be compassionate…":

The secret art of inviting happiness
The miraculous medicine of all diseases

Just for today,
Do not anger,
Do not worry
Be humble
Be honest (in your dealings with other people)
Be compassionate towards yourself and others

In every morning and evening join your hand in prayer,
pray these words to your heart and chant these words with your mouth:

"Usui Reiki Treatment (for) Improvement of body and mind"

The Founder, Usui Mikao

You may find that some versions of the precepts include an extra item: "honour your parents, elders and teachers". This is not original and seems to have been added by Mrs Takata to make the "list of rules to live by" more acceptable to her (largely) Christian American audience.

Incidentally, you may find some commentators saying that negative affirmations are not a good idea: such things are said to be more effective when framed in positive terms. What we have presented to us in the precepts is just a quirk of translation from Japanese to English: the precepts are actually a recommendation that we exist in the moment in a state where we are free from anger and worry, a 'worry-free, anger-free' state.

The importance of the precepts

These Reiki 'precepts' are Mikao Usui's guidelines for living and are perhaps the most important part of his system. They were the baseline, the foundation of his teachings, and it was said that as much spiritual development would come through following the precepts as would come through carrying out any of the energy work.

In 'Gakkai practice the Reiki principles would be chanted three times by his students at their weekly training sessions, and every day, towards the end of their Hatsu Rei Ho. It was said within the 'Gakkai that if a student wanted to progress on their spiritual path, they needed to:

1. Receive Reiju empowerments on a regular basis
2. Practice Hatsu Rei Ho
3. Live the Reiki principles as part of their lives: they would live their lives in accordance with these principles

For me, Mikao Usui's precepts represent both some of the beneficial effects that Reiki can produce in your life if you work with the energy regularly, and they represent a set of principles that we need to follow to enhance our journey of self-healing and self-development with Reiki.

The Reiki precepts are important.

What do the precepts mean to you?

I do not want to provide a lot of commentary about Mikao Usui's precepts because I want to ask you what these principles mean to you and how you think you can apply them to your life. I want you to consider carefully how each precept impinges on your daily life, on your thoughts and emotions and on the way that you react to and deal with other people. I want you to reflect on the way that you consider your past, imagine your future, and the way that you journey through life.

Just for Today

This line is not just preamble: it is one of the most important phrases. "Just for Today" exhorts us to be fully engaged in the moment, to be mindful. All we have is now; our life consists of an endless stream of moments that we can only experience in the now: the past is gone and we can do nothing about it and the future is not here yet so there is no need to worry about it. The only gift of life we have is now. We can learn to become fully aware of our existence in the moment, to enjoy the moment, to appreciate and to be content in the now. We deal more with mindfulness later in this section.

Do not Anger, do not Worry

For me the instruction not to anger does not mean that you should be suppressing anger (not a very good thing to do according to the principles of Traditional Chinese Medicine, which were adopted by the Japanese). But we should not get wound up by things that are really of no consequence. The first two instructions – do not anger do not worry - tell us to try and live in the moment. We should put things in their proper perspective. We should not dwell on the past and beat ourselves up for things that have happened which we cannot change, and we should not focus on the future and worry now about things that may never happen. These precepts help to reinforce "Just for Today", or to reflect that exhortation, because living your life fully engaged in the moment means existing in a state where anger and fear do not exist. All is illusion and fear is a distraction.

Be Humble

The instruction to be humble has been interpreted as an exhortation to remind ourselves of the many blessings that we have in our lives, the many positive things. We are reminded that we should focus on those things and be grateful. And we should try and restrain our ego, because no one knows everything. No one has all the answers. We all can learn from others.

Be Honest in your dealings with people

The 'honesty' principle is I suppose self-explanatory. But can we be honest with ourselves and with those close to us, as well as to strangers? Can we say what we really think and feel, opening up to reveal the real us to other people?

Be Compassionate

The compassion principle applies as much to us as to others. Can we be gentle with ourselves? Can we forgive ourselves for not being perfect, for perhaps not achieving what we thought we could achieve, or for not behaving in the way that perhaps we ought to have behaved? Can we extend that same forgiveness to others? We can be gentle with ourselves, light hearted and forgiving? Forgiveness sets us free.

We can echo the original Japanese practice of contemplating the principles each day. Put the precepts on a post-it note and stick them on your fridge or your PC. Frame them and hang them on your wall. Mentally review them a couple of times each day. Maybe on Monday you might focus on being free from anger, on Tuesday you can be free from worry, on Wednesday you can remind yourself of the many blessings in your life, on Thursday you can make sure you are honest with yourself and others, on Friday you can forgive yourself and forgive others, you can care for others and care for yourself.

Here is a copy of the Reiki principles, drawn for me by talented Japanese calligrapher Eri Takase:

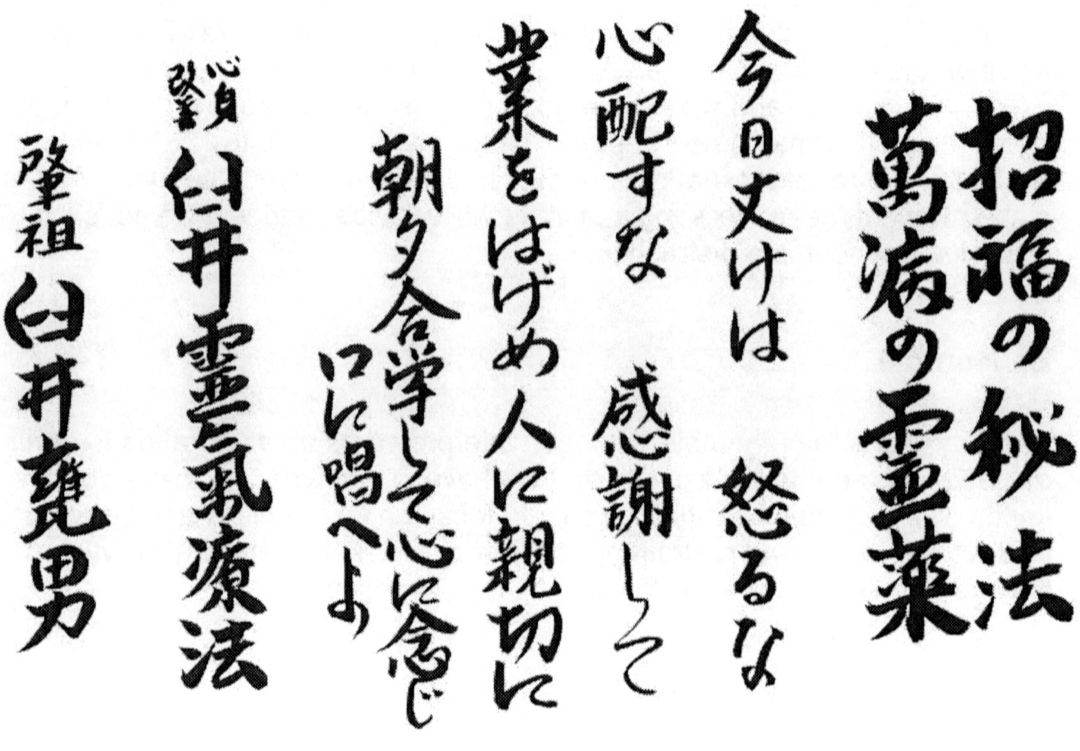

“Releasing” exercise

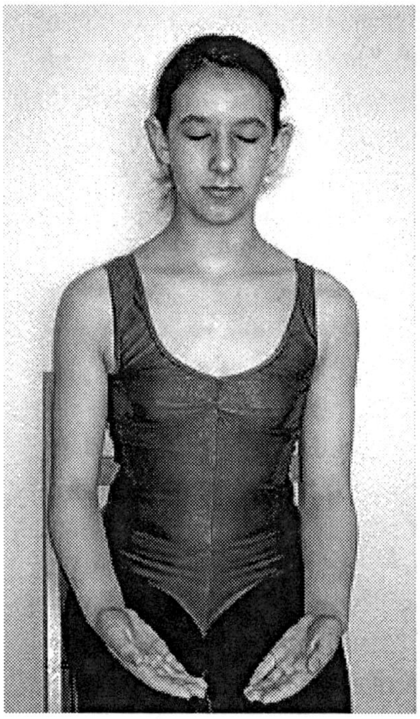

Here is an exercise that you can practise on a regular basis – say weekly. It gives the first two precepts an ‘energetic edge’ by allowing Reiki to help us to release the anger and worry that are hindering us from being content in the moment. This is not a practice that has come from Usui Sensei’s system. This is something that I have developed myself.

Stage One

Sit comfortably with your eyes closed and your hands resting in your lap, palms up. Take a few long deep breaths and feel yourself becoming peaceful and relaxed. Your mind empties. Say to yourself “I now release all my anger…”; say this three times to yourself if you like. Allow energy to be released through your palms, and be still until the flow of energy subsides. This may take a little while, particularly the first time you try this exercise.

Stage Two

Now say to yourself “I now release all my worry…”; say this three times to yourself if you like. Again allow a flurry of energy to leave your hands and be still until it subsides. Again this may take a little while, particularly the first time you try this exercise.

Alternatively, try carrying out the releasing exercise in time with your breath. Breathe in gently, say to yourself “I now release all my anger…” and then breathe out, allowing your anger to flood out of you on the out breath. Gently breath in, and repeat.

Mindfulness and Mikao Usui's system

Mikao Usui introduced his students to the concept of mindfulness at First Degree level, and emphasised this more at Second Degree level. According to the Concise Oxford Dictionary (9th Edition), to be mindful is to take heed or care, to be conscious. Mindfulness or being mindful is being aware of your present moment. You are not judging, reflecting or thinking. You are simply observing the moment in which you find yourself, fully aware. Moments are like a breath. Each breath is replaced by the next breath. You are there with no other purpose than being awake and aware of that moment.
Like precepts, mindfulness is largely associated with Buddhism and it is a meditative practice that is not reserved for special meditation sessions: it is a practice that you can embrace as part of your daily life and when carrying out routine and mundane tasks. It is really beyond the scope of this course – and all Reiki courses in fact – to teach mindfulness, but we can suggest resources that you can consult to investigate this area further.

To give you an idea of what mindfulness is all about, I have quoted below two small passages from "The Miracle of Mindfulness" (Thich Nhat Hanh, Rider, London, where the practice of mindfulness is explained by reference to two simple daily activities: doing the washing up and drinking tea:

> *"While washing the dishes one should only be washing the dishes, which means that while washing the dishes one should be completely aware of the fact that one is washing the dishes. At first glance, that might seem a little silly: why put such stress on a simple thing? But that's precisely the point. The fact that I am standing there and washing these bowls is a wondrous reality. I'm being completely myself, following my breath, conscious of my presence, and conscious of my thoughts and actions. There's no way I can be tossed around mindlessly like a bottle slapped here and there on the waves."*

> *"...there are two ways to wash the dishes. The first is to wash the dishes in order to have clean dishes and the second is to wash the dishes in order to wash the dishes. We should choose the second way. If while washing dishes, we think only of the cup of tea that awaits us, thus hurrying to get the dishes out of the way as if they were a nuisance, then we are not "washing the dishes to wash the dishes." What's more, we are not alive during the time we are washing the dishes. In fact we are completely incapable of realizing the miracle of life while standing at the sink. If we can't wash the dishes, the chances are we won't be able to drink our tea either. While drinking the cup of tea, we will only be thinking of other things, barely aware of the cup in our hands. Thus we are sucked away into the future – and we are incapable of actually living one minute of life"*

For further information about mindfulness you can search for this term on the Internet, and there are books written on this subject that can be found easily by consulting Amazon.co.uk. Here are two books that I can recommend:

The Miracle of Mindfulness
Thich Nhat Hanh, Rider, London

Mindfulness in Plain English
Bhante Henepola Gunaratana
Wisdom Publications, Boston

Some people also recommend this book:

The Power of Now
Eckhart Tolle
Hodder and Stoughton

Mindfulness and the precepts

The Thich Nhat Hanh passage quoted above reminds us that if we are forever living in the future (or dwelling on the past) then we are incapable of actually living even a minute of life. And what do we find in Mikao Usui's precepts? We find that the first three lines exhort us to live in the moment, to focus on the moment in a state where the future and the past do not concern us, a state free from anger or worry. Everything is illusion and fear is a distraction. If we can live for a moment, fully aware of the present, fully mindful, then we can live for a whole series of moments, fully aware and fully present, fully engaged in whatever task we are carrying out. Our life consists of a never-ending series of individual moments, and the precepts tell us just for this moment to be mindful, to be content, to be compassionate, honest, humble and forgiving.

REIJU

What are empowerments?

Whether you have attended one of our live Reiki courses, or have learned Reiki through one of our home study courses, you will have received a series of “Reiju empowerments”, either in person or sent at a distance.

In fact, no matter what sort of Reiki course you choose to follow, you will go through a series of rituals which can be seen as a way of ‘connecting’ you to Reiki, a way of hooking you up to something that you were previously not connected to. But perhaps it is more useful to say that an empowerment is a ‘ritual permission’, a permission to recognise something that is within, something that has always been there.

The effect of an empowerment is to allow you to channel energy for your own benefit, and for other people’s benefit, in a way that was not possible for you before you received the empowerment from your Reiki teacher.

You can write the word "Reiju" in two different ways using Japanese kanji, one way meaning "accepting the spirituality" and the other meaning "giving the spirituality"; spirituality in this case means ‘connection’ to the Reiki energy. In fact the word Reiju has been interpreted in several ways, for example “giving of the five blessings” and “the union of mind and ki”. The line in the Reiki precepts where it says “the secret method of inviting happiness through many blessings” may actually mean “the secret method of inviting happiness through receiving many Reiju empowerments”.

The empowerments that Mikao Usui used with his students can be referred to as “Reiju” and these were equivalent to a Tendai Buddhist blessing, a blessing that a Tendai teacher would bestow on a student with the intention that the student should receive what they need. Usui Sensei gave the blessing using intent only, but within Tendai Buddhism there is also a physical ritual that can be carried out which conveys the Reiju blessing; details of this ritual were passed to the West from Usui’s surviving students in the late 1990s and it is this ritual that we use on our courses.

Repeating your empowerments

While the effects of empowerments do not wear out, there are definite benefits associated with receiving Reiju repeatedly, and Usui Sensei's students received Reiju from him again and again throughout their training at all levels. We echo this approach by making distant empowerments available for all our students to tune into at any time on a Monday, and you can read more about this in the "Daily Energy Exercises" section of this manual.

Receiving Reiju regularly helps to 'reinforce' your connection to the source. It enhances self-healing, it helps the student to develop spiritually, it enhances intuition and increases sensitivity to the flow of energy.

What are "attunements"

You may have seen the word "attunement" mentioned in association with Reiki courses and perhaps you are wondering what attunements are and how they differ from the Reiju empowerments that we use.

Attunements are used in the vast majority of Reiki courses, and most of the Reiki Practitioners and Masters in the world will have received attunements rather than Reiju empowerments.

Until approximately 1999, everyone within the world of Reiki will have been 'attuned' using some sort of variation of the connection ritual that Hawayo Takata taught to the Masters that she initiated in the 1970s. Since the '70s Reiki has spread throughout the world and the rituals used have evolved as they have been passed from one teacher to another down the line. Some attunements are quite complicated affairs, while others are fairly simple, though there are some common themes that seem to run through most methods, for example the placing of the Reiki symbols into different parts of the student's body (head and hands for example).

But of course Mikao Usui did not perform what we would understand as 'attunements'. so where did the attunements used on most Reiki courses come from? Interestingly, it seems that the Imperial Officers had not been taught how to carry out the Reiju ritual by Usui Sensei, and after his death they put together a ritual that replicated the feelings or the experiences that they had when being empowered by Usui. Dr Hayashi passed on such a ritual to Mrs Takata, and then variations of this ritual spread throughout the world.

Are distant 'connections' effective?

Some people are taught that empowerments or attunements are only effective and valid if they are carried out in person, with the student sitting before the teacher. At the same time, people are also taught that it is possible to send Reiki from one side of the planet to another – through distant healing – with just the power of thought. These two sets of statements make uneasy bedfellows, and it takes a particular set of mental gymnastics to believe both that Reiki can be sent effortlessly at a distance, no matter what the distance (as indeed it can), but that for an empowerment or attunement to 'take', the student has to be right there in front of the teacher. This is not the case. Attunements and empowerments do not follow the inverse square law (like gravity, where the further away you are, the less strong the force). Distance is irrelevant to Reiki; distance does not exist for the purposes of the practice of Reiki or for the purpose of conveying attunements or empowerments.

Distant empowerments and attunements work. There is no difference between distant attunements and 'in person' attunements at all. When you attune, when you empower, you are not going in with an invisible spanner to adjust someone's energy system – to retune their antenna – you are simply 'making the introductions' between the student and the source, you are helping the student to notice and utilise something that is already there... and this can be done no matter what the distance.

We have extensive experience of teaching Reiki through home study at all Reiki levels.

Why do we need attunements or empowerments?

I mentioned above that the effect of an empowerment is to allow you to channel energy for your own benefit, and for other people's benefit, in a way that was not possible for you before you received the empowerment from your Reiki teacher. To expand on this a little, I would like to quote (with permission) an e-mail message sent in July 2004 by an American Reiki Master, Elizabeth King, on a now defunct Reiki Internet discussion group called "URRI". This is what Elizabeth had to say about attunements and the difference that attunement to Reiki has made to her. Her comments are equally applicable to Reiju empowerments:

> *"Every human being and I would venture a vast majority of animals have the natural ability of using "Reiki" which is a Japanese word for "Universal Energy." The main difference is that without Attunement, the energy is not as strong, nor is it as steady in flow. As an energy healer for nearly 30 years before hearing about and studying and being attuned to Reiki and becoming a Reiki Master and a Gendai Shihan, I found that my healing ability was very*

dependent on a number of variables - how I was feeling physically, how I was feeling emotionally, etc., and I had to "draw" on my own energy resources and then had to take time to regenerate it, so to speak. The gist is that after 30 years I was forced to stop my work as a healer, something I found is very common with many energy healers, and had to go to strictly teaching because my own physical strength and health had been compromised.

"When I was attuned to Reiki the first thing I noticed was that I was not longer having to draw on my own reserves, but that I had become a "flute" if you will, an instrument through whom Reiki flowed, healing me and healing the person upon whom I was working. What a huge difference! I also noticed very quickly that the energy was steady, strong, and very invigorating - to me~!

"So that is why Attunement is critical to the Reiki practitioner - it is what literally plugs us into the Universe (you can call it God, the Force, The Goddess, Creator, whatever you want to call it, it's all the One), and because of that, I have recovered much of my own health (those who know me and my story know what I mean, this miracle of Reiki), and since being attuned 6 years ago I have resumed my life - I have gone from housebound to teaching 10 and 11 classes of English each year for the Community college, I teach Reiki, practice as a Reiki practitioner, work as a hypnotherapist and teach classes in Hypnosis - and I'm 66 years old.

"That, in a nutshell is what Attunement is all about! Makes perfect sense to me."
Elizabeth K

What will I feel when I receive an empowerment?

There is no way of predicting what an individual will experience when receiving an empowerment, whether in person or at a distance. You may have an amazing experience, or you may feel very little or nothing. It is not uncommon for people to see some colours or feel some heat or tingling or pulsing or pressure in various areas of their bodies. For some people an empowerment is a unique experience, profound, emotional, an experience that is almost unbelievable. For others very little happens.

What a student experiences when they receive an empowerment is no guide to the effectiveness of that empowerment. In fact what a student experiences is irrelevant. Empowerments always work. Of course it is nice and reassuring to have the "bells and whistles and fireworks" – it helps you to believe that something definite has happened - but someone who has noticed all these things has not been more effectively empowered when compared with a student who felt nothing.

Experiences are interesting, but not important. They don't mean anything in terms of whether or how well an empowerment has worked, because empowerments always work, no matter what the student feels or doesn't feel.

Students' Experiences: receiving Reiju empowerments

"I have been tuning in to the empowerments, which have varied in the experiences that I have had. To begin with they seemed quite long, and then a couple of short ones and then longer again. Interestingly, the shorter ones were the ones where I then felt dizzy afterwards. Quite often I also get a pulsing white light across my eyes, but after each one I have felt a lot calmer and also that things can wash over me a lot easier. I have found that when I have been stressed and then done my exercises, it has certainly helped to realign my thoughts and actions. I even used them the other night when I woke up in the middle of the night and couldn't get back to sleep !"
"T.B." from Norfolk

"The empowerment began as something small and then really built up. My feet tingled, almost like pins and needles. Especially so on the toes of my left foot. Also a tingle on the back. The whole thing lasted for about 10 minutes."
Jason Brown from North Wales

"This feels like standing under a warm water fall in the sunshine, the energy i get from you seems to wash over me taking any negativity with it, i feel cleansed and refreshed afterwards."
Niki Leach from Tyne and Wear

"On receiving the attunement I felt a sense of spaciousness and peace but not much in the way of tingling or anything, as if a path had been cleared."
Susan Naylor from West Yorkshire

"I moved into the prayer position to receive my first reiju empowerment and to start with it felt like nothing was happening. However, after the first few minutes, my hands felt very hot (not warm) and tingled whenever I breathed in. It was a very strange experience as when I exhaled, they felt cool again. This continued to happen for approx 10 to 15 minutes and included my feet getting hotter and hotter. This sensation did not just disappear but slowly died down with my hands getting less and less hot on each inhalation. After 15 minutes or so the sensation completely disappeared.

Also, during my empowerment I felt, again upon inhaling as though I had a 'pulling' sensation in my head. It was as though a plunger was sucking up and something was pulling up inside my head. Upon exhaling it sunk back down. It was not unpleasant at all, in fact it was a deeply relaxing feeling.

After empowerment everything disappeared. My hands went cool, my ball of energy dissipated and I felt extremely calm, relaxed and serene.

The second empowerment was much the same as the first but did not last as long as the first. The energy exercises produced more heat in the hands and feet and felt like more than just energy was being pushed away on exhaling."
Sarah Quinn from Kent

"I found this week to be very interesting. I am a scientist by training, and I have found I need to guard against my gullible nature. So I found myself questioning everything, trying to determine if it was "just my imagination" or if there were other explanations for things I noticed while doing the exercises. At the same time, I kept trying to just relax into the experience and trust in it. Very conflicting situation which probably affected my impressions of the experiences.

The first time I did Joshin Kokkyu Ho I felt almost tearful (didn't have that again). I sometimes felt hand and foot tingling as well. My experiences when I asked for my empowerment varied. Sometimes I noticed nothing. Several times however I noticed something odd: a feeling of weight and pressure on my upper back, shoulders and head. Sometimes it felt strong enough to cause me to lean forward. I would also see "lights" in my closed eyes, sometimes blobs of light dripping down, or flashes."
Karen Small from America

EXPERIENCING ENERGY

Reiki is all about working with energy, and the idea of energy may seem a little strange at first. Energy is all around you, though. Your body is composed of it, energy flows through you, energy surrounds you; it is right under your nose. But in the West we don't even spend five minutes trying to experience energy. When we do change our focus, though, when we change what we are focusing our attention on, we can start to experience something that has always been there.

What we notice may be quite subtle to begin with, and that's not a problem because this is all very new, it is the early stages for you. Our experience of energy usually develops with time and practice, so if you keep on working with energy then you are likely to become more sensitive to it. What you experience on the day of a Reiki course, or in the first few weeks of a home study course, is not representative of what you will experience once you have had the opportunity to work with Reiki regularly.

In this section I am going to describe some exercises that you can carry out to start to experience energy. You will need a partner for some of them. Work with them regularly and you will build your sensitivity to energy. You may well be surprised by what you can notice!

Feel Energy Between your Hands

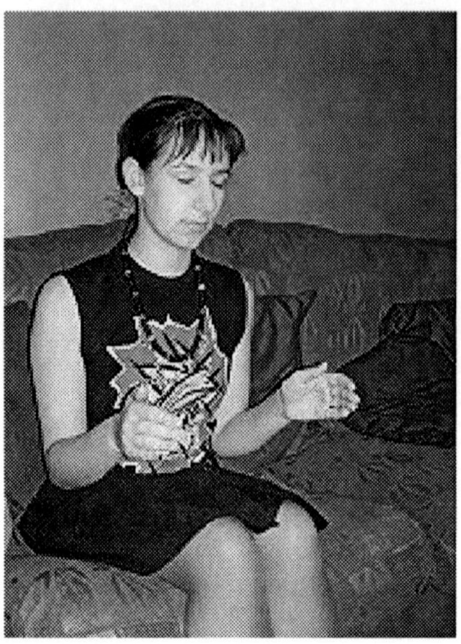

Rub your hands together for half a minute, rather like you are warming your hands up after being out in the cold. Now hold your hands out in front of you, shoulder width apart, with your palms facing each other, rather like you were holding the sides of a very large ball.

Now slowly 'bounce' your hands together until you have an impression that there is something tangible between your hands. You may feel something squashy like a marshmallow, a balloon or a rubber ball; you may feel a surface, a layer, some resistance, some magnetic repulsion… some 'thing' that your hands are resting on that prevents them from touching.

Now obviously you can move your hands all the way together, but with a few attempts most people can feel something between their hands that they can rest their hands on, bounce their hands against. Sometimes you can find a position where your hands don't want to come any closer, but equally they don't want to move away from each other either, a position of balance.

You are feeling your energy field. You have always been able to do this. It has always been right there in front of you. To experience it you have simply changed your focus.

Feel Energy on a Partner's Hand

You will need someone to do this exercise with you. Sit fairly near to each other.

Both of you should rub your hands together for half a minute, rather like you are warming your hands up after being out in the cold. Now hold one hand out in front of you, at shoulder height, with your palm facing your partner's palm, rather like you were about to push his/her hand away from you.

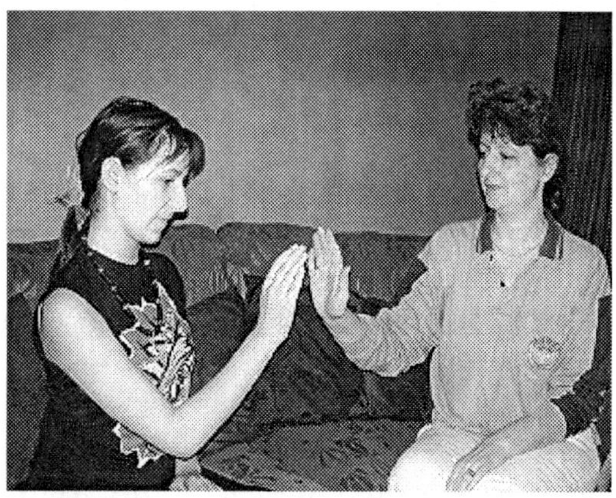

Now slowly 'bounce' your hands together until you have an impression that there is something tangible between your hands. You may feel something squashy like a marshmallow, a balloon or a rubber ball; you may feel a surface, a layer, some resistance, some magnetic repulsion... some 'thing' that your hands are resting on that prevents them from touching.

See if you can agree between yourselves about the point where you can both feel that 'contact', that layer or surface, that magnetic repulsion or resistance.

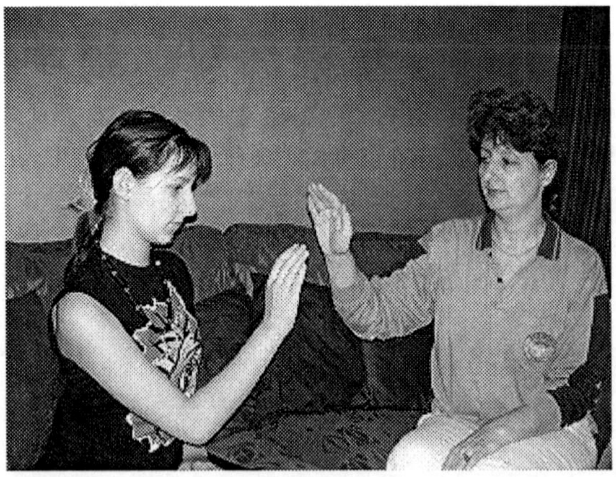

Now one person should keep their hand still while the other person slowly moves their hand vertically up and down, from side to side, and slowly towards and away from their partner's palm. How does this feel? What sensations are you experiencing? How do the sensations change?

Now swap over. The person whose hand was moving should now keep their hand still, and the other person moves their hand around (as described above). Again, how does this feel? What sensations are you experiencing? How do the sensations change? Now both move your hands, together and away from each other. How does this feel? What sensations are you experiencing? How do the sensations change?

You are feeling the other person's energy field, and you are feeling the reaction of your energy field top the other person's energy field. You have always been able to do this. It has always been right there in front of you. To experience this you have simply changed your focus.

Feel Energy on a Partner's Head & Shoulders

You will need someone to do this exercise with you.

One person sits in a dining chair and closes their eyes. They are the 'guinea pig' and just sit there throughout the exercise. The other person stands behind them.

The person standing up starts with their hands raised, hovering about 12" (30cm) above the subject's head, palms down. Now bring your hands slowly down, bouncing them down until you feel that your hands are resting on the subject's energy field. Now move your hands away again and 'bounce' them down onto an adjacent area above the head. Feel the energy field over different parts of the subject's head, the forehead, the back of the head and the temples. Is the energy field the same distance away all round the head? Does it feel the same in all places? Feel the energy field over the shoulders, above, behind and in front. How does the energy field feel here?

Push Someone off Balance using Energy

You will need someone to do this exercise with you.

Your 'victim' should stand up, standing still with their eyes closed. They should not stand stiff and rigid, but simply stand in a relaxed way, and they should be told that if they feel that their body wants to drift either forwards or backwards then they should not resist: they should simply allow their body to drift, and if they need to take a step back to steady themselves then they should do that.

Stand about 2m (6ft) behind the person with your hands in front of your chest, palms facing away from you and towards the victim, as if you were going to push their shoulders. Slowly move towards them until you have an impression that your hands are resting on the person's energy field. You may have some physical sensations – maybe the same or similar to the sensations you experienced when you were feeling the energy field in the above exercises – or you may simply 'know' that your hands have made contact with the person's energy field. Now you are going to alternate between doing two things:

Deliberately 'squash' the person's energy field for 20-30 seconds, moving your palms closer and closer to their body intending that you are compressing their energy field against them.

Deliberately pull their energy field away from their body for 20-30 seconds, by moving your palms away from their body. You can take a step back. You can take several steps back, and you imagine that their energy field is being stretched out like elastic, being pulled away from their body.

Do not alternate quickly between pushing and pulling. That won't work. You need to be either squashing their energy field for a while, or pulling it away from their body for a while. Alternate between the two.

What happens? Most people will find that they lean forward or backwards. People lean back more readily than they move forward. Some people will resist and although you cannot see any movements, they can feel the pull. Some people are pulled backwards so powerfully that they have to take a step back to steady themselves.

Your body is used to being in the centre of its energy field, and if you distort that then your body seems to want to drift into a position of balance.

Play with 'Energy Balls'

You will need someone to do this exercise with you.

Hold your hands approximately 9" (22cm) apart and imagine that energy is flooding through your palms into the space between. You are building up a ball of energy between your hands. Bounce your hands against this ball of energy and feel it become stronger and denser over a period of a couple of minutes. When you feel ready, slowly pass the energy ball to someone sitting next to you and place it gently in their hands. They will be holding their hands together, palms cupped, ready to receive the ball from you. As you place the ball in their hands and release it, what can they feel? Many people can feel pressure, heaviness, or fizzing; sensations vary. Can that person now build up and intensify this energy ball and then pass it back to you? What do you feel?

Students' Experiences: playing with energy and scanning

"I have tried out my scanning on people, my cat and a horse ! With each one I have felt pretty much a constant tingling in my hand but then also a heat in the base of my palm when over certain areas, which seems to be where there is a 'problem'. Again like last week, I seem to be able to feel things better with my right hand and it feels right to use this hand more than the left"
"T.B." from Norfolk

"Energy exercises (individual) carried out. Feel more of a pull on my hands when I part them rather than too much when I put them together. Strong feelings on the lower thumb (the fat part!) as if lines anre attached to them and when pulled apart there is resistance.

Tried again, tingles in fingers. Still don't really feel anything tangible between my hands, but a strong pull and drag is felt when I move my hands to and fro."
Jason Brown from North Wales

"Feel energy on a partner's hand: During the first stage, my hands were very hot and there was a tingle on my fingertips. My partner felt this from me. Nothing tangible between our hands but there was 'something'.

Worked on both hands. My partner said that with the left hand he felt like I was sending an electric shock to him, a very weak current.

During the second stage, my partner again felt a very strong electric sensation. I felt my fingers to be hot and tingly. Still difficult to discern if there is anything tangible between us (so to speak!).

Moving my hand up and down, side to side, my partner again felt the electric flow, whereas I felt a difference between when my hand was over his or not. My partner commented that he felt most of the energy coming from my fingertips, rather than from the whole hand. Again, for much of it my fingers were tingly.

On my own: Tingly hands and fingers, with even the wrists beginning to tingle. Again, feel a drag effect as I pull away my hands. Still can't really feel 'something' between my hands."
Jason Brown from North Wales

"Every day I have tried to feel the energy between my hands and friend's hands and body. I was not feeling much most at the beginning and sometimes was finding it hard to concentrate but the last couple of days I can feel like a bouncy substance, the most fascinating one was pushing my friend off-balance and he could really feel like a push."
Bruno Cassani from Essex

"I have practiced my energy exercises with friends and colleagues. The experience is so different from one person to the other : sometimes it is a strong tingling sensation or warmth, other times is just like foam between our hands, once we did not feel anything at all."
Bruno Cassani from Essex

"I have been playing with energy and can feel it between my hands. My hands feel tingly, almost a 'fizzy' feeling, and it feels like there is actually an object there. I have practised with my partner feeling each others energy force and we could both feel the energy moving along with our hands on alternate turns."
Emily Cook from Oxfordshire

"Energy play - I have had two volunteers for my practice one being my dog who loves me giving him 15mins direct attention, with my dog I found the energy quite quickly and especially around the back legs and lower back. The heat I felt above and around his face and ears was incredible and he didn-t seem to enjoy the play so much around these area's but go across his back and legs and he was away, fast asleep.

I also practiced scanning on my partner around the head and shoulders initially I felt no energy around the shoulders and upper arm and yet after a short period playing with these area's my partner felt the heat. Not as much as she did when I was around the top of the head and forehead where my fingers seemed to tingling strongly.I bounced with the energy around these area's and felt comfortable approx.
1" above the body even around the back where I thought I would need to actually touch to feel anything.

Finally.. I was intrigued to find out what the energy would feel like in a tree so having plucked up courage and made sure no one was watching I began to scan different tree's. I found the older tree's difficult to feel anything but the younger ones were fantastic my hands were buzzing from the moment I put them near the trunk."
Paul Harrison from Hertfordshire

"The hand energy exercises have produced a ball like feeling between my hands and my partners hands (although he says he can't feel anything i can) when i moved my hands up and down the feeling was like rolling a ball between them."
Niki Leach from Tyne and Wear

"With the "playing with energy" exercises I felt the energy most when doing the solitary exercise. I could definitely feel a ball of energy and was able to play with it and bounce the energy backwards and forwards. While feeling the energy with a partner's hand, we both felt the energy when our hands were about 2 inches away from eachothers. We could feel heat, and I felt a fuzzing in my hands. I did find it harder to feel the energy while moving my hand up and down away from my partner's hand. I seemed to loose the energy a bit. My partner had the same experience. We could bounce the energy between us if our hands were a few inches away but further away it was more difficult.

Scanned partner. The energy field varied around the head and shoulders. The energy felt most dense around the temples. Felt a magnetic repulsion there. (Went back there later and still felt it). Partner said he felt buzzing in his ears while I was scanning his temples, and it carried on buzzing after the exercise for a few minutes.

Scanned sister. Felt heat about 2 inches from crown and around shoulders, but surprised to find a wall of energy around throat area. It was very dense and the energy felt very strong. When I bounced the energy the sensation was unpleasant for my sister. She said she felt a pressure on her throat and found it hard to breathe, so I stopped pushing and pulling the energy. (She is very stressed at the moment and also has an underactive thyroid). I went back to the energy around the throat later and the enery was still very heavy and dense all around the area."
Lindsay Long from Surrey

"I had no problem feeling the energy between my hands and around my partners hand. I experienced tingling and heat in my hands some areas felt warmer than others. I also could feel some pulsing in my hands like a magnetic pull. When my partner moved their hand around mine I could feel tingling and this pull. I did these exercises everyday for 10-20 mins. The exercise where your partner is stood up and you move the energy backwards and forewards behind them I did 3 times that week. I felt that I could move the energy in and out slowly and my partner felt a bit wobbly."
Susan Naylor from West Yorkshire

"I have performed the scanning exercises and hand positions on my partners and friends head and shoulders this week. I can feel different levels of energy around them some areas seem to pulsate. My husband said that after treating his head and shoulders this week he felt tingling and heat in his forehead

much more than he had before. My friends could feel some tingling but in different places, Neck for one person and left shoulder for the other.

I tried feeling the energy around my small elderly dog who has arthritis there were quite a few areas where the energy felt like someone was sticking pins in my hands and I had to stop after five minutes, although it hadn't slowed down yet.

I was able to feel the energy around one of my house plants, it was much stronger than I thought it would be for a small plant .

Trees- Wow very powerful the energy they radiate could Knock you of your feet. The pulsing in my hands was incredible."
Susan Naylor from West Yorkshire

"Energy between hands - Firsty my hands became all fizzy. As I moved them together they felt drawn together, it was as though they were being pulled towards each other by a very strong magnet. As I moved them apart again I came to a point which felt inbetween the magnatism, where they didnt want to move in either direction.

Energy Hands - During this exercise my partner felt warmth and tingly in his knuckles. We both felt real heat when moving close, the closer we got the hotter the sensation and my partner felt pressure in his wrist. The feeling got cooler and cooler as each of us took turns in moving away. I could feel a sponge sensation around his hand which got lesser as I moved in different directions and stronger in others. At the bottom of his hand, my hands became extremely warm but the sensation died down when I moved position.

I practised this exercise with two other people and although I had the same spongy, warm sensation which varied as to where my hand was, they only felt a warm tingling when our hands were facing.

Energy between hands - As the week has gone on I have felt that my ball of energy has grown considerably. It is much bigger now than it was at the start of the week. I can feel a real bounciness with a big distance between my hands. The further away I move them the lesser the strength in the bounciness until there is nothing at all. When I move my hands closer again the fizzing, bouncy, spongy feeling returns stronger and stronger."
Sarah Quinn from Kent

DAILY ENERGY EXERCISES

Doing energy work on yourself, regularly, is the foundation of your Reiki practice. In this section you are going to discover how to practise the exercises that Mikao Usui taught at First Degree level, and you are going to find out how those simple exercises were developed and expanded upon in the Usui Reiki Ryoho Gakkai – the Usui Memorial Society in Japan.

The energy exercises that you will be practising have the following effects. They will:

1. Clear and cleanse your energy system
2. Help to move your energy system more into a state of balance
3. Help to ground you
4. Help to build up your personal energy reserves
5. Develop your ability as a channel for Reiki
6. Help to develop your sensitivity to the flow of energy
7. Help to develop your intuitive side

The energy exercises will focus on an area of your body called the "Tanden" ("Dantien" or "Tan T'ien" in Chinese) which is an energy centre located two fingerbreadths (3 – 5cm) below your tummy button and 1/3rd of the way into your body. You will be imagining that you are drawing energy – or light – into the Tanden and then moving the energy on elsewhere.

The Tanden

The Tanden point is seen as the centre of our selves from the Oriental point of view, a seat of power, the centre of our intuitive faculties, the centre of life. Drawing energy into your Tanden is drawing energy into the centre of your life and soul. This area acts as a power centre that allows the amazing feats of martial artists to be performed, but also acts as the source of inspiration in Oriental flower arranging and calligraphy. Meditation, exercise techniques like Tai Chi and QiGong, martial arts and Usui Reiki can all develop the Tanden.

The Tanden is thus seen as your personal energy store, the focus of your personal power. In energy cultivation techniques like Tai Chi and Qi Gong the Tanden is the place where you store the energy that you are cultivating.

Conversely, martial artist might draw down energy from the sun to store in their Tanden before moving on to spar with an opponent.

The Tanden is also seen as the centre of your intuition and your creativity, so when people carry out Japanese calligraphy, or Ikebana (flower arranging) or the Tea ceremony, they are focusing their attention on the Tanden, the centre of their being.

Two Simple Energy Exercises

Mikao Usui taught his first degree students two simple exercises that they would carry out daily. The exercises are called “Kenyoku” and “Joshin Kokkyu Ho”.

Kenyoku

This means 'Dry Bathing' or 'Brushing Off'. Kenyoku can be seen as a way of getting rid of negative energy. It has correspondences with Taoist massage, or meridian massage. Here is what to do:

Place the fingertips of your right hand near the top of the left shoulder, where the collarbone meets the bulge of the shoulder. The hand is lying flat on your chest.

Draw your flat hand down and across the chest in a straight line, over the base of the sternum (where your breastbone stops and your abdomen starts, in the midline) and down to the right hip. Exhale as you do this.

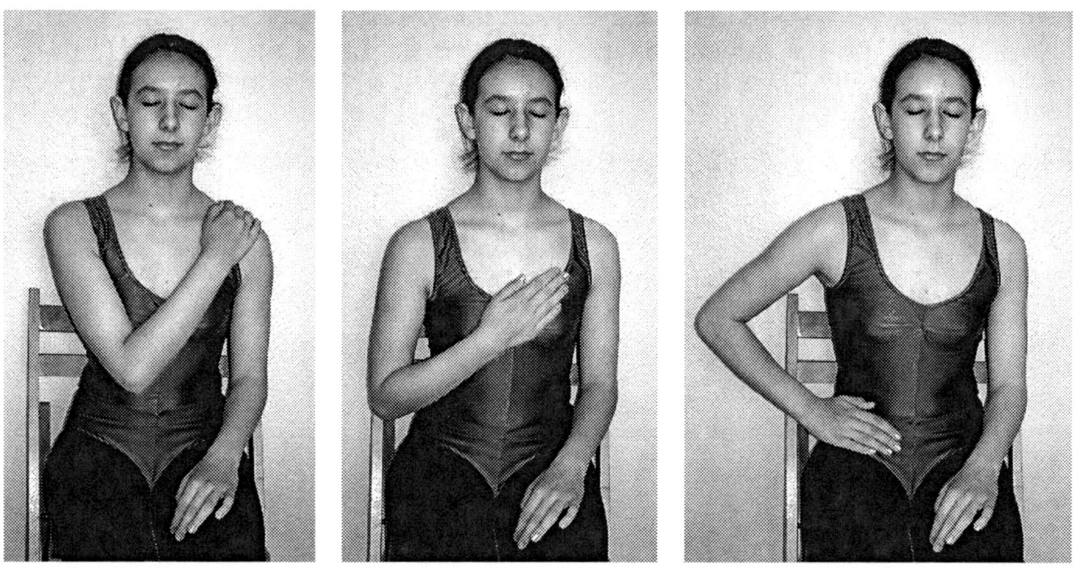

Do the same on the right side, using your left hand. Draw your left hand from the right shoulder, in a straight line across the sternum, to the left hip, and again exhale as you make the downward movement.

Do the same on the left side again (like you did at the start), so you will have carried out movements with your right hand, left hand, and right hand again.

Now put your right fingertips on the outer edge of the left shoulder, at the top of your slightly outstretched left arm, with your fingertips pointing sideways away from your body.

Move your right hand, flattened, along the outside of your arm, all the way to the fingertips and beyond, all the while keeping the left arm straight. Exhale as you do this.

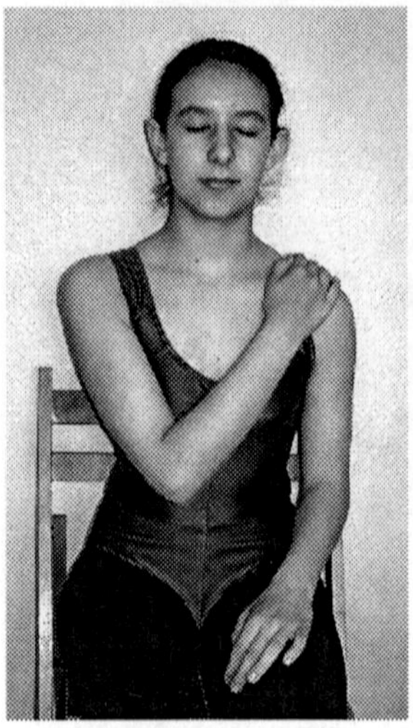 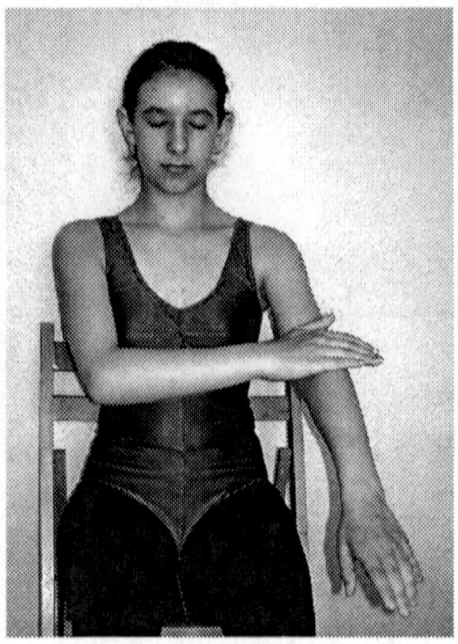 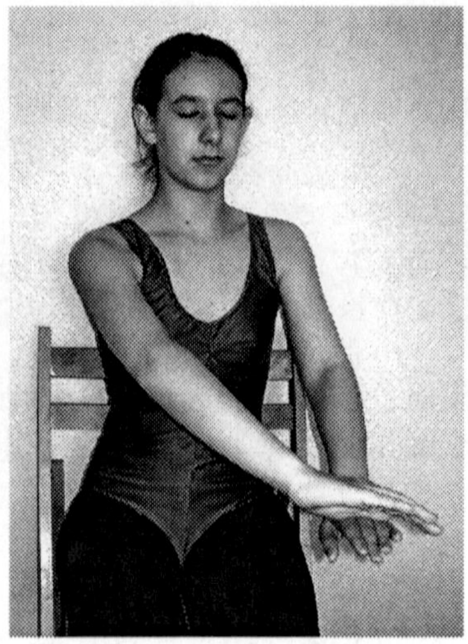

Repeat this process on the right side, with the left hand placed on the right shoulder, and move it down the right arm to the fingertips and beyond. Exhale as you do this.

Repeat the process on the left side again, so you will have carried out movements with your right hand, left hand, and right hand again, like before.

Joshin Kokkyu Ho

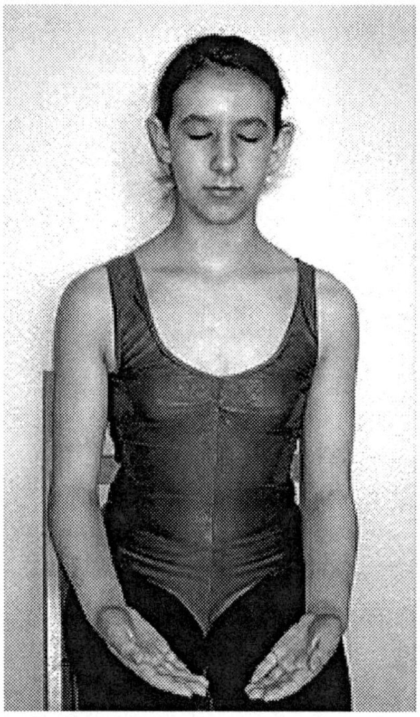

This means 'Technique for Purification of the Spirit' or 'Soul Cleansing Breathing Method'. This is a meditation that focuses on the Tanden point.

Put your hands on your lap with your palms facing upwards and breathe naturally through your nose. Focus on your Tanden point and relax.

When you breathe in, visualise energy or light flooding into your crown chakra and passing into your Tanden and, as you pause before exhaling, feel that energy expand throughout your body, melting all your tensions.

When you breathe out, imagine that the energy floods out of your body in all directions as far as infinity. You should soon feel energy/tingling in your hands and even in your feet, as the meditation progresses!
It does not matter how you actually visualise the energy. Some people can visualise really easily, while others find it very difficult to 'see' a visual image in their mind's eye. This is not a problem because it is the underlying intent that is the important thing. The energy moves in response to your intent. For many people, visualising is a good way of focusing your intent in a particular way, but even with no imagined visual images, the energy will still move as you intend it to... so instead of visualising you might 'have in mind' or 'feel' that the energy is moving to a particular place, and that will work just as well.

So the energy will follow your thoughts, follow your focus. If you focus your attention or focus your awareness on your Tanden then you will be placing energy there. It is said that Ki is moved by the mind: where the attention goes, ki flows"

On a more esoteric note, by directing your attention towards and moving energy to the Tanden, the integration of body and mind is deepened and strengthened, and the Spirit is dynamically grounded in the Present Moment.

A simple sequence

Follow these instructions to put together a short sequence of energy exercises:

1. Close your eyes and take a few long deep breaths
2. Focus your attention on your Tanden point
3. Perform Kenyoku
4. Perform Joshin Kokkyu Ho for 5-15 minutes
5. Be still for a while

If you are not used to meditating then you are likely to find that your mind wanders sometimes. This is normal and this is human, and you do not need to be perfect in order to achieve great benefits from using Reiki on yourself. If thoughts intrude, pay them no attention; let them drift past and simply bring your attention back to what you were doing: focus your attention on your Tanden and again be open, and empty, feel yourself merging with the energy and becoming one with it, imagine yourself disappearing into the energy.

With practice, over time, you will find that your mind will intrude less.

'Hatsu Rei Ho'

In the Usui Reiki Ryoho Gakkai – the Usui Memorial Society – a longer sequence of energy exercises has been used: a sequence called 'Hatsurei ho' which is clearly based upon the simple exercises that Usui Sensei taught at First Degree. Kenyoku reappears, as does Joshin Kokkyu ho, but there are a few other simple stages to follow.

'Hatsu Rei Ho' seems to originate in Tendai Buddhism, and the exercises have correspondences with Tibetan Buddhist purification rituals, Taoist or meridian massage, and QiGong too. It was only in Autumn 1999 that the techniques were revealed in the Western world by a man called Hiroshi Doi who is a member of the Usui Reiki Ryoho Gakkai. Hatsu Rei Ho is designed to be carried out every day for at about 10-15 minutes.

The Japanese word 'Ho' means 'technique', so you will find it attached to a number of Reiki techniques used in the 'Gakkai. 'Hatsu Rei' means 'start up Reiki', and 'Hatsu Rei Ho' can be taken as meaning a technique to start up and strengthen your Reiki.

You can see this method working with the Reiju empowerments to allow the student to develop: Reiju can be seen as transmitting the Reiki ability to another person, and Hatsu Rei Ho can be viewed as a way of strengthening that connection and purifying the Reiki energy that passes through the student. Reiju and Hatsu Rei Ho are a way of enhancing the student's intuitive abilities and accelerating their spiritual development.

This is How to do Hatsu Rei Ho...

Stage One: Relax

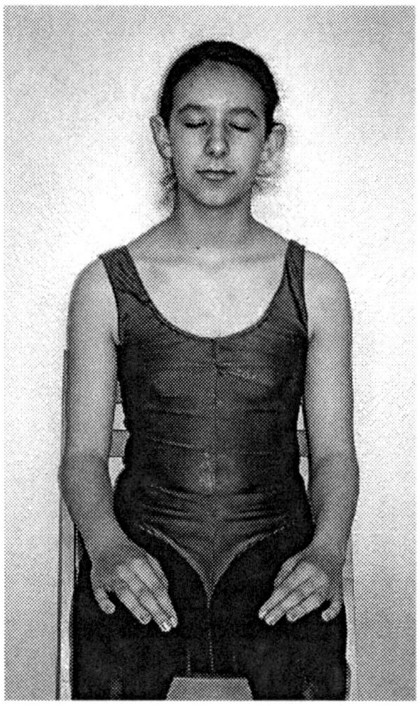

Relax and close your eyes, and place your hands palms down on your lap.

Focus your attention on your Tanden point: an energy centre two fingerbreadths (3-5 cm) below your tummy button and 1/3 of the way into your body.

Stage Two: Mokunen (Focusing)

Say to yourself "I'm going to start Hatsu Rei now".

Stage Three: Kenyoku

This means 'Dry Bathing' or 'Brushing Off'

Kenyoku can be seen as a way of getting rid of negative energy. It has correspondences with Taoist massage, or meridian massage. Here is what to do:

Place the fingertips of your right hand near the top of the left shoulder, where the collarbone meets the bulge of the shoulder. The hand is lying flat on your chest.

Draw your flat hand down and across the chest in a straight line, over the base of the sternum (where your breastbone stops and your abdomen starts, in the midline) and down to the right hip. Exhale as you do this.

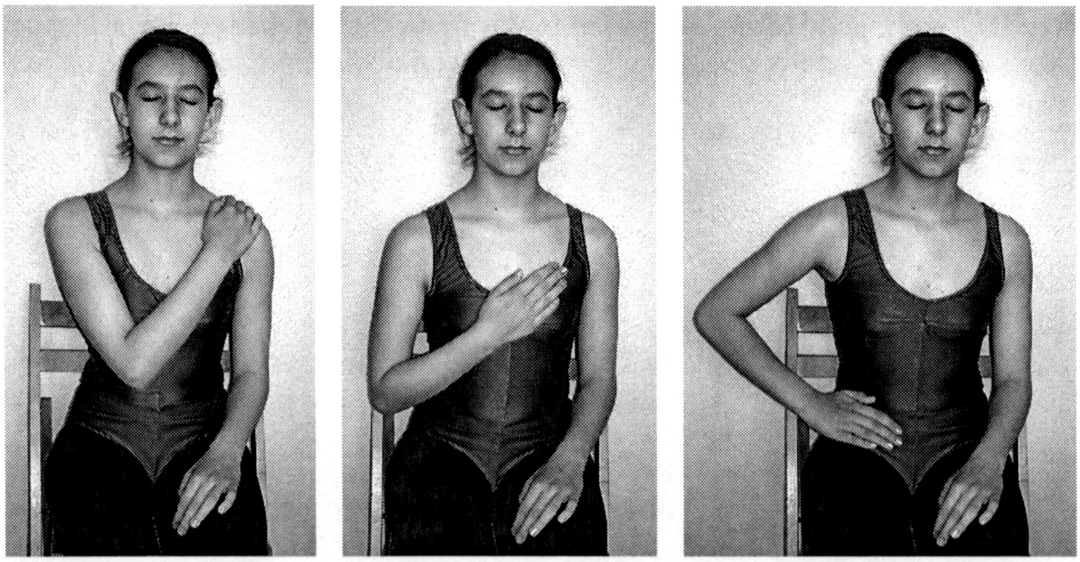

Do the same on the right side, using your left hand. Draw your left hand from the right shoulder, in a straight line across the sternum, to the left hip, and again exhale as you make the downward movement.

Do the same on the left side again (like you did at the start), so you will have carried out movements with your right hand, left hand, and right hand again.

Now put your right fingertips on the outer edge of the left shoulder, at the top of your slightly outstretched left arm, with your fingertips pointing sideways away from your body.

Move your right hand, flattened, along the outside of your arm, all the way to the fingertips and beyond, all the while keeping the left arm straight. Exhale as you do this.

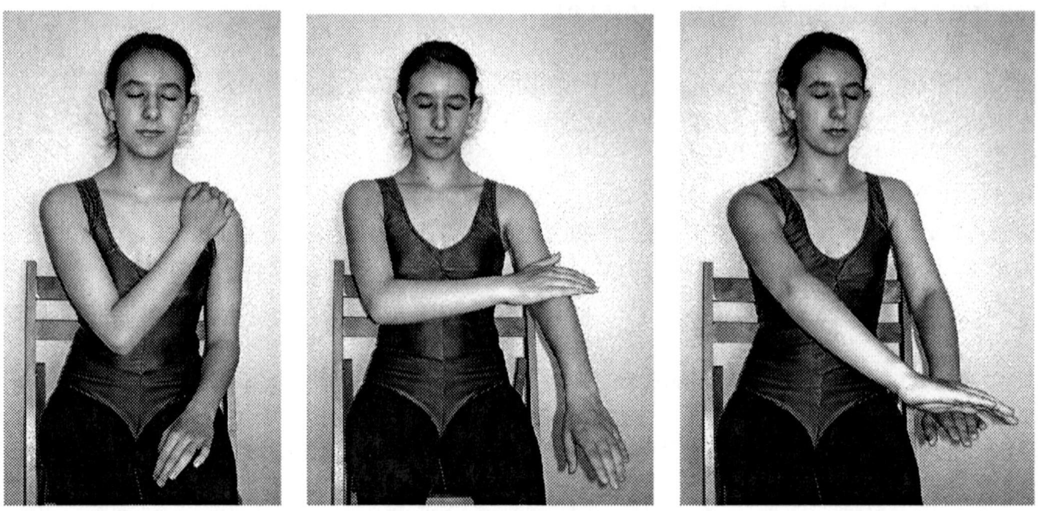

Repeat this process on the right side, with the left hand placed on the right shoulder, and move it down the right arm to the fingertips and beyond. Exhale as you do this.

Repeat the process on the left side again, so you will have carried out movements with your right hand, left hand, and right hand again, like before.

Stage Four: Connect to Reiki

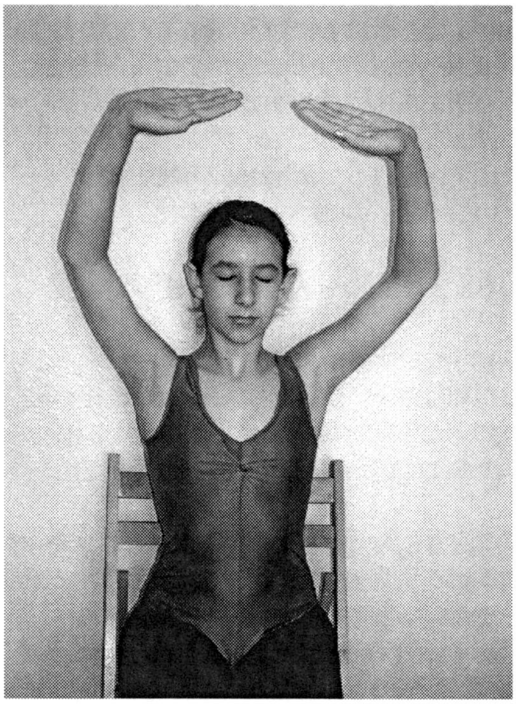

Raise your hands high up in the air on either side of your head, with your palms facing the sky and your fingers pointing towards the midline.

Connect to Reiki by visualising energy or white light cascading into your hands and running through your arms into your body. Feel the sensations.

As you become aware of Reiki flowing, slowly lower your hands.

This position is the first of the 'Eight Brocades' in QiGong: connecting heaven and earth.

Stage Five: Joshin Kokkyu Ho

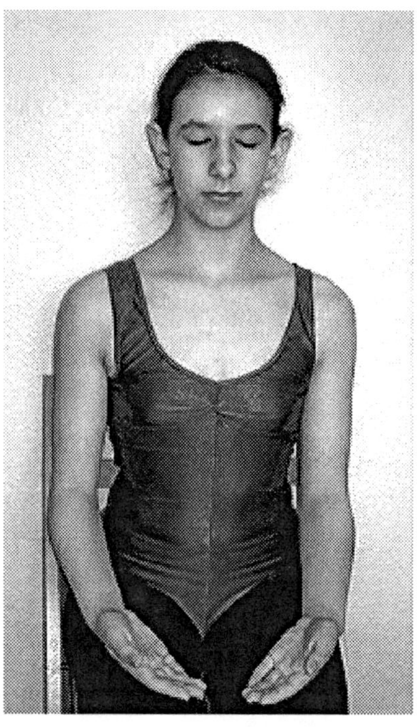

This means 'Technique for Purification of the Spirit' or 'Soul Cleansing Breathing Method'. This is a meditation that focuses on the Tanden point.

Put your hands on your lap with your palms facing upwards and breathe naturally through your nose. Focus on your Tanden point and relax.

When you breathe in, visualise energy or light flooding into your crown chakra and passing into your Tanden and, as you pause before exhaling, feel that energy expand throughout your body, melting all your tensions.

When you breathe out, imagine that the energy floods out of your body in all directions as far as infinity. You should soon feel energy/tingling in your hands and even in your feet, as the meditation progresses!

Stage Six: Gassho

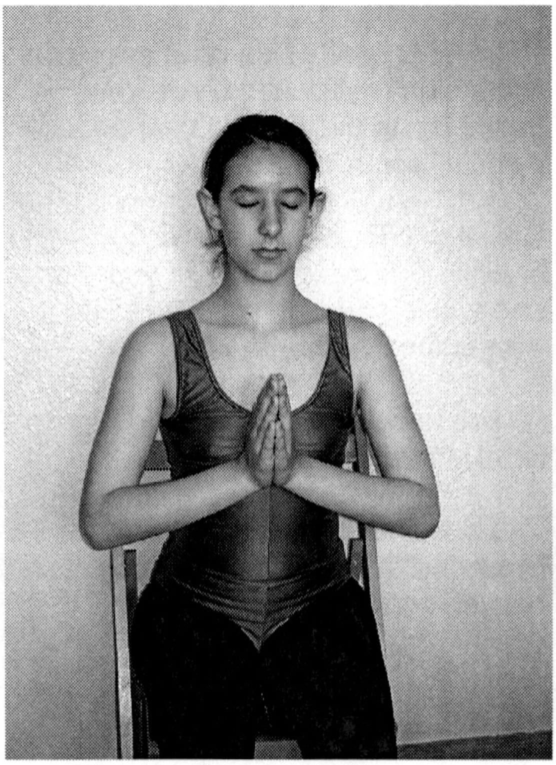

Gassho means 'hands together', and the correct position to hold is to have your hands together in front of your chest (like praying hands) a little higher that your heart, so that you could breathe out onto your fingertips if you wanted to.

Hold this position for meditation.

An important aspect of this meditation is that you should focus your awareness on the point where your middle fingers touch.

You might try putting your tongue up to touch the roof of your mouth with each in-breath, and release the tongue on each out-breath, and see if this makes any difference to your experience of this stage.

Stage Seven: Seishin Toitsu

This means 'my mind is focused' or 'my spirit is gathered', and is the stage when Reiju is given by teachers in the Gakkai.

Stay in the Gassho position.

When you breathe in, visualise energy or light flooding into your hands and passing into your Dantien: breathe in through your hands.

Feel the energy accumulating and building there.

When you breathe out, visualise that the energy stored in your Dantien floods out through your hands.

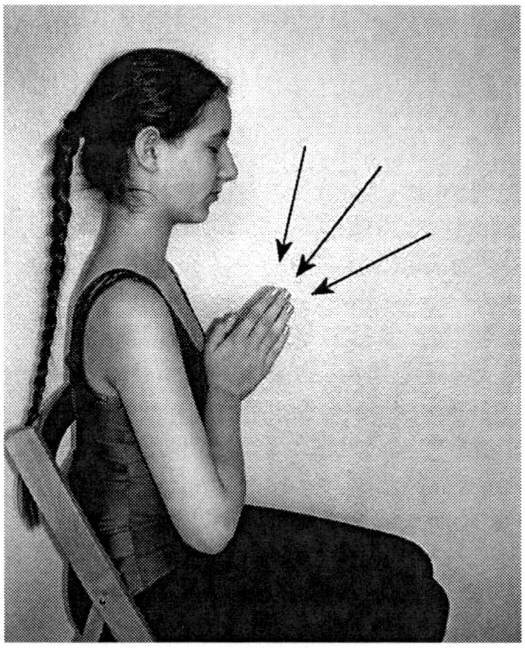

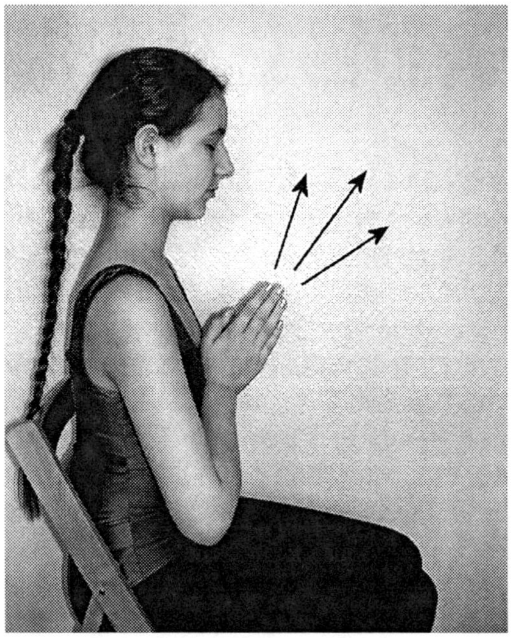

Stage Eight: Gokai Sansho (optional)

Say 5 Principles aloud three times.

> *Just for today*
> *Do not anger*
> *Do not worry*
> *Be humble*
> *Be honest*
> *Be compassionate towards yourself and others*

Maybe you would like to mentally review the principles, and dwell on their meaning for you.

Stage Nine: Mokunen

Put your hands back on to your laps with your palms down. Say to yourself that "I've finished Hatsu Rei Ho now" to your sub-conscious.

Open your eyes and shake your hands up/down/left/right for a few seconds.

Essay on Seishin Toitsu

To give you an insight into the sort of state that is being cultivated when you practise Hatsurei ho, and particularly the stage called "Seishin Toitsu", here is an article written by Eri Takase, the Japanese Master Calligrapher who does all our calligraphy work. Eri Takase is ranked as Shihan in Japan's most prestigious calligraphic society, the Bokuteki-kai. She is among the few to have won several best of category awards in national competitions and her work has been displayed in the Osaka Museum of Arts. Master Takase has been teaching Japanese Calligraphy for more than twenty years and for the past ten years has been teaching Japanese and non-Japanese speaking students in the United States. The article is reproduced with Eri's permission.

> *"When in Japan I will visit Zen temples for what is called Seishin Toitsu which my dictionary says means "concentration". While this definition is true, it is also unsatisfactory.*
>
> *By stepping through the temple gate, I am transported to a world of harmony and tranquillity. The temple will be, perhaps, covered in early autumn. Around me the multi-coloured leaves will fall like jewels to the dew covered ground. Here there is no male and female. There is no age. There is no social standing.*
>
> *It is this place and this state of mind I come to when my spirit (Seishin) is gathered (Toitsu), when my mind (Seishin) is one (Toitsu). Gone are the myriad distractions and all that remains is myself, focused and attentive on the here and now. All is equal and in harmony and this transcends all.*
>
> *I first met with Japanese Calligraphy when I was just six years old. I can say it did not appeal to me then. Especially the part where I would have to tediously grind the sumi ink against the ink stone for what seemed an eternity. And it helped not at all that my instructor would say mysteriously that the essence of calligraphy can be found in the grinding of the ink.*
>
> *It is the grinding of the ink, a metaphor for the process and the form, that takes one from the myriad distractions of life to that Zen temple in early autumn. To the state of Seishin Toitsu. As the water takes the ink and as the colour approaches the subtle shade, I am possessed of a strong energy that is focused and flowing. There is no hesitation and no doubt. When the ink is complete, my spirit (Seishin) is focused (Toitsu) in the here and now. And my mind is one with the task. This is Seishin Toitsu. This is the mindset that without which there would be no calligraphy.*
>
> *Only when one is centred and focused can one can act.*
>
> *In contrast, one might imagine someone arranging flowers by choosing one flower and putting it this way. Then after some thought replacing it with another flower placed another way. And continuing in this manner. Trying this and then trying that. Looking at it from this angle and that. Perhaps even asking the opinion of someone nearby. While flower arranging does not condone this style, one can certainly arrange flowers in this manner and*

stumble upon a very lovely combination. The final arrangement does not reflect every detail of the creation.

And despite all the fussing, one can still end up with an exquisite end product. But with the calligraphy brush, as with the sword, one cannot escape from the effects of indecisiveness and hesitation. One cannot start over. One cannot change what has already been done. With calligraphy as with the tea ceremony as with the Martial Arts, all movements are visible and an integral part of the art. The speed with which the line is drawn. The pause. The fluidity of one movement into the next. A powerful line. A gentle line. All visible. All an integral part of the art.

This is the nature of Japanese Calligraphy and the Martial Arts. It has been this way in ancient times and it is this way today. The end result is not the point. The end result will happen only by focusing on the process. Only when the mind (Seishin) is one (Toitsu) will the end result flow from the act. And so it is the process: the planning, the grinding of the ink, the mental preparation, the Seishin Toitsu that is all important.

And so it is not out of place for individuals to practice several of these arts. Miyamoto Musashi (1584-1645), who authored "The Book of Five Rings" in the last year of his life, is renowned today for not only his swordsmanship, but also for his calligraphy and painting. Japan's most famous generals of the 16th century Toyotomi Hideyoshi and Tokugawa Ieyasu were known both for the uniting of Japan and for their fine skills in the Tea Ceremony. The common thread being Seishin Toitsu."

Receiving distant empowerments

If you are following one of our home study courses, you will be receiving a series of distant empowerments during the early stages of your course, and then you will be tuning into our weekly distant Reiju empowerments, which you can tune into at any time on a Monday, during the course and subsequently. We recommend that you tune in every week.

If you are attending a live course you will receive some empowerments on the day of your course, and we recommend that you then tune into our distant empowerments each week, some time on a Monday.

Tuning into the empowerment is simple. While you can simply sit down and call in your empowerment, we recommend that you tune into your weekly empowerment at the end of your daily energy exercises.

So if you are performing Kenyoku/Joshin Kokkyu ho, stop the visualisation of Joshin Kokkyu ho and bring your hands into the prayer position; say to yourself "I'm ready to receive my empowerment from Taggart now...". See what you notice, and stay in that position until you feel that the empowerment is basically over. Then bring your hands down into your lap, palms down, take a few deep breaths, and then slowly bring yourself back.

If you are performing Hatsurei ho, after the Seishin Toitsu stage you should keep your hands together in the prayer position and stop the visualisation of Seishin Toitsu. Say to yourself "I'm ready to receive my empowerment from Taggart now…". See what you notice, and stay in that position until you feel that the empowerment is basically over. Then bring your hands down into your lap, palms down, take a few deep breaths, say to yourself "I'm finishing Hatsurei now…" and then slowly bring yourself back.

Other uses for parts of Hatsu Rei Ho

Kenyoku (Dry Bathing)

Kenyoku can be carried out at the beginning and end of every treatment by way of disconnecting you from your surroundings, disconnecting you from your patient, and disconnecting you from your thoughts. It can be used to protect yourself from worrisome or stressful situations, to stop things from bothering you, to stop you from 'bringing work home'.

Joshin Kokkyu Ho

You can use a variation of this technique before you start a treatment, by way of 'getting the energy flowing', and during a treatment to increase the flow of Reiki through you. Try visualising that the energy is not flowing out of you in all directions, but just through your hands and feet, to get things flowing nicely before you start a treatment. Then just send the Reiki through your hands once you are treating someone. Try this variation of Joshin Kokkyu Ho throughout a treatment, or only on selected areas, for example 'hotspots', where there is a greater need for energy.

Also, you can use a variation of this technique to send Reiki through your body to areas of need - without using your hands on yourself. For example, draw energy into your Dantien, feel it intensify, and then move the energy to your forehead, or your back, or your stomach, and see what you notice.

Gassho

Frank Arjava Petter recommends that this method can be usefully carried out for 20-30 minutes each day, in the morning or evening. At the end of your long Gassho session, Petter recommends that you 'enjoy the silence in your heart'.

Other ways of making your Reiki Strong

Apart from carrying out Hatsu Rei Ho, and treating yourself regularly, there are other ways that you can ensure that you are a clear channel for the energy.

Treat Other People

Whenever you treat another person you are sending Reiki through your energy channels, and the more you do this the more smoothly and intensely the energy will flow, particularly in the early stages after having been attuned.

The first time I treated five people in a day I was so, so clam, content, serene... I almost floated home. Treating others can be an extremely relaxing experience, and you may find that you have difficulty keeping awake yourself!

Practice Other Energy Cultivation Techniques

Oriental energy cultivation techniques like Tai Chi and QiGong deal with essentially the same sort of energy as Reiki practitioners. Reiki people who practice these systems are likely to be more effective channels than Reiki people who don't, all other things being equal.

If you already practice Tai Chi or QiGong you are likely to experience the energy flow more intensely once you have been attuned to Reiki. Reiki practitioners who take up these techniques are likely to be more sensitive to the energies they are working with than their non-Reiki compatriots at the same stage as them.

Yoga again deals with essentially the same energy that is channelled when you practice Reiki, and being attuned to Reiki can enhance your experience of this energy exercise system also.

Students' experiences: Hatsurei ho

"On the first day that I did my exercises, I felt really drained and felt like I was coming down with a cold, and then yesterday and today I have come down with a full blown cold ! But the interesting point to this is that it is all in the right hand side - my right eye is running, my right nostril is blocked and the right hand side of my throat is very sore. When I do my exercises, I feel lots of energy in my right hand but very little in my left"
"T.B." from Norfolk

"This week I have found the Hatsurei ho really strengthening for me in terms of it bringing me a great deal of calm which has been good for me as I have had a very stressful week. I seem to be able to think a lot clearer afterwards and also I seem to have a lot more patience and the ability to see through the 'fog'. Also when I join my hands and do the breathing, I can feel the energy between my palms in like the marshmallow effect that you talk about, and feel my hands moving apart as I do the breathing."
"T.B." from Norfolk

"The daily energy exercises are brilliant and i can definitely feel a lot, especially on the first time. I had been doing joshin kokkyu ho for about 20minutes and was very relaxed. I moved on to the gassho position and could feel it straight away. I felt like i was zooming out of my body and floating, this lasted a couple of minutes. I then seemed to come right back down again very quickly, then back up again. It was almost like an out of body experience. I do not know exactly how long this lasted, and i kept my eyes closed throughout. My hands were together in the prayer position and the top half of my fingers were tingling, but this was more of a pulsing sensation. Through the whole of this i had a sensation on my forehead, like someone had their finger pressed in the middle above my eyes. I have also recently been finding out about chakras, so i take this as a good sign! When i did open my eyes i just had to sit for about 5 minutes and absorb everything in the room, everything seemed clearer and brighter. I have been practising this every day and feeling the effects, although the first time was the most intense."
Emily Cook from Oxfordshire

"I have been practising hatsurei ho every day and i feel that my connection with the energy is becoming stronger and clearer. I can sometimes feel the sensations coming to me almost as soon as i sit down to practice. sometimes it may take a while longer, but i feel that it is definitely becoming easier for me to connect"
Emily Cook from Oxfordshire

"The first time I did the Joshin Kokkyo ho , i felt like i had sunshine behind my eyes and I couldn't stop smiling. My hands were red hot and my feet became very tingly. The Reiju empowerment felt like being under a warm shower or waterfall with energy running down my insides and outsides in big droplets. These feelings have happened in all the exercises so far until the fifth time and then a very strange feeling happened. When i was breathing the energy in through the crown of my head i could actually feel a soft breath in through my head. When i finished and touched the top of my head it was red hot."
Niki Leach from Tyne and Wear

"On the 4th Dec. woke late (slept 10 hrs rather than my usual 8 hrs). Did my energy exercise. Whilst visualising light entering my crown I was aware of a coolness around my head and was more aware of that area than usual. Then I felt complete calmness and serenity. I saw flashing colours of blue and green and my eyes were twitching uncontrollably. Tears flooded down my face, and I felt total peace (it reminded me of how I had felt while having a Reiki treatment a few weeks previously). It was as if a peaceful presence was surrounding me. This all lasted about 10 minutes."
Lindsay Long from Surrey

"With the Hatsurei I can feel energy flowing in and out of me as channels are being opened. My hands start to tingle, and feel warm as do my feet. I feel connected to all things in the Universe by this energy. It is also incredibly peaceful and relaxing."
Susan Naylor from West Yorkshire

"One evening, while doing my energy exercises my hands again became very warm and mildly tingly but I had a strange sensation in my mind. It was almost like drifting in and out of something. On completion of this my daughter came to say goodnight to me. I placed my hands on her face to pull her closer and kiss her goodnight and she actually recoiled away from me in shock proclaiming that my hands were to hot! I was extremely surprised by this reaction and placed my hands on my partner who also agreed they were radiating a vast amount of heat."
Sarah Quinn from Kent

"During stage four (connecting to Reiki) my hands felt warm when breathing in. However, throughout the rest of the exercise my hands felt hot when exhaling. Hands felt tingly and hot throughout and almost felt unattached from the rest of my body at the end of the exercise. Never felt hands so hot, they have always been cold throughout my life!"
Sarah Quinn from Kent

"Felt fantastic tonight and was really easy! Found I stayed completely focused throughout and the visualisation was much, much easier than normal. Came naturally tonight, didn't have to work at it. Hands grew very hot during Joshin Kokkyu Ho (stage 5) and Seishin Toitsu (stage 7). "
Sarah Quinn from Kent

"I'm feeling more confident about my hatsurei ho practice and self-treatments. Visualizations are coming more easily. I have less of the "monkey mind", and the energy flow is more apparent to me."
Karen Small from America

"This week has been a mixed one for me.. I have had a lot of emotions going on again, felt low and depressed, unsettled with things in general Have been doing the exercises and even they have been a damp squid, nothing happening, not even the fizzing in fingers. I have had headaches when I have come out of the exercises for a while, and head felt very heavy.. I have felt no heat at all but very cold with a cool breeze thru my hands and body

.

.

.

This week have done my exercises as you advised me to do. Will continue next week with the same. I have felt the energy coming back to me and it seems to be a lot stronger than before. I still get this cool breeze that seems to cover my hand and face when doing certain exercises, still have headache when I have completed the exercises. My emotions have calmed down. I am also getting better at focusing too. I find that your CD really helps me to do the exercises"
Christine Weston from Spain

REGULAR SELF-TREATMENTS

Doing energy work on yourself, regularly, is the foundation of your Reiki practice. In this section you are going to learn how to treat yourself, using methods that Usui Sensei taught to his students at First Degree level. You are also going to discover how one of these approaches was formalised during its journey to the West.

No matter what method you use, when you self-treat you are creating what you might describe as a "healing space", a place where your energy system has the freedom, the space, the time to move more into a state of balance, releasing things that do not serve you: releasing things on all levels, from your physical body and from your thoughts and emotions.

Mikao Usui taught his students a range of approaches that could use to further their self-healing. Students could:

1. Meditate with the intention to heal.
2. Meditate by visualising that they are treating themselves – their head - using a set of simple standard hand positions.
3. Carry out a hands-on self-treatment, using intuitively-guided hand positions.

In the following sections we will be describing each of these approaches. Over time you should become familiar with each method and decide upon the method that feels most comfortable for you. You do not need to choose only one method to use, though. You may feel prompted to use one method on a particular occasion, whilst using another approach routinely. Do what feels appropriate on each occasion.

Healing meditation

This is the simplest approach to self-healing, involving no visualisation and no resting of your hands in different positions on your body. A simple scheme could be as follows:

1. Rest your hands in your lap, palms up
2. Close your eyes and take a few long deep breaths
3. Focus your attention on your Tanden point

4. Imagine that energy floods down to you from above and builds in your Tanden; maintain your attention on your Tanden
5. Your intention is to heal on all levels; be open, and empty, feel yourself merging with the energy and becoming one with it, imagine yourself disappearing into the energy
6. Remain in this state for 10-15 minutes

If you are not used to meditating then you are likely to find that your mind wanders sometimes. This is normal and this is human, and you do not need to be perfect in order to achieve great benefits from using Reiki on yourself. If thoughts intrude, pay them no attention; let them drift past and simply bring your attention back to what you were doing: focus your attention on your Tanden and again be open, and empty, feel yourself merging with the energy and becoming one with it, imagine yourself disappearing into the energy.

With practice, over time, you will find that your mind will intrude less.

Self-treatment meditation

This is again a simple approach to self-healing, involving no resting of your hands in different positions on your body. It can involve some visualisation though. A simple scheme could be as follows:

1. Sit comfortably on a chair and close your eyes.
2. Imagine a carbon copy of you sitting in front of you, maybe on the floor, with its back towards you.
3. Imagine that you are treating yourself, by resting your imaginary hands in a series of hand positions on the head (see the diagrams below).
4. Imagine yourself holding each imaginary hand position for about 5-6 minutes.
5. While holding each hand position, focus on imagining yourself channelling Reiki through your hands into the imaginary you that is sitting in front of you.

The standard hand positions are as follows (illustrated overleaf):

(1) Front of forehead along the hairline, with your hands held with fingertips touching each other in the midline, and your palms facing towards you.

(2) Hands hovering by the temples.

(3) One hand cupping the back of the head, with the other hand resting on the forehead.

(4) Both hands at the back of the neck/base of skull. Thumbs are joined from the tips to the base, pointing upwards. The rest of the palm and the fingers gently curve round the sides of the base of the skull/upper neck.

(5) Rest both hands on the crown, overlapping one another.

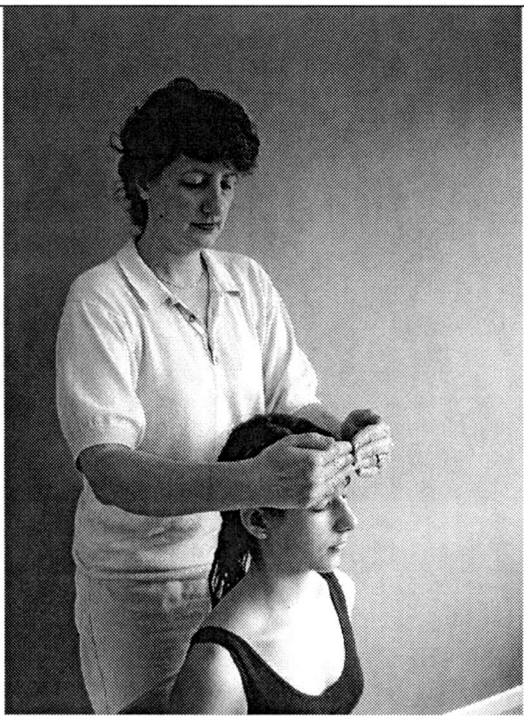

(1) Front of forehead

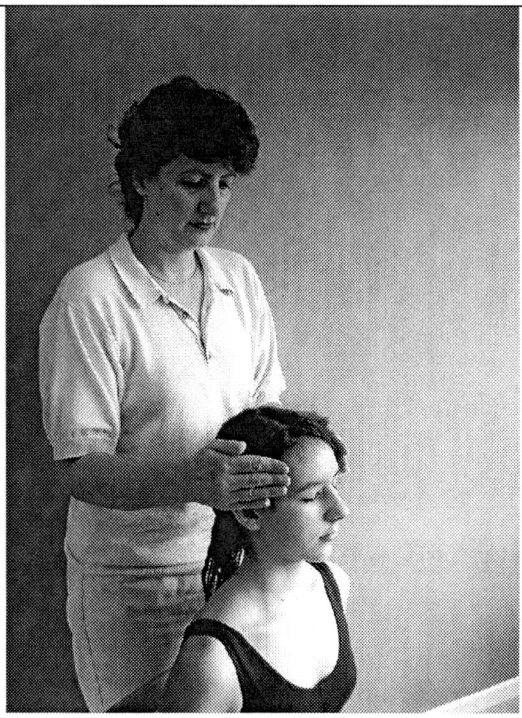

(2) Hands hovering by the temples

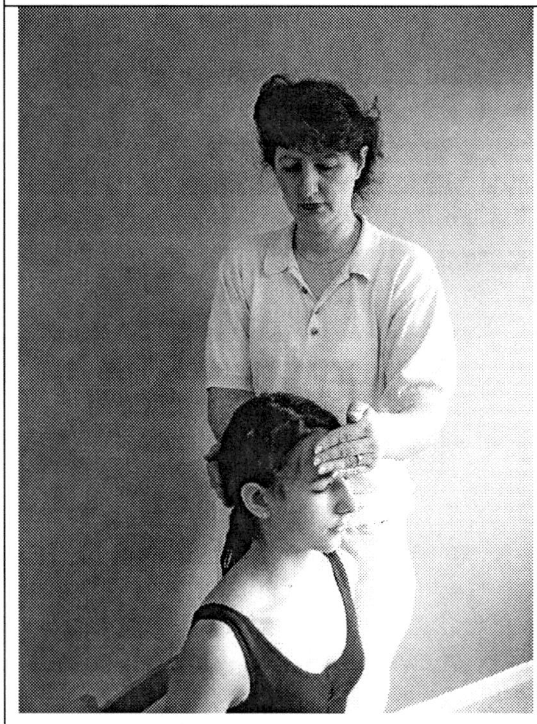

(3) Back of head and forehead

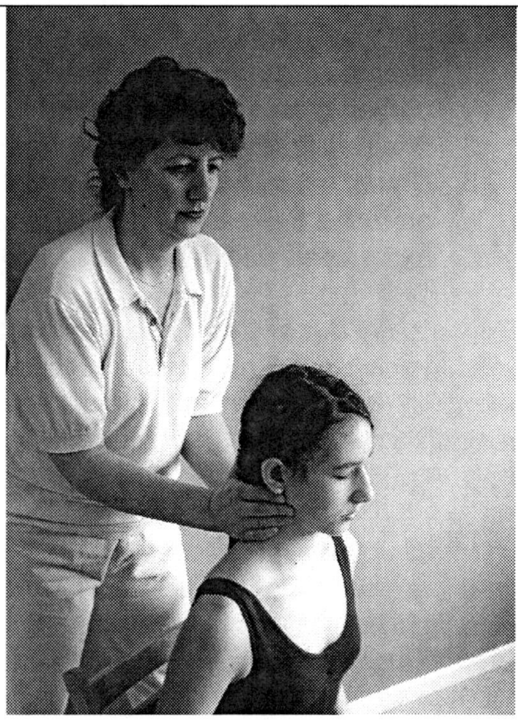

(4) Back of neck/base of skull

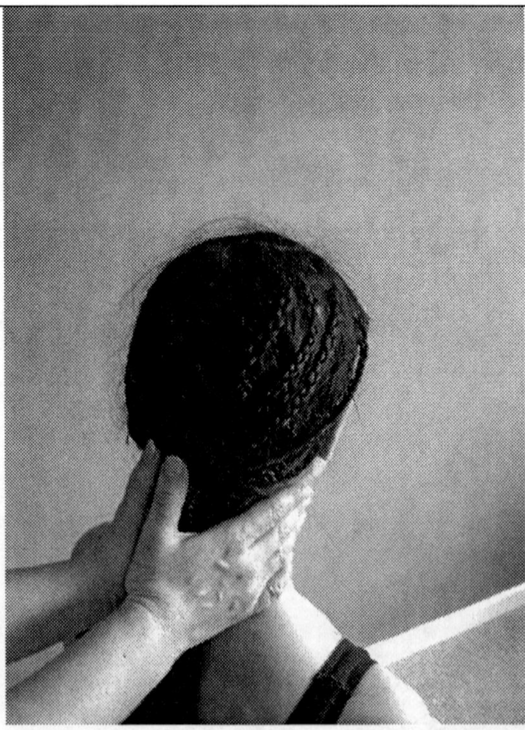

Stage (4) hand position in more detail

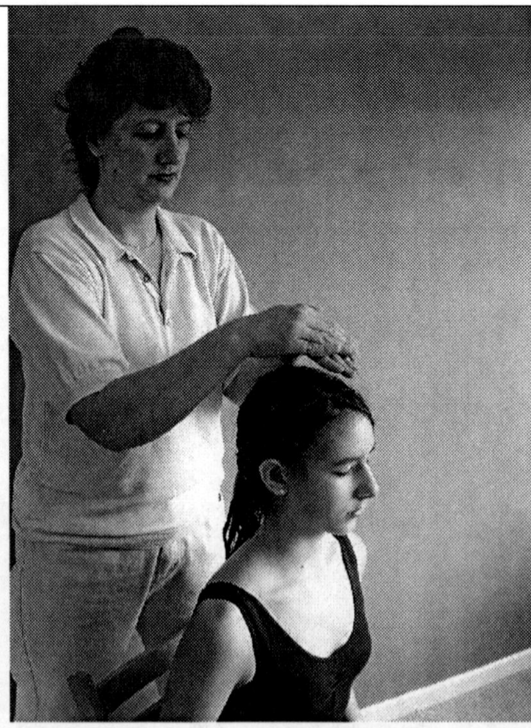

(5) Rest both hands on the crown

Alternative approaches

The scheme above is not the only way that the self-treatment meditation can be carried out. As alternative approaches, try the following:

1. Imagine that the 'real' you is being treated by the carbon copy, with the carbon copy standing behind you in your imagination
2. Imagine that you are being treated by disembodied hands
3. Do not visualise anything: simply allow your attention to rest or to dwell on those five areas of your head. The energy will follow your focus ans focus itself where your attention is directed

As you carry out any of these approaches, you may well feel 'hands' on your head in some or all of the positions, or heat, pr tingling, or pressure. This is normal. You may even find that there is a bit of a headache in a particular position, and that the headache dissipates when you move on to another area. Again, this is no problem.

The third suggestion above demonstrates to us that if you find it difficult to visualise you do not need to worry because Reiki will still work for you. Your visualisation may develop with practice, but you can simply 'intend' that the energy is passing into you in those various positions, and it will do so, without you having to visualise clearly.

Why these particular hand positions?

These hand movements (facing, opposed, away from you) are mudras from a specific Boddhisattva, a senior disciple of the Buddha who was renowned for his healing abilities: someone called Binzuru (see picture on the right). These hand positions are invoking the healing powers of Binzuru at an unconscious level.

Advantages of the Self-treatment meditation

One big advantage of the self-treatment meditation is that it is something that you can do unobtrusively when sitting with your eyes closed anywhere: on a train or a bus, as a passenger in a car, or waiting in the departure lounge of an airport.

If you don't have 25-30 minutes to do the full session, then just cut down on the amount of time you spend in each imaginary hand position, but do go through the sequence of five.

What is exciting about this technique is that it demonstrates that Reiki will simply follow your thoughts; it will follow your focus. You simply use a visualisation to focus your intent in a particular way, and Reiki does what you intend!

Students' experiences: Self-treatment meditation

"The first time I did it, I completely did not hear the second part of the track on the CD as I think that I went too deep into it. It was strange as I was definitely not asleep but I certainly did not hear the instructions to do the last three hand placements at all. I also felt quite strange when I did eventually come to which was because the CD changer kicked in ! So the next time I did the self treatment I tried to keep myself on a more conscious level and I did manage to finish it completely which I have done each time since. I am guessing that this is what a patient would feel though?

Doing the self treatments has given me a great motivation to want to do it more which is both good and odd - I feel on an entirely different plane when I have completed it and that I could almost turn around and do the whole treatment again there and then. I look forward to doing these each day and will continue to do them as I get so much from them. "
"T.B." from Norfolk

"Carried out the Self treatment meditation, which was amazing! The visualization confused me a little, but felt tingles on my forehead and temples, that lasted all session and beyond. The other positions carried out were not so strong. Throughout, my hands became progressively more tingly, as did my feet.

Tried another Seft Treatment later in the day, with the carbon copy behind me. This was much stronger. Hands and feet very tingly. Time also was 'quick' throughout."
Jason Brown from North Wales

"I could not feel much when trying to use a carbon copy of myself in front of me being treated by a carbon copy. I was having real difficulties with it. So I have tried the other method thinking that a carbon copy is treating me directly. So far it has worked: I do feel the warmth especially on my temples, I do "see" some kind of shadow in front of my eyes when treating the forehead. The strongest feeling is at the back of my neck, I get very sensitive, it is not tickling but it does get uncomfortable as if someone is using the tip of a feather.

I have been nicely surprised with the vision of colours: at the beginning it was just plain white but so bright hard to explain then it went to deep purple and violet. It was so amazing !

I feel more relaxed, less anxious and more easy-going with every one. My mum says that I don't look tired as always do because of the flying."
Bruno Cassani from Essex

"I have definitely been feeling the difference after the self treatments, I feel happier and healthier and my head feels clearer, especially after the meditation. I am currently injured and waiting for an operation on my ankle which has been giving me a lot of problems, and so have also been focusing on this. Whilst i know it cannot be healed without surgery i have become a lot more comfortable on it, have experienced less pain and am feeling generally more positive about it. This has emphasised the meaning of Reiki treatments to me."
Emily Cook from Oxfordshire

"I have been doing self treatments as well, and this has benefited me in a big way. I have had an injured ankle which i am on a hospital waiting list for an operation. I have suffered with this for over a year but since I started this course the improvement has been incredible. Before sometimes i would not be able to put full weight on the foot and would walk with a limp but now I have hardly any pain and can walk as normal."
Emily Cook from Oxfordshire

"In the self healing visualisations I feel slightly different sensations when I imagine myself sat on the floor in front of me as opposed to standing behind me. While carrying out this series of visualisations and hand positions, my real hands are hot and tingly, sometimes pulsating in my lap. I can feel different areas in my body popping as energy flows through. Sometimes afterwards my existing back problem feels a little worse."
Susan Naylor from West Yorkshire

"This has been the most amazing experience of my life. I didn't initially expect this to work the first time as I have all my life struggled to visualise. However, the first time I did it I immediately managed to visualise an imaginary me, standing behind myself, treating myself. I didn't actually feel the hands on my skin but I did feel real pressure where ever I visualised my hands to be. Not only did I feel pressure I felt a tingly, numb floating sensation in my head. My hands became really hot which was weird as I could feel myself both treating and being treated at the same time. It was an absolutely amazing sensation. I have always had problems relaxing but I actually felt resentful when the meditation moved onto the next hand position as I was enjoying it so much. After I had finished I had the most amazing feeling of health, well being and relaxation which lasted and lasted. Everything tingled, felt numb and I felt really distant. For the rest of the week I have found it easier to visualise my imaginary self standing behind me and I have really had to work to pull myself back to reality. Last night I also felt a pulling or drawing in sensation through my temples."
Sarah Quinn from Kent

Intuitive Hands-on Self-treatments

A further approach that Usui taught to his students was to treat themselves by resting their hands on themselves, and allowing the energy to flow through their hands into their bodies. There were no standard hand positions to follow, though. Usui Sensei's approach to such things was intuitive, so he expected his students to place their hands wherever was appropriate for them on that occasion. Each time a student treated themselves in this way the hand-positions might well change, as the student's energy needs changed from one self-treatment to another. Here is a suitable scheme for you to follow:

1. Rest your hands in your lap, palms up
2. Close your eyes and take a few long deep breaths
3. Focus your attention on your Tanden point
4. Imagine that energy floods down to you from above and builds in your Tanden; maintain your attention on your Tanden
5. Be still, and be aware of any impression about where the energy wants to go
6. Rest your hand or hands on, or near to, the area that has drawn your attention
7. Stay in this position and allow the energy to flow out of your hands into your body for as long as feels right for you; if you can't comfortably rest your hands in a particular position, hold them nearby and have in mind that the energy is flowing from your hands to the area you want to treat
8. Now move your hand or hands to another position, and stay in the new position for as long as feels right for you
9. Continue for up to 30 minutes, or bring the session to a close earlier than that if you feel that the session has come to an end

"Western-style" Hands-on Self-treatments

The three approaches that we have covered so far are not common within the world of Reiki. The vast majority of Reiki people on the planet treat themselves "Western style", a procedure that is based on the teachings of Hawayo Takata and her Master students.

"Western-style" self-treatments are based on resting your real hands in a series of standard hand positions on your head, shoulders and torso, and letting Reiki flow into you. We know that Chujiro Hayashi, and the other Imperial Officers, were interested in learning a hands-on healing method from Usui Sensei, and we know that Dr Hayashi put together a range of standard treatment sequences that could be used on patients, based on their particular medical condition. So we can see how a simple and intuitive approach, that of Usui Sensei, came to be changed into a treatment system based on following standard sets of hand positions, and the idea of standardised hand positions came to be applied to self-treatment too, as Reiki was taught in the West.

You can see the hand positions for giving yourself a Reiki treatment in the diagrams below, but of course they are not set in stone: they just give good overall coverage of the head and torso, and depending on who teaches you Reiki, you are likely to be taught different sets of hand positions. They are all just variations on a theme. In practice you will find your own preferred combinations, based on what you find comfortable, and based on where you need to send the energy. This is you, so you can put your hands wherever seems appropriate! You are not obliged to always do a “full” hands-on self-treatment, either, going through every hand position and treating yourself for 30 minutes. You can do 'informal' self-treatments using very few hand positions, for whatever period of time you have available. It doesn't have to be 'all or nothing'. If you have just sprained your ankle, then just treat your ankle!

While you are relaxing for a few minutes, or even watching television, you could have hands on your heart and solar plexus, or your stomach – see what feels most comfortable. Try resting your hands one-over-the-other in front of your Tanden. While it is better to treat yourself in an un-distracted state, because the energy will flow more intensely, some self-treatment – even while watching television - is better than no self-treatment and it can be fitted into the busiest routine if you want it to be. Here are the hand positions, which you can see illustrated below:

Shoulders
Temples
Crown
Back of Head/Back of Neck
Front of Face
Throat
Heart and Solar Plexus
Navel
Hips

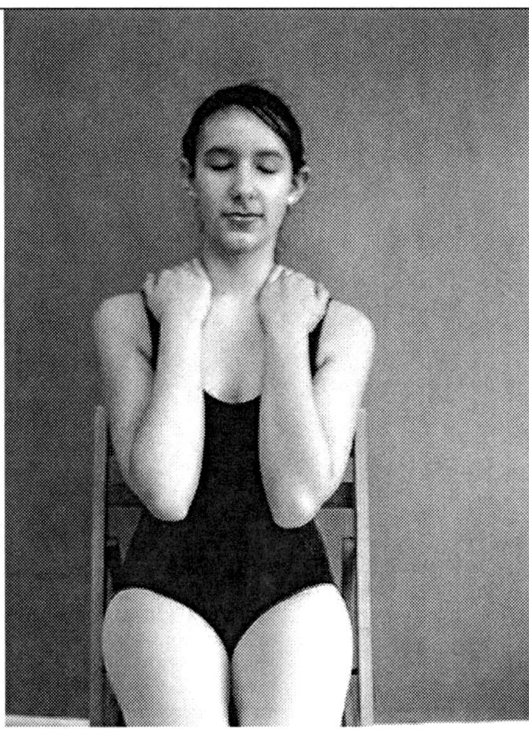
Shoulders

Temples

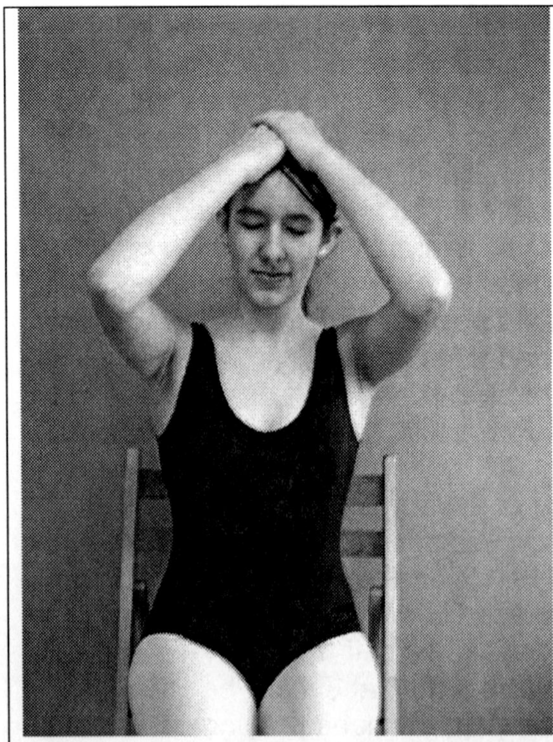

Crown

Back of Head / Neck

Front of Face

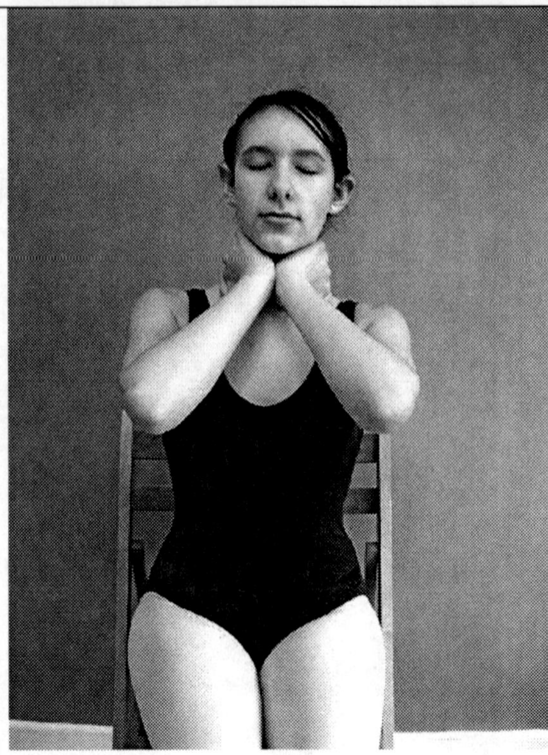

Throat

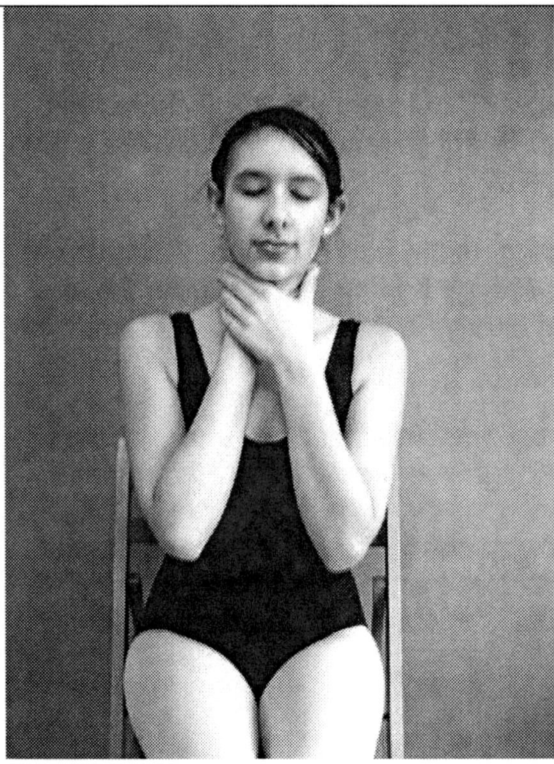

Throat (alternative position)

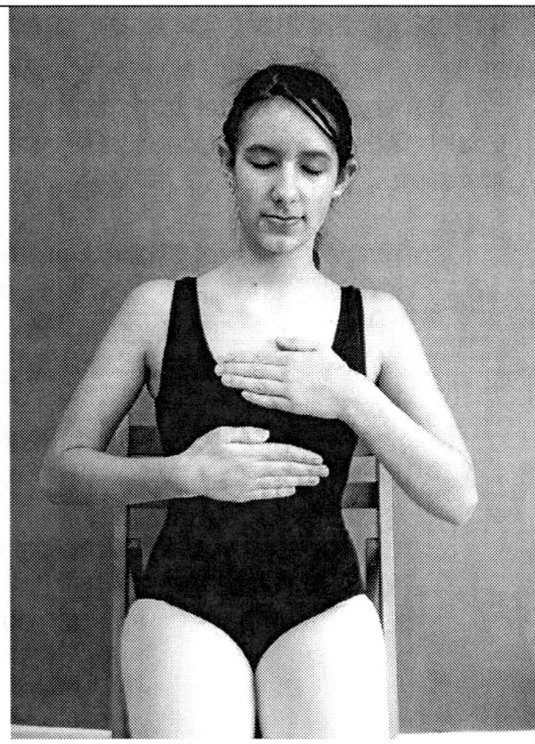

Heart & Solar Plexus

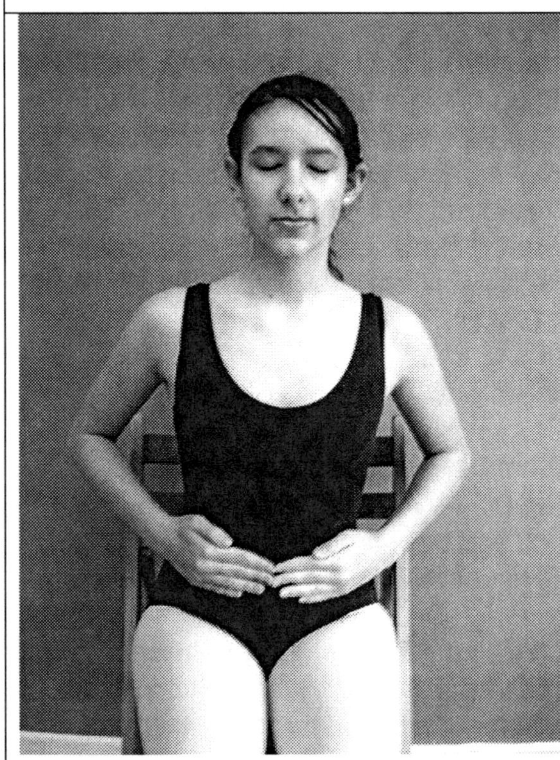

Navel

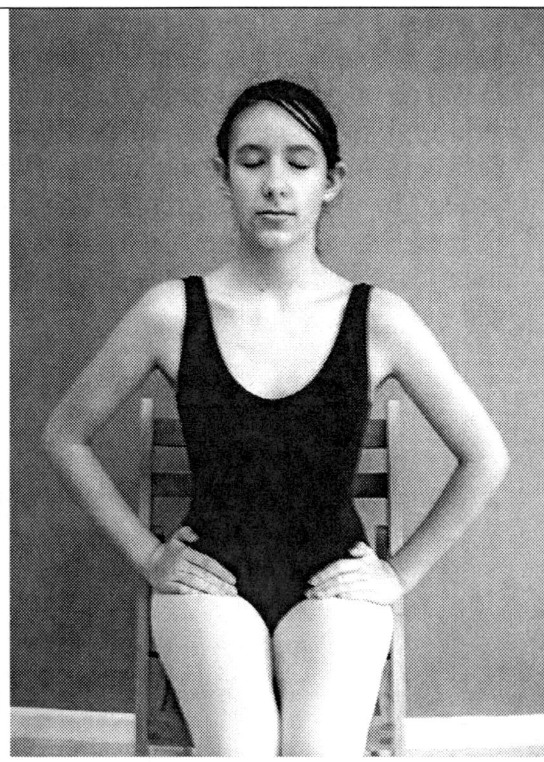

Hips

Treating 'difficult-to-reach' areas

If there are parts of the body that you would like to treat, but you cannot get your hands to them because they are awkward to reach, then there are a few choices:

1. Imagine that your hands are resting on the part of the body that you cannot quite reach, and imagine energy flowing into you from these imaginary hands, or imagine that energy is flowing from your hands to the area you want to treat.

2. Rest your hands on your navel, and imagine that Reiki energy builds up in that area and then flows through your body to the area of need.

3. Imagine that you are drawing energy down through the crown of your head, and that the energy flows through your body directly to the area of need, without using your hands. This can be done anywhere, anytime.

Using Western self-treatments in practice

Most people find it easiest to carry out Western-style self-treatments first thing in the morning upon waking up, or last thing at night in bed, before falling asleep. It might even be worth waking up a little earlier each day to ensure that time is available for a self-treatment! Alternatively, what better way to get you off to sleep! Many people use self-treatment as a way of getting themselves of to sleep. One lady wondered if there was a problem in never using hand-positions below the heart, because whenever she got to the heart area she would fall asleep!

A few disadvantages of the Western system are:

1. You can't do this sort of self-treatment in a public place without attracting a certain amount of attention to yourself, and you may not have room for the contortions if you are on a crowded train.
2. Some of the hand positions can feel uncomfortable to hold for any length of time.
3. A lot of people feel very little when doing Western self-treatments (that doesn't mean that nothing is happening, just that you aren't so aware of it happening, but it can be a little disheartening in the early stages).
4. There is a tendency to fall asleep quite quickly, and you tend to 'drift off' rather than keeping your mind on the job at hand, which seems to lessen the flow of energy when compared to the original method.

Combining Japanese and Western approaches

It is possible to combine the Japanese and Western approaches to an extent. The Japanese approach emphasises to us that you do not have to rest your hands on yourself to do a self-treatment: your intention is enough. If you intend (through your visualisation) that Reiki enters your head from a particular point then it does so. Reiki will follow your thoughts and your intention.

To combine the two approaches, sit with your hands resting on your heart and solar plexus (the most comforting of the Western self-treatment hand positions) and visualise imaginary hands going through the standard five hand positions described above.

The effects of Self-treatments

You can read in the section 'The effects of Reiki attunements' about the effects that Reiki is likely to produce in your life. You can intensify these effects and maximise the benefits that are available to you through Reiki by treating yourself on a regular basis, and by treating others too.

WORKING ON OTHER PEOPLE

Experiencing treatments

It is clear now, as we have mentioned earlier, that the treating of other people was not really a part of the system that Usui Sensei taught at First Degree, and even at Second Degree the treatment of others was not emphasised or focused upon; it was not what his system was all about. It was only when the Imperial Officers approached Mikao Usui to be taught a treatment method that "Reiki" as a hands-on treatment method came into being, in the last few years of Usui Sensei's life, and of course that system was passed from Dr Hayashi to Mrs Takata to the group of teachers that she initiated in the 1970s.

Now, although the treatment of others was not a big part of Usui's system, and would not have been carried out at First Degree, there is no reason at all why we should not treat people at First Degree level. Treatments carried out by First Degree practitioners are effective and beneficial both to the giver and the receiver, and you will be amazed by the feedback that you receive from the people that you work on. Treating others as soon as you can will help you to develop your ability as a channel for the energy, and will help to build your confidence.

Treat as many people as you can, and not necessarily full-length hour-long treatment sessions (though it would be good if you could arrange some). Go with the time that you have available: treat someone's painful knee or shoulder for 5-10 minutes, treat someone's head and shoulders while they are sitting in a straight-backed chair for 15-20 minutes. The important thing is to get the hands-on practice on a variety of people, and to become comfortable with treating others.

What I am going to do in this section is to begin by describing the sorts of sensations and experiences that you might have while treating others, and also to describe the sorts of sensations and effects that might be experienced by the people you treat. Then I will move on to give you step-by-step instructions so it is completely clear to you how to treat other people in a variety of situations.

What you will feel when treating others

We can generalise to a certain extent about the sorts of sensations that Reiki people experience when treating themselves and others. Generally, you will notice a lot more going on in your hands when you treat other people, compared to what you will feel when you treat yourself hands-on: hands-on self-treatments are usually a lot more subtle and gentle.

Reiki people vary greatly in terms of the sort of sensations they have when treating others, and particularly in the early stages the intensity of those sensations will be greater in some people than in others. Sensitivity to the energy develops over time, through practice, so what you notice when you first start to treat people is usually not representative of what you will notice when you are more experienced.

A few people feel very little, and will always feel very little, when they treat others, though this is not common. This does not mean that Reiki is working for them and the people that they treat: it means that they are not noticing as much going on in their hands when compared with the average. Feedback from the people worked on will help to reassure people in this situation.

Here are the main sensations that Reiki people experience when working on others:

1. Tingling in the palms of your hands, or fingers, or both.
2. Heat in the palms of your hands, or fingers, or both.
3. Tingling that becomes hot if there is a lot of energy flowing.
4. Heat that starts to tingle if there is a lot of energy flowing.

So the main sensations are either heat, or tingling/fizzing, in different combinations. Some people have heat as their main experience of the energy, while others feel very little heat, favouring tingling/fizzing.

Less common sensations

1. Coolness, though this can have different meanings for different people.
2. Magnetic attraction or repulsion.
3. Some sort of vibration or pulsing, or a 'breeze' blowing under your hand.
4. An experience of 'colour' of some sort, in your hands, or in your head, as the energy flows.
5. Something that is difficult to explain, but you know what it is when it is happening!
6. Not very much at all.

This last outcome mentioned above is infrequent. My first Reiki teacher said that had attuned one person who feels nothing at all when she gives Reiki treatments – as far as her hands are concerned, nothing is happening. However, when she treats people they experience all the sensations that are common to people having Reiki treatments, and they experience all the benefits that Reiki can produce.

I have attuned a couple of people who did not feel very much at all after Reiki First Degree. One lady in particular was not convinced that much was going on (though her husband was: seeing coloured lights, feeling loads of heat from her hands, falling asleep after 15 minutes, and asking for Reiki at every possible opportunity!). When she went through Reiki Second Degree, all the more 'standard' feelings came through for her, and she felt greatly reassured. I have found that the Japanese empowerments that I now use seem to enhance people's sensitivity to the energy very early on, more so than Western attunements.

How much you get out of Reiki depends on what you are prepared to invest in it: practice your Hatsurei Ho and do regular self-treatments in the early stages, and treat people. You will find that the energy will get stronger and you will become more sensitive to the flow of energy with time.

The Early Stages

When you first practice Reiki, it is possible that you will feel simple tingling from your hands (or heat, or whatever sensation is 'the one' for you), maybe with no great variation in its intensity. With practice, though, you will develop more sensitivity in your hands and you will be able to feel variations or gradations in the sensations you experience, as the energy flows to a greater or lesser degree. Some people are quite sensitive from the start. There is a lot of individual variation.

The importance of being able to detect variations in the flow of energy is that if you can feel that there is a lot of energy flowing into a particular area of the body, you should leave your hands there for a lot longer than the average 3-5 minutes. After a while you will feel the flow of energy subsiding, as that area of the body has taken as much as it can on that occasion, and you know that it is ok to move on. So you can use the sensations in your hands as a guide to how long you spend in each treatment position.

Aches and Pains

Occasionally you may find that your hands ache when channelling Reiki in a particular hand position, and sometimes the tingling can extend into your forearms. This can be indicative of intense energy flow. Pain is uncommon; tingling in the forearms is much more common. Occasionally pain can be caused by holding your hand and arm in an awkward or tense position. With practice you will find the most comfortable position for you to hold your hands and arms when you treat.

If your hand does ache, move it away from that area for a few moments, and then move your hand back again; if pain develops again, treat the area in short bursts, or alternate brief treatments of the 'painful' area with the treatment of other hand positions. This sensation is unlikely to recur should you treat the recipient on another occasion.

Nausea and Queasiness

Sometimes during your first few treatments you might find that you feel a bit queasy at some stage during the treatment; this can happen during the treatment that you give on the day of your live course. What is happening is that you are not yet accustomed to having energy flooding through you – sometimes quite strongly – and the first few times that this happens with a recipient who is drawing lots of energy it can be a bit of a shock to your system. But this sort of reaction is temporary. With a bit of practice you'll get used to channelling energy strongly and you'll be fine.

Infrequently, when placing your hands on the solar plexus area (usually), you may start to feel nauseous. This seems to relate to long-term emotional turmoil, or unresolved issues which are held in the solar plexus area of the person you are treating. The nausea relates to the release of the emotional problem. The feeling will subside once you have moved your hands away from the area, but while you are treating that area you may just have to put up with it! You might choose to treat this area in short bursts (see the comment above about pain in your hands) if you really feel that you need to move away from that area, but the feeling won't last long.

Coolness

Sometimes you may feel coolness in a particular hand position (make sure it is not just your client exhaling through their nose onto your hand, in which case the coolness will come and go regularly!), or you may feel a coarseness, or harshness, in the energy. This seems to me to relate to physical trauma - for example I felt it over the site of a recent mastectomy, but the sensation of coolness seems to have different implications for different people. You may not be the same as me, and you will have to work out for yourself what the various sensations means for you. We should remind ourselves, though, that Reiki is not a diagnostic therapy, so you do not need to work hard to try and interpret the different sensations that you experience.

An Absence of Sensations

Finally, you may feel like your hands have 'switched off'. Once you are reasonably sensitive to the energy, you can usually feel tingling (or heat or whatever) in most places, and when the sensations stop altogether then this is indicative of something, for example an 'emotional block'. I have felt this in the heart area, for example in the case of a young girl who had been through a bad relationship break-up. When I came to the heart area I could feel no sensations in my hand. In this situation, just like when you feel a 'hot-spot', you should stay there for longer to give an opportunity for the Reiki energy to deal with the block. After two treatments, the girl spent the next day crying and the block was released. She went back to being an open, demonstrative person, and went through Reiki First and Second Degree herself!

Effects noticed after the treatment has finished

When you treat someone, you receive the benefit from the energy that you are channelling; to an extent, you are also giving yourself a Reiki treatment as you treat them. So at the end of a treatment session it is likely that you will feel calm, peaceful, content, serene, maybe even on a high, blissful. We know that Reiki treatments can bring things to the surface to be released or dissipated, and since when you treat someone you are also treating yourself then it is possible for you to experience something by way of a healing 'crisis' (a bit of an extreme term, actually).

I am sometimes contacted by people who have just started to give some Reiki treatments to friends and relatives and they think that the treatments are draining them because they feel that they have no energy. What is happening is that Reiki is relaxing you; giving treatments is relaxing you. You will know that if people are busy, on the go, on the go, they can sustain this frantic activity. But when they finally sit down to relax the tiredness hits them and they feel exhausted. A similar thing can happen with Reiki: you treat people and you receive some benefit from the energy you have been channelling. The Reiki starts to work on you and relaxes you. You are relaxed and all your accumulated tiredness hits you, and you don't want to do anything other than sleep.

Such an effect is temporary, and as you continue to work on yourself and other people these effects will disappear, and will not be part of your routine experience of Reiki.

What people feel when they are treated

So what is happening on the receiving end of a Reiki treatment? Well, the sensations experienced by people having a Reiki treatment vary enormously. There is no 'correct' set of experiences, but you can generalise to an extent. While there are endless individual variations, I can say that men seem to notice or experience a lot less than most women, who seem a lot more ‘in touch’ with their bodies and able to experience more subtle variations.

The most common feelings are these:

Relaxation, sometimes very deep relaxation

It is not uncommon for people to fall asleep and start snoring within 15-20 minutes (usually men!). People quite often drift in and out of consciousness and are surprised that so much time has elapsed on the treatment table. It is quite common for people to make some involuntary twitches, too, as you might do when you go off to sleep sometimes. People may become more relaxed on a subsequent treatment session when compared to the first. This is either because the energy penetrates more deeply on subsequent sessions, or people are more relaxed with you as a therapist after the first session, or a bit of both.

Falling asleep during a treatment is not a problem. The recipient does not need to stay awake in order to receive the benefits of the treatment.

Heat or warmth from your hands

This is commonly felt over the forehead, and people have described feeling like they were under an angle-poise lamp or an electric heater. Frequently the recipient’s sensation of intense heat will follow the sensations you are getting in your hands, so if there is a lot going on in your hands, and thus a lot of energy flowing, the recipient will feel a lot of heat.

Interestingly, your hands are not actually getting hot, so it is not ‘temperature’ heat that the recipient is feeling. The main way the body seems to be able to interpret or experience the energy is as heat: if your hands were really that hot, you would have to be treated in a casualty department for burns! Interestingly, a minority of people experience the energy as coldness.

Seeing colours

Some people see a 'light show' against their closed eyelids, sometimes rainbow colours, sometimes individual colours like violet or green, sometimes a flickering white light. Blue, and violet/purple/mauve, are quite common, the latter being the traditional colour associated with the healing energy. The practitioner can see this colour quite often too.

Men's experiences are usually limited to the first two sensations mentioned above, occasionally the third, but there are more.

Floating or sinking

People describe feeling as if they are floating, or sinking, or both, or 'melting' into the treatment table, or they may feel as if they have no limbs at all or as if their limbs have turned to wood or stone.

'Movement' or 'drawing'

There can be a feeling of something travelling along the length of the body or the limbs, by way of tingling or heat sensations, or a localised spot can feel as if it is 'drawing'. When there are back problems, holding the ankles can result in a feeling of heat extending up the back/spine, for example.

Disorientation

Sometimes there is a feeling of the head swimming or of 'movement' along a dark tunnel when you are treating the head, especially the temples.

Memories coming to the surface

One lady recalled different stages of her life dependent on what hand position was being held. One lady who had an extended series of treatments seemed to be going through a past life experience, with each 'episode' carrying on from where the last one left off in the previous treatment.

Pressure or difficulty in breathing

Not a very common reaction, but it can happen sometimes. This may happen when you are treating the throat area, and usually ties in with a person's inability to express themselves. The effect is transitory, and occurs as the energy is starting to deal with the problem, but it can be a little worrying for the recipient.

A feeling of intense cold

Not a very common reaction, but it can happen sometimes. This seems to tie in with a big shift of energy on the part of the recipient. Once or twice I have had to interrupt a treatment to go and get a blanket to cover someone up, so it would be a good idea to have one to hand just in case.

Emotional release

This is quite common and if it is going to happen it is likely to happen on the first treatment, with maybe some repercussions into the second treatment, possibly the third. As an emotional problem is being dealt with by the Reiki energy, perhaps the release of an emotional block, or the release of a long-standing unresolved issue, a quite 'primal' welling-up of emotion can occur. The recipient is not usually thinking of anything in particular, but the pure emotion is released, and lets this be known as it goes past! A change in the breathing rate, eyes 'filling up', or a tear running down a cheek, are quite common, and can even happen in men sometimes.

It is a positive step though, since the block or problem is being pushed to the surface and dissipated, and it is usually experienced as a positive thing too. Reiki can reach deep and even deal with childhood emotional issues dating back many decades; this would be likely to take a lot of treatments though, and most short courses of treatment would not necessarily have the opportunity to deal with this.

When someone has an emotional release in front of you it can be a little disturbing at first. If they seem quite distressed, do not stop the treatment, but you can go back to the head of the table and rest your hands gently on the shoulders for a while until things have subsided. They will be fine, and the release just seems to happen for a few minutes during the course of the treatment. By the end of the session they will have retained their composure and be feeling a bit better.

In extreme cases, the person may find that they are quite emotional – on and off - for a few days after a treatment, as the block is dealt with and released.

'Physical release'

There is a physical counterpart to the emotional release, and this usually shows itself as an intensification of a physical problem while being treated, or shortly afterwards. For example, I have treated some people with arthritis who felt their joint pains get worse during their Reiki treatment, but the pains eased subsequently; they then came back for another treatment, whereupon the pains would intensify during the treatment, and improve again subsequently.

Other examples would be a headache or back pain appearing or intensifying during the treatment, or shortly afterwards.

It is quite common for people to experience a 'healing crisis' when being treated with complementary therapies in general, for example using homoeopathy, where the symptoms intensify before they are dissipated. But with Reiki any such healing crisis seems to be short-lived and not very intense. Reiki seems to 'damp down' such a strong reaction in most people, but not all.

The effect of Reiki on people you treat

Over the years it seems that Reiki has made a real difference to people suffering from an amazing variety of medical conditions and problems, even very serious ones, but all the evidence is patchy and anecdotal: there are no proper 'clinical trials' as far as I am aware, and I think it is unlikely that there will be. It is not possible to say with any confidence, backed up by hard data, that Reiki will produce a particular effect for a person suffering from a particular problem. So in this section I am just going to talk about some of the people I have treated, to give you an idea of the sort of things that Reiki can do, based on my personal experience of treating people with a wide range of conditions and problems.

Sometimes when a treatment has been successful I ask the patient to write a letter of recommendation for me, so I have included some of these so you can hear what they have to say, too. Obviously I don't have personal experience of all conditions and diseases, but it appears to me that Reiki has the potential to make a difference to most problems that people could experience. In my experience the majority of people who have come to see me have had their problems sorted out so long as they stayed for a full course of treatments.

Four healing sessions at weekly intervals seems to be enough to deal with most cases of stress, tension, anxiety, and sleeplessness - even where this has been continuing for a long time, even for years. Emotional blocks and emotional turmoil, feelings of being unable to cope, seem to shift just as quickly. Physical problems can take longer, but I have had success with things like long term back pain, sciatica, post-operative pain, and the pain of arthritis and scoliosis, after only a few sessions.

We need to remember, though, that Reiki is not a cure-all, and as a practitioner we have no way of knowing what effects Reiki will produce in a particular person, though we might generalise about the sort of things that Reiki tends to do for a lot of people. We cannot guarantee that Reiki will resolve a person's problems, and we have no control over what the treatments will do for the recipient, or indeed in which order – if any – the person's problems will be dealt with or resolved.

Here are some examples of the sort of things that Reiki can do for people:

Physical Problems

Sports Injury

I treated an aerobics instructor who had been doing a lot of 'high impact' aerobics. This had resulted in her developing stress fractures in both lower legs and painful knees. When I treated her I felt huge amounts of tingling over her knees and lower legs, and spent a large portion of the treatment working on that area. It had become so painful for Keily that she could barely walk, let alone do her job. After two Reiki treatments over consecutive days she was able to go back to the gymnasium, and ran for two miles on the treadmill without pain. This amazed me because I had only just been through Reiki First Degree and was wondering whether it was all a load of nonsense. It slowly dawned on me that there might me something in this Reiki business!

This is what Keily had to say:

> *"Dear Taggart,*
>
> *I am writing to thank you for all the time and effort you have spent on treatments for my legs. Reiki was a totally new experience for me up to about a month or so ago, and I really didn't know what to expect to begin with. But I didn't have anything to lose because all the other treatments I had had to try to cure my shin splints hadn't worked at all.*
>
> *They had become so painful that I was unable to participate in any high impact sport and because it is my profession it came to pose quite a large problem - but after a number of treatments they now seem to have completely vanished.*
>
> *I can't put it down to anything else but Reiki! A month ago putting weight on my legs was painful, let alone exercising as I am used to, but now I feel confident that I could do what I want without any problems."*
> ***Miss K.Heard, Braintree, Essex December 1997***

Long term back pain

James had suffered with back problems for decades. He had worked on a farm when he was a teenager, and had done huge amounts of heavy lifting without taking care to do the lifting properly. As a result, any heavy work led to his back 'going out'. He had received treatments from an osteopath, which gave some relief, and he had been taught various exercises to do, but it was a real problem for him. James does a lot of work in his large garden growing food, and has a couple of fields where he was doing heavy work grubbing up tree roots etc. The first couple of times I treated him, he had been doing heavy digging the day before, and his back had 'gone' each time. Within half an hour of completing the Reiki session, his back 'clicked in' of its own accord. After half a dozen treatments, the problem seemed to have disappeared and over the next year James did a lot of heavy work renovating a house, without any back problems. This is what he had to say:

> *"Dear Taggart,*
>
> *I am writing to thank you for your help in solving my problem. I have to say that I had just learned to live with it until you suggested the Reiki solution.*
>
> *To think that after all these years and the worry, all it took was some mystical mumbo-jumbo and hand waving. It's a puzzle to me. How it works defies my logic, but the fact that it has for me is indisputable.*
>
> *My back usually became painful after a few hours heavy work, something would come out of line. If I didn't stop, rest and do some special exercises until my spine would click then I knew I would be in for three or four painful days, until I could click things back. An osteopath had explained that my problem was muscular, the muscles causing the spine to distort. He claimed that stress probably caused the muscles to tension up.*
>
> *After just four sessions it became much easier to 'click back in'; now a few months later I have done some tremendously hard and heavy work and my back seems to have stopped clicking out altogether.*
>
> *So thank you once again for all your help. I would recommend Reiki to anyone. I don't think that there is much doubt that it has helped me.*
>
> *Kind regards,"*
> ***Mr J Wheatley, Bulmer, Suffolk   June 1998***

A Painful Limp

David had a painful limp. He had been to a Doctor and had tried a variety of conventional treatments including physiotherapy, but to no avail. This was a real problem for David because he had several large dogs that he loved to take for long walks in the countryside. His painful limp prevented him from doing this.

Five treatments seemed to improve things quite a lot, and I bumped into him six months later, doing Christmas shopping in Sainsburys in December 1998. The limp had gone, and not returned, and most of the pain had disappeared. He now walks his dogs happily again!

Postoperative Pain

Helen had undergone an operation on her face and cheek, to remove the Parotid (salivary) gland. The problem in carrying out this operation is that the main facial nerve and its various branches travel through this gland, so when the gland is surgically removed the surgeon has to dissect out the gland very carefully in the hope of leaving the facial nerve undamaged. It is quite common for the facial nerve to be damaged as a result of this operation, and this can lead to long-term facial pain, which is what had happened here. Helen had tried acupuncture, and had experienced some limited improvement in her condition, but she was far from happy. Her face hurt all the time, and the pain was made worse by talking or eating – the facial movements seemed to trigger off an increase in the pain that she was experiencing.

When I treated her, the hand that was over the affected area went crazy, with extremely intense tingling, tingles extending into my forearm, and pain in my hand that led me to move my hand elsewhere for a while, and treat the face in short bursts. We carried out perhaps 4-5 treatments, and Reiki made a real difference: the pain lessened greatly, and was no longer made worse by eating and talking. Helen happily went out socialising with her friends in December 1998.

Scoliosis

Scoliosis is a degenerative back problem that causes ongoing pain. Georgina worked in a Health Food shop where I was running healing sessions, and she popped in for occasional 20-minute 'blasts' of Reiki, when I was in-between bookings. She said that the pains she experienced had lessened generally, though they had not disappeared.

Low Energy Levels: ME (myalgic encephalomyelitis)

Janet had M.E. for 3 years and when I first saw her in April 1999 she was grey and lifeless and in a lot of pain. Over the year that I treated her I have seen her pains disappear by the end of the first treatment session and not return, I have seen her energy levels rise dramatically, and her self-confidence and feelings of self-worth improve greatly. Over her course of treatments, Reiki has helped her to release emotional problems reaching back to childhood, and she seems a different woman: bright and perky, enthusiastic and positive, calm and serene, with a real stillness and confidence. She says that she feels that she no longer has M.E., and feels better than she did before she had M.E., because the energy has dealt with all the 'emotional baggage' that she had been carrying around for all of her adult life.

Janet has now gone through Reiki First and Second Degree, and now Reiki Mastership, and this has helped to accelerate her progression back to health.

This is what Janet had to say in Autumn 1999:

> *"My son and I have M.E. and my daughter is recovering from a long-lasting virus. The situation was hard for the whole family and I had reached a low point when a friend suggested Reiki. I dug out a newspaper article I had been given 12 months earlier about Taggart King. I had no real knowledge of Reiki but the results that were to follow far exceeded any hopes I might have had.*
>
> *The first treatments brought about a great improvement in the aches and pains in my arms, legs and back, and a boost in energy levels. With further treatments specifically to treat M.E., migraine headaches reduced, sleep*

improved, energy levels and good spirits were sustained and a gradual process of recovery was underway. As well as the great physical improvements, the Reiki treatments that Taggart has given me have helped me relax, sleep, be patient, laugh, lose the anger and stress the illness has imposed, and brought the sparkle back into my life."
Mrs J Butchart, Essex ***September 1999***

Note: Janet's treatments started with weekly sessions for 6 weeks, followed by further treatments at fortnightly, three-weekly and monthly intervals. The treatments were carried out using a special technique taught on the Second Degree course that is designed to boost personal energy levels.

Mental and Emotional problems

Margaret came for a Reiki treatment just to give it a try to see what would happen, and was quite sceptical. She decided on the treatment on impulse. It made a tremendous difference to her, and she ended up going through all the Reiki training up to Master Level. This is what she said:

"Dear Taggart,

I would like to take the time to tell you about the changes that Reiki has brought about in my life.

I came into the shop in Florence Walk to purchase some potato flour, smelt the incense you were using and asked the assistant what was going on. I was informed about Reiki and although I had never heard of it in my life I decided to give it a try. I had been feeling depressed, listless, sleepless and generally under the weather for some time. As well as this I was living under a great deal of stress and had been like that for four years since my husband's death.

After the first hour-long session I felt strangely calm and relaxed and slept that night for the first time in weeks. After a few days I began to feel more energetic and started running and exercising.

Each subsequent session left me feeling calmer than I'd felt in years. After four sessions I can honestly say that I am a much more relaxed, balanced, energetic person. I sleep soundly almost every night and I am able to cope with everyday worries and problems in a way that I never thought possible. Thanks to you and your influence I am learning to become a Reiki healer myself. Much love and thanks"
Mrs M.Taylor. Bishop's Stortford, Herts ***March 1998***

Yvonne was suffering from a great deal of stress and worry revolving around her daughter's relationship, and problems with the attitude and behaviour of her daughter's future mother-in-law. It was all getting too much for her and her daughter, so they came to see me in quite a desperate state. I treated both mother and daughter, and both felt that they could view things more positively, take control, and cope in a difficult situation. This is what Yvonne had to say:

"Dear Taggart,

I would like to thank you for the difference you and the Reiki treatment has made to the lives of my daughter Annie and I.

I can hardly believe the difference between the tense, weepy and insecure person I was when I first came to you, and the more relaxed and confident lady I am now.
My confidence continues to grow, as does the feeling that I can now 'listen' to my body, relax and help make it and my mind better.

I would not hesitate to recommend you to my friends and acquaintances.
Once again, a big thank you. Kindest regards"
Mrs Y Freestone, Sawston, CambsJune 1998

Ewan came to see me because he was suffering from a great deal of stress at work. He works as a money trader in the City, spending his day on several telephones and yelling at people. Most traders burn out in their 20s and have to change job, but Ewan was still doing it in his mid-30s. He found that he could not sleep properly, he could not wind down on weekends, and 'bad days' would take him days and days to recover from.

While treating him I experienced a huge wave of nausea as the stress and emotional effects of his job were released (an occasional sensation that you may experience when giving a treatment – fortunately not a very common one). After five treatments, Ewan is sleeping better and does not find that stressful days take him a long time to get over. There are limits to what Reiki can achieve if a person's lifestyle is 'toxic'. Reiki can made long-term positive changes, but in the end Ewan's problems will only be solved by changing jobs.

Anorexia

I had the opportunity to treat a teenager who was suffering from anorexia. I only carried out four treatments, and I was not able to follow her up subsequently, but Reiki produced a marked effect even over that short period of time. This young lady had put her life on hold, deferred her A-Levels, and despite having been through the conventional method for dealing with her problem, things had still not been resolved. Though she had lots of ideas about what she wanted to do, she woke up not looking forward to each day and was too fearful to put any plans into effect.

However after just a couple of treatments she started coming back into the world: she started working in the afternoons as a primary school classroom assistant (her mother was a teacher); though she was fearful of doing this, she managed to get over her resistance and actually do something. She enjoyed herself, felt good about herself, and started looking forward to each day.

Multiple Addictions

I treated a lady who had been addicted to painkillers, sleeping pills and tranquillisers for many years. She had decided that 'enough was enough' and tipped all her pills down the toilet, and she came to see me in the middle of her 'cold turkey' phase. Amazingly, after her first treatment she also gave up smoking - though this has relapsed subsequently. Now Lesley's self-confidence has changed quite remarkably. She seems to be enjoying life, and has fallen in love. A friend of hers who I spoke to said that she was amazed with the changes that Lesley's treatments had brought.

A whole range of problems

Brooks had an auto-immune condition that gave her joint pains, she had low energy levels, and sciatica. She was extremely stressed at work and going through a difficult period with her ex-husband (a Director of the company she still worked for). Over a course of 6-7 treatments the sciatica disappeared, the joint aches eased, and energy levels rose. Brooks started to redecorate her house, something she just would not have done before because she ached and had no energy. She felt a lot better about her work, with all the office politics and bitchiness washing over her instead of getting her down as it had done, and her encounters with her ex-husband were no longer the problem they had been. This is what she said:

> *"Dear Taggart,*
>
> *I came to see you by chance originally, suffering a long-term chronic illness, with an open mind, prepared to try anything once. I have had five sessions with you now and I am managing my condition so very much better and feel fitter and healthier than I have for years. The most marked effect is on my 'spirit'. My stress level has decreased dramatically and I feel so calm, and more able to cope. I don't know what you do or why it works, but I am so glad that I came to you. Kindest regards,"*
> ***Mrs B.Crossman. Finchingfield, Essex March 1998***

Note: Brooks went on to learn Reiki First and Second Degree, and the last time I saw her she reported that she no longer had the 'abnormal protein' that characterised her autoimmune condition.

Treating a Dog

Tracy (mentioned above) met me when she was looking for someone to treat her dog. The dog had some sort of developmental disorder in its back leg which led to the leg crossing over the other one. The muscles were wasting and the dog was not putting pressure on it. I carried out four 20-minute treatments and Reiki made a real difference over a short space of time. Interestingly, whereas the dog would usually ricochet off the walls when someone new came to visit, within a couple of minutes she was flopped out on my lap snoring, and I felt a great deal of tingling over her rear leg. This is what Tracy said about it:

> *"I met Taggart when I was looking for a healer for my dog, 'Star'. She had a misplaced patella, and although she is not in any pain, her right back leg was crossed over her other back leg, and she was walking with a terrible limp. The vets told me that there was nothing they could do for her.*
>
> *After 2 sessions with Taggart, Star was beginning to sit like a normal dog, instead of sweeping her leg under her; after 6 sessions she now sits properly all the time, she runs using all four legs, and she doesn't cross them at all anymore.*
>
> *Thank you Taggart for all you've done for my 'Star'."*
> ***Miss T Burrow, Braintree, Essex August 1998***

Giving Reiki treatments

Once you have been attuned to Reiki, you only have to place your hands on someone and the energy will flow automatically. The energy is drawn according to the recipient's need, and you act as a necessary bystander in the healing process: you need to be there for the process to take place, but your role is simply to be a channel for the energy. You are not the source of the healing; you are not 'a healer'. You are simply the conduit through which the energy flows, like a hollow bamboo tube. The best way that you can approach being a channel is by 'getting out of the way': you do not direct the energy; you let it flow as it wants to flow and with experience you can learn to work in partnership with the energy, by working intuitively, for example.

So Reiki flows automatically to the areas of need. It knows where to go to a large extent, and in what amounts. If you try to 'force' the process by 'willing' the recipient to get better, or if you give the treatment with the strong goal of resolving a particular medical condition, then your ego starts to get in the way and there may be a general lessening of the balancing effect of Reiki.

Because you are a channel for the energy and not the source of the energy, any treatments that you give will not drain you, but should actually replenish and invigorate you, as you receive a benefit from the energy that you are channelling. It is not your energy that you are dealing with when you treat, so your state of health or state of mind will in no way 'taint' the energy that you are channelling..

Just trust that Reiki will work, and let it do what it needs to do.

Situations when you should not treat someone

Basically, there are no situations where a Reiki treatment is contraindicated. That is not to say that there are not lists of 'situations where you should not use Reiki' taught in different Reiki lineages, but such lists have no basis; there is no evidence to back up restrictions on the use of Reiki. Some contraindications seem to have been 'lifted' from lists used in other complementary therapies, and some contraindications have been arrived at by thinking too much, thinking irrationally, worrying too much, and feeling that we need to restrict ourselves 'just to be on the safe side'. Restrictions are passed on from Master to student and are then passed on in good faith by new teachers, but it is groundless scaremongering.

Reiki is safe. There is no way that we can mess up a Reiki treatment because we are not really doing anything: it is the recipient that is drawing the energy and we are there to allow this to happen. Reiki gives the recipient what they need on each occasion, it creates a 'healing space' where balancing of the recipient's energy system can occur.

By way of demonstrating how irrational and nonsensical Reiki restrictions can be, I will mention two Reiki 'contraindications'. The first is that we should not treat pregnant women. One problem with this restriction is that there is not a shred of evidence – even anecdotal – to suggest that Reiki causes problems for pregnant women at any stage of their pregnancy, and all the anecdotal evidence demonstrates that Reiki is safe and beneficial. There is also a problem with this restriction in that there will be women coming for Reiki treatments who are pregnant but who do not know it yet. Thus to be 'safe' we need to make sure that we do not treat any woman of childbearing age, to make sure that we aren't treating anyone who is or might be pregnant.

In reality, Reiki is hugely beneficial and safe for pregnant women, new Mums and newborn babies.

Another contraindication that is taught sometimes is that we should not treat people with cancer (or that we should not use a particular Reiki symbol when treating people with cancer) because the Reiki energy (or the symbol) will 'feed the cancer'. The problem with this restriction is that everyone has cancer cells in their bodies, all the time. Cells are going haywire all the time and our immune systems clear up and deal with cancerous cells continually. If we were to heed this contraindication then we would not treat anyone!

There are further restrictions taught: we should not treat people with pacemakers, we should not treat diabetics or people taking steroids, or people with hearing aids. Again, there is no rational basis for or evidence to justify such restrictions. Reiki is safe.

One thing I will say, though, is that there seems to be some anecdotal evidence that some diabetics' blood sugar levels may alter – jiggle up and down - after having a Reiki treatment, in the same way that a person's emotional state can jiggle up and down following a treatment or course of treatments. This doesn't mean that you shouldn't treat diabetics, though. It means that the recipient should be told of this possibility and advised to keep an eye on their blood sugar levels (which they should be doing anyway). There is some evidence that Reiki may alter long-term the insulin requirement of some Diabetics.

Different treatment approaches

When you visit a Reiki practitioner it is likely that you will receive a treatment lasting approximately an hour. This is a 'full treatment'. You will be carrying out a full treatment during your live course, or carrying out several full treatments during your home study course.

But you are not obliged to always treat someone for an hour, going through all the hand positions that you will find described later and treating the head and shoulders, the torso and the legs. Such treatments are appropriate for people working as Reiki practitioners, dealing with the general public, but if you are treating friends and family – and we recommend that you do so as soon as you can – then you can treat for shorter periods if you like. You might treat a painful knee or shoulders for 5-10 minutes, or treat someone's head and shoulders for 15-20 minutes, for example.

So we have three possibilities for you:

1. Short blasts
2. Head and shoulder treatments
3. Full treatments

The following sections of the manual will deal with these treatment possibilities, we will consider the treatment of people's backs, and touch on treating animals and plants. We will also talk about various 'techniques' that you can use if you like, for example feeling the recipient's energy field, "scanning", and we will also touch on "freestyle" practice (based on the use of intuition).

For all the different treatment approaches we will follow a simple scheme, which can be summarised by these few words:

1. Affirm
2. Connect
3. Build
4. Merge
5. Flow

Keep these few words in mind as you read the following sections of the manual, which will explain in detail what these stages are and how to carry them out.

“Short Blasts”

Reiki treatments are ideally carried out in nice peaceful surroundings, with dimmed lights and gentle music, maybe some candles and incense burning, during a treatment session that lasts for up to an hour. But we can carry out brief Reiki treatments in a very informal way, and in locations and situations that are not ideal.

So if you are visiting family members and someone complains of a painful knee, just sit yourself down on the floor next to them and rest one hand over the other on top of the knee to treat it for 10 minutes or longer. If they have a painful back then they could lie on a bed or a sofa, for you to treat their back for 15-20 minutes or longer. If they have a headache they could sit in a straight-backed chair and you can treat their head for 15 minutes or longer. Treat for as long as feels right. Treat for as long as you have time available.

The energy will not have an opportunity to deal with the recipient’s entire energy system, and heal at all levels, but it should deal with the immediate problem, and that may be all that is wanted.

We should remember that when we use Reiki on someone we are not pushing for a particular end result: the recipient may want their headache to disappear – and it may well do – but we do not focus on that, we have no expectations. We are neutral in the process and simply allow the energy to flow; we allow the energy to do whatever is appropriate for the recipient. You might say that this approach involves dedicating the treatment to the recipient’s “highest good” or “highest healing good”.

We can follow a very simple ritual to start the treatment and to get the energy flowing. Here is my suggestion:

1. Close your eyes and take a few long deep breaths to still your mind
2. Remind your self that you are neutral in the process – **Affirm** that the treatment is for the ‘highest good’ of the recipient.
3. Imagine energy/light passing down to you from above, flowing through your crown down to your Tanden: **Connect**
4. Imagine/feel the energy building up in your Tanden; we work from the Tanden: **Build**
5. Rest your hand(s) on the recipient
6. Feel yourself merging with the energy and with the recipient: **Merge**
7. Let the energy flow for as long as feels appropriate: **Flow**

To bring the treatment to a close, you could take a long deep breath, bring your attention back to the room, back to reality, and take your hands off the recipient. Rest your hands in your lap and just be still for a few moments.

Seated Reiki treatments

Probably the 'ideal' way to carry out a Reiki treatment is for the recipient to be lying on a treatment couch. They can relax completely and in a safe way. But perhaps you do not have a treatment couch available to you, or with you, so the next best thing is to carry out a treatment with the recipient sitting in a straight-backed chair. For the recipient this will not be quite as comfortable as a padded treatment table, and they will not be able to relax as much as they would when supine, but a seated treatments can work well and can be a lovely experience for the recipient.

Below you can find a series of 'standard' hand positions that you can use to treat someone who is seated, but first I would like to talk in general about your approach to treating in this way.

Firstly, we should remember that when we use Reiki on someone we are not pushing for a particular end result: the recipient may want their headache to disappear – and it may well do – but we do not focus on that, we have no expectations. We are neutral in the process and simply allow the energy to flow; we allow the energy to do whatever is appropriate for the recipient. You might say that this approach involves dedicating the treatment to the recipient's "highest good" or "highest healing good".

Secondly, the hand positions that you can find illustrated below are just there for guidance. They are not set in stone. If when you give the treatment you feel drawn to a particular area of the body then you should accept the impression without trying to rationalise it, and treat the area that you feel drawn to, adding an extra hand position or adjusting the hand positions as seems appropriate. Also, while most hand positions are held for 3-5 minutes each, if you can feel that there is a lot of energy flowing through your hands into a particular position, stay in that position for longer until you can feel the flow of energy subside; then move on.

Starting the treatment

We can follow a very simple ritual to start the treatment and to get the energy flowing. Here is my suggestion:

1. Close your eyes and bring your hands into the prayer position
2. Take a few long deep breaths to still your mind
3. Remind your self that you are neutral in the process – **Affirm** that the treatment is for the 'highest good' of the recipient.
4. Imagine energy/light passing down to you from above, flowing through your crown down to your Tanden: **Connect**
5. Imagine/feel the energy building up in your Tanden; we work from the Tanden: **Build**
6. Rest your hands on the recipient's shoulders
7. Feel yourself merging with the energy and with the recipient: **Merge**
8. Allow the energy to flow, and move on to other hand positions when ready: **Flow**

Merging with the energy

Once the energy is building in your Tanden you can feel yourself merging with the energy that is flowing down to you. You can do this by imagining yourself disappearing into the energy, blending with it, becoming one with it. You can 'bliss out' on the energy. Still your mind and be neutral and empty.

Merging with the recipient

When you feel yourself or imagine yourself merging with the recipient, what I mean is that you can imagine a 'closeness' or a 'connection' between yourself and the person sitting on the chair. Imagine or feel your energy field and that of your client beginning to merge, coming together. Feel yourself becoming 'one' with the recipient. There is no you and no them, just the energy. Still your mind and be neutral and empty.

Finishing the treatment

To bring the treatment to a close, there are couple of things that you can do. Firstly you can smooth down the person's energy field, a way of boosting and energising and settling their energy field at the end of the treatment. Make some sweeps from the crown down towards the feet, using one hand or both hands, stroking the energy field with your palms. Do this a few times, but you need not go overboard. Cover the front, sides and back of the person.

Now you need to 'disconnect'. You felt yourself merging with the recipient at the start of the treatment, and during the treatment; now you need to take a ritual 'step back' from them, so you might rub your hands together, or blow through your hands held in the prayer position in front of your mouth, or shake your hands by your sides a few times, or even carry out Kenyoku. Some people recommend that you need to wash your hands after a treatment to fully disconnect from someone, but I think that this is unnecessary for the purposes of 'disconnection'.

Hand positions for seated treatments

Here is a basic scheme. I have not included arms and hands in this sequence, but treat them if that seems appropriate. You could rest one hand on the shoulder or elbow, and the other on the wrist, or hold their hand. This can feel really comforting. You could also treat the Liver and Spleen areas when you are working on the torso, if you like.

Please refer to the images below when reading this note: when treating the heart, solar plexus and navel, you could rest one hand on the shoulder all the time, and treat these areas with the other hand. Alternatively, you could treat these positions from the front and back of the body at the same time, and this would be made easier if the recipient was sitting in a 'Director's Chair' with a cloth back.

The practitioner, standing with a fairly straight back, can comfortably carry out the hand positions on the head and shoulders – and the heart. The hand positions on the torso and legs can be carried out while the practitioner kneels on the floor, or sits on another chair next to the recipient while treating the torso. Again, you can be in a reasonably comfortable position when you do this.

It is important that you are comfortable when you give a Reiki treatment. If you find that your arms or your back are aching then you distracted and you will not be as clear a channel when compared to a situation in which you are comfortable, still, and merged with the energy as it flows through you. With practice you should be able to work out the right way to hold your arms and body when you treat, to make sure you are comfortable and relaxed.

Here are some suggested hand positions for treating people sitting on a chair. Most of them are illustrated below...

Shoulders
Temples
Crown
Back of Head and the Forehead
Throat
Heart

Solar Plexus
Navel
Hips
Upper Leg
Knees
Ankles

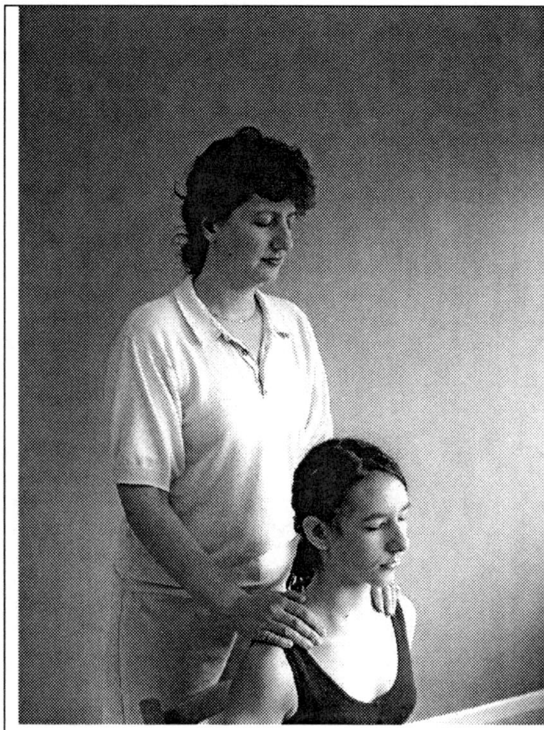

Shoulders

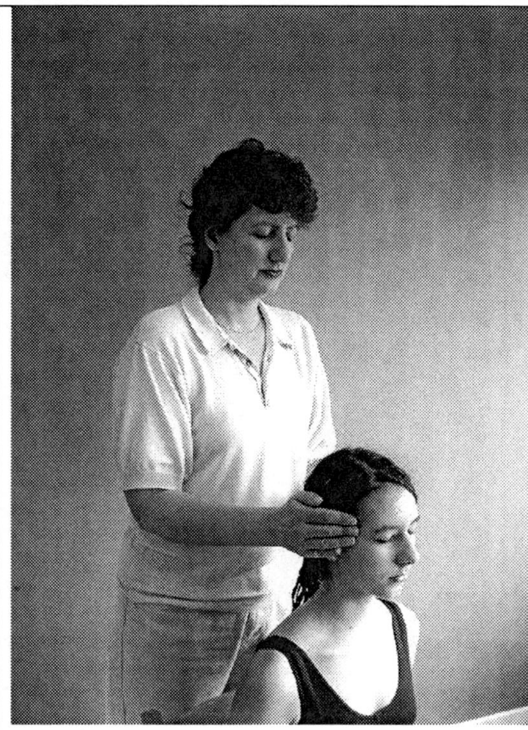

Temples

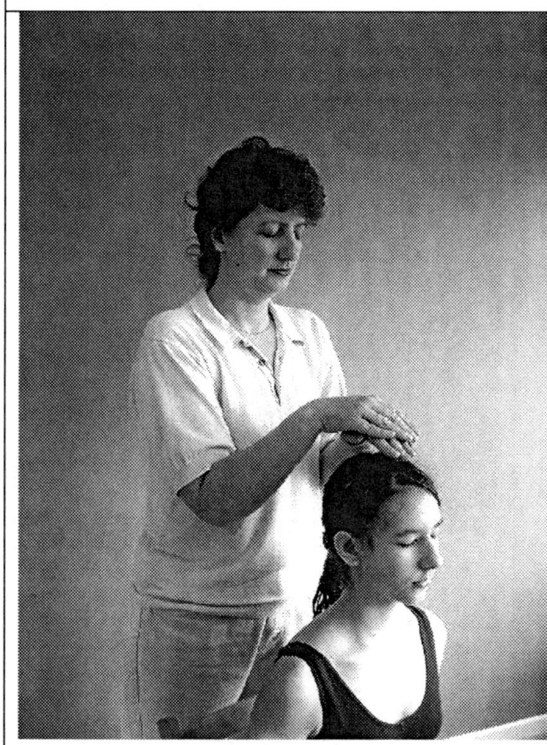

Crown

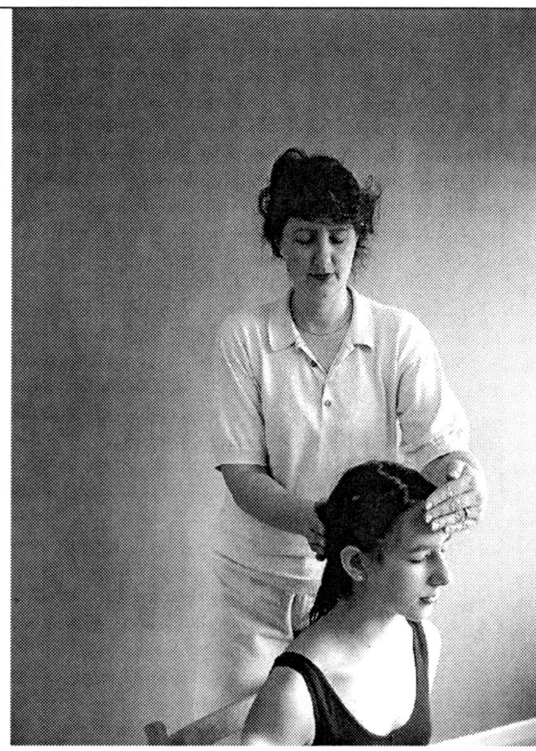

Forehead & Back of Head

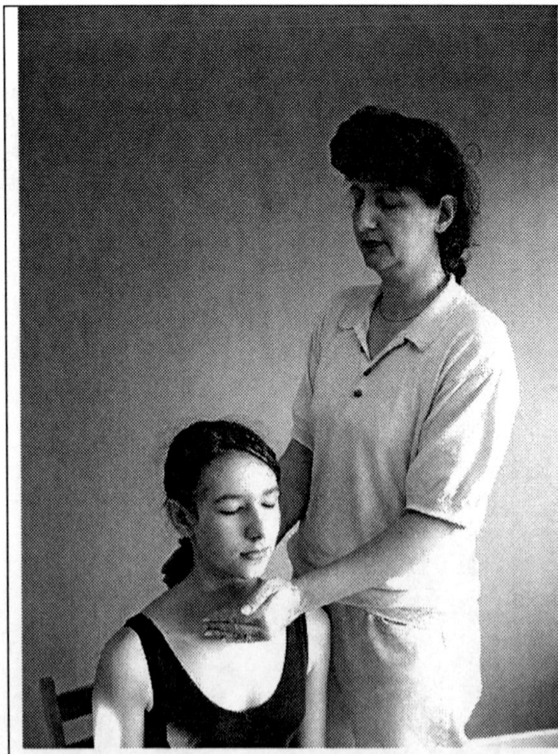

Throat

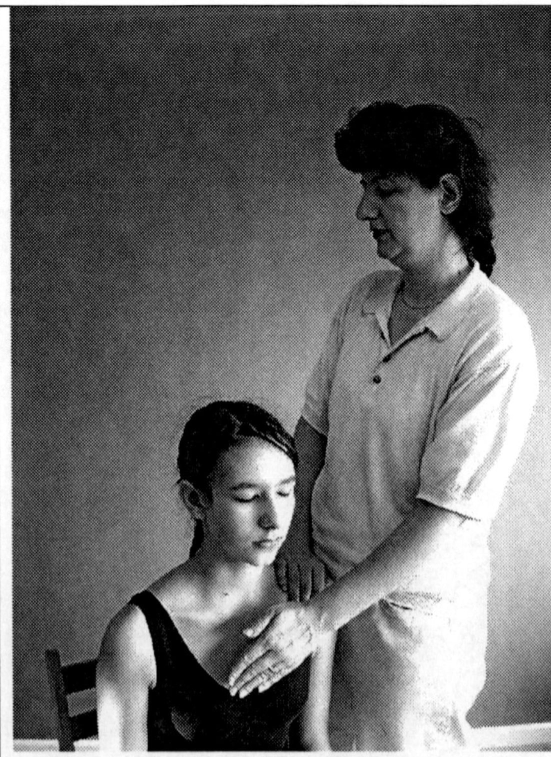

Heart

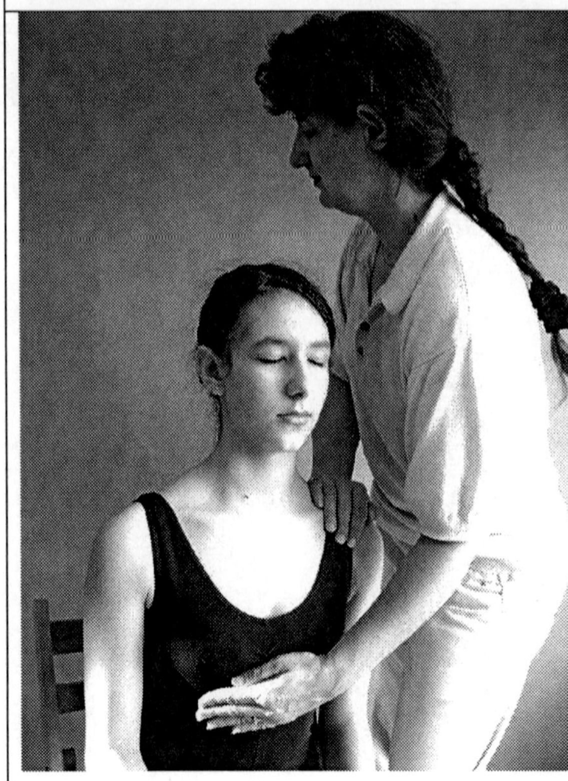

Solar Plexus

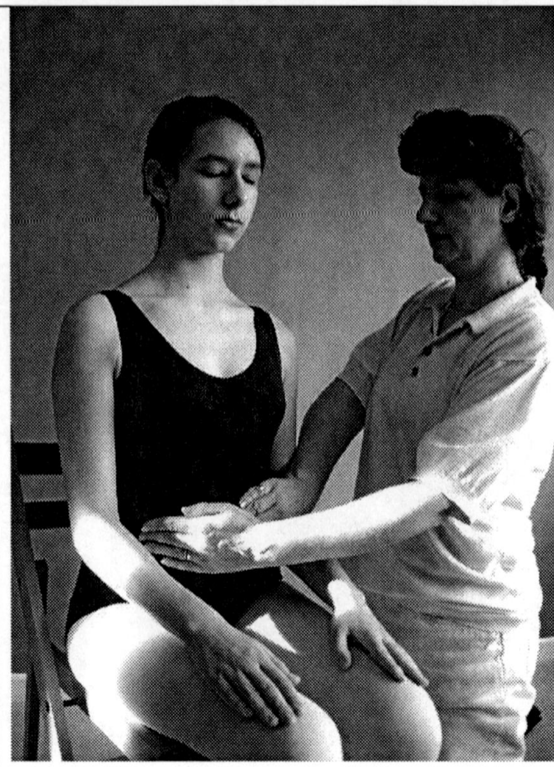

Navel

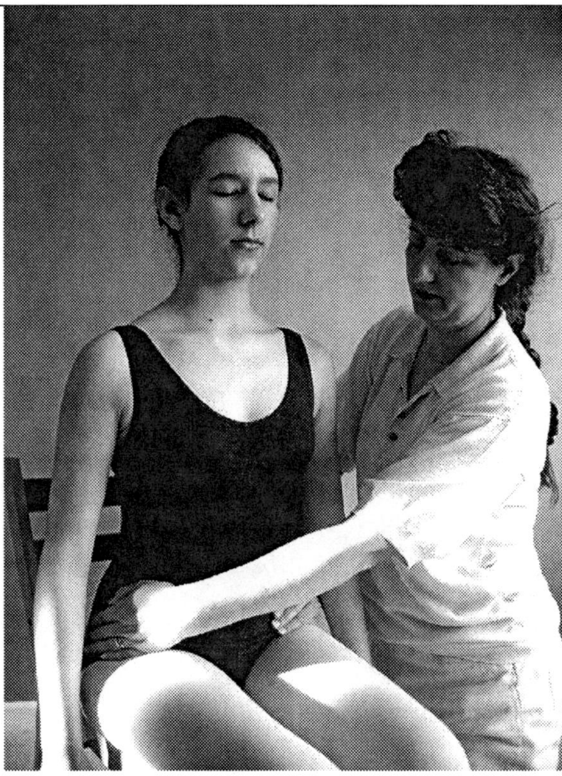

Hips

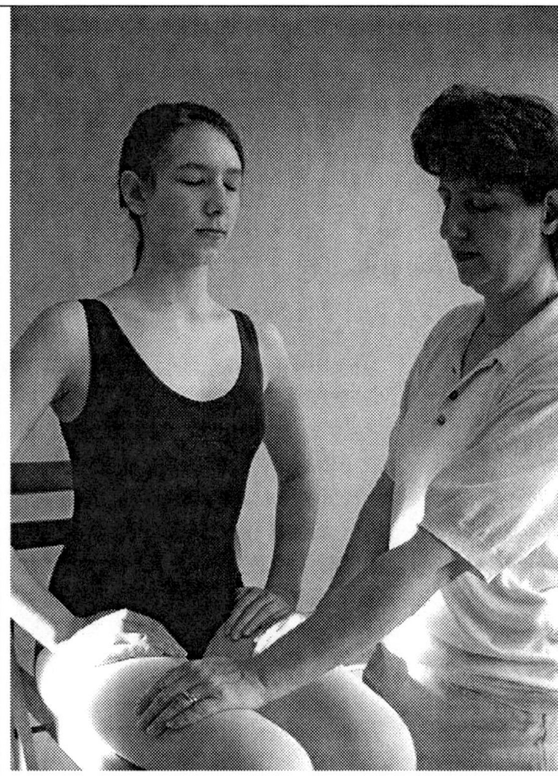

Upper Leg

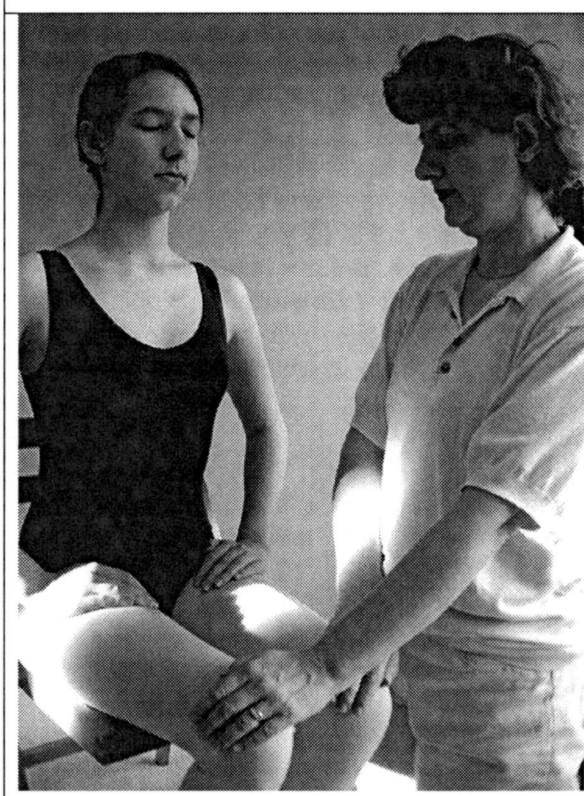

Knees

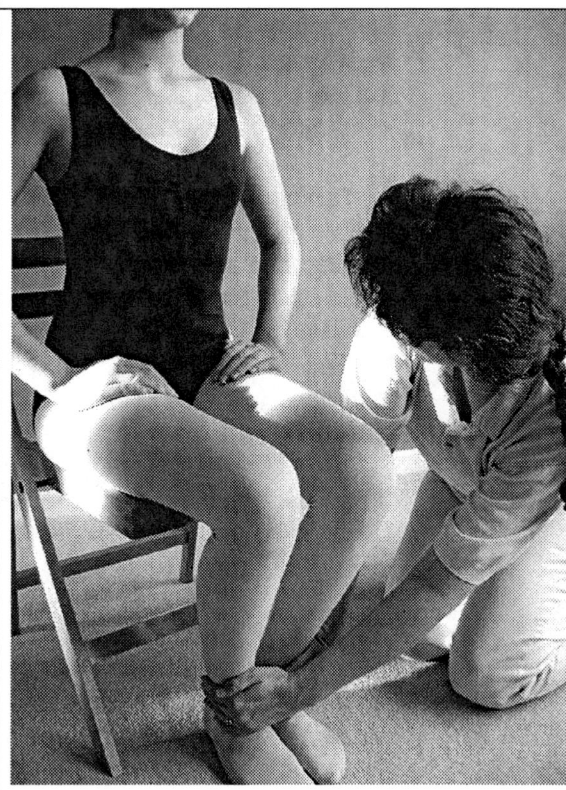

Ankles

Students' experiences: treating head and shoulders

"The human side of things has been interesting as both my patients and I have felt a wide variety of sensations. My strongest sensations have been whilst treating one person where I had a very strong fizzing in my hands around her temples, and she said afterwards that she had felt a very strong reaction in her head at that time too. Also when treating her shoulders my right hand went very heavy almost to the point of feeling numb, and it turns out that she has a lot of problems through her shoulder, back and pelvis down her right side. The other patients that I did felt a variety of sensations, but again mostly to me it is a strong fizzing"
"T.B." from Norfolk

"The first treatment took a while to get going but gradually got stronger. Throughout the treatment I kept in mind the strong connection to reiki and that really helped. On the sholders I felt more a few cm away from the person rather than touching?

My partner felt tingling through his body, down from his neck to his legs, and tingling in his fingers, and also a creeping sensation on his forehead, as if an ant were crawling on it, which progressively got stronger. He also felt something on his crown.

The second time I treated him, he felt as if someone were holding the back of his head, and he had tingling sensations down his back and accross his face. He also had a feeling of sinking down. But when I put my hands on his sholders to mark the end of the session he felt as if he were rising up.
For me, I was very tingly from the word go. Interestingly, in some positions the flow seemed to stop abruptly. Again, I felt more when my hands were at a distance."
Jason Brown from North Wales

"I had the opportunity to treat head and shoulders of 8 different member of my family, also done energy exercise with some of them : mainly a strong tingling feeling and also repulsion.

They could feel the heat and a tingling sensation. My aunt could see the following colours : dark yellow turning to green then back to yellow, back to green and so on. My sister in law only saw a deep violet colour. Strangely enough, a colleague of mine I treated could see red then green then red on a regular interval and was feeling a slight discomfort with my palms on the front of the forehead. My mum felt like she was floating and my sister in law said she thought her body was lifting. I don't know if these are common sensation.

My cousin did not like being sitting as he felt like falling to sleep but the chair made it uncomfortable. He also could feel a little bit of pain during the treatment.

All of them said they'd rather lye down then sit as they were getting so relaxed and mellow."
Bruno Cassani from Essex

"I've been treating my husband and mother in law with the head and shoulder technique and have experienced hot and tingling hands in area which have needed treatment. My mother in law has fibromyalga so she has a lot of fatigue and sleep problems, after both treatments she has felt rested, slept well and has had more energy.

My husband has slept better than normal and has said he feels very chilled after the treatments i have given him.

Some of the feed back i have had whilst performing the head and shoulders treatments has been amazing, one of my friends saw the colours of red, orange and yellow at the same time as i saw them, she also had a tingling feeling around her face area and said she felt extremely relaxed when i had finished."
Niki Leach from Tyne and Wear

"I could feel a difference in the energy around the head and shoulders of all four of the people I practiced on. In both the people I practiced on who had sore necks I could feel increased pulsation and heat in my hands when they were over the sore areas and it took about 10 mins over each area for the pulsation to ease off, but tingling and heat remained. The people with neck pain also had a change in energy in the forehead region and they told me afterwards that they had been having headaches. On one of the other people I could feel a change in energy at the top of their head, I felt this in my hands has a pulsation, heat and tingling. On the 4th person I couldn't feel any change in their energy, although I did feel heat and slight tingling in my hands, this is the person who felt nothing.

While I was carrying out the treatment I felt very peaceful and relaxed, I felt like I was a channel for the energy and that space had been made in me in order that it could flow, I felt light."
Susan Naylor from West Yorkshire

"In the evening I set the scene to do my first head and shoulders treatment, starting with treating my partner. I turned the lights down, burned some incense and played some relaxing meditation music to set a relaxing, non distractive atmosphere. Immediately upon starting the treatment I felt my hands become very hot which then ran down my arms and within about 2 minutes my entire body became very hot. Even my feet felt as though they were almost burning into the floor.

I decided to meditate during the treatment to try and increase the flow of energy for my first time. I visualised the energy entering my crown, moving down my torso into my Dantian, strengthening and then floading through my hands.

As I proceeded to visualised, the stronger the visualisation, the strong the heat became. Although I was hot at all times I experienced very hot heat waves travel through my body to the point where it was actually slightly umcomfortable. The temperature of the room was the same as it had been during the day.

I only treated for 20 minutes as I was uncomfortably hot and my partner was very fidgety!!! After the treatment he said that he was sorry for fidgeting so much but he was very very hot! He said it started as soon as I laid my hands on him and hit him in waves through his body which made it difficult for him to be comfortable especially sitting in a chair. He said he felt a tingling feeling on his head but he just felt so so so hot!

.

.

.

Thank you for your advice last week. You were quite right, my next experiences with giving head and shoulder treatments was completely different. I actually felt like I was able to control the energy during the next 4 treatments on different people. I again meditated whilst giving treatments as I found that it was easier to keep my mind from wandering if I meditated. I have a very busy, active mind and can sometimes struggle to keep it clear so mediation has been the perfect way for me to enable it to empty and allow the energy to flow. When I have felt a real surge of energy that has brought the intense heat I have ceased to meditate and just let the energy flow by itself for a while.

My experiences with treating this week have been lovely. It has been extremely relaxing for myself but all 3 people that I have treated also fell asleep during the treatment. They said they felt real warmth from my hands and a fuzzy kind of feeling and were unable to stay awake during the treatment. Upon waking they were amazed at how fast the time had gone and commented that it was not like a normal sleep where they would wake up feeling really groggy. They did indeed wake up feeling fresh, relaxed and really good in them selves. This was so encouraging for me!"
Sarah Quinn from Kent

"I gave neck and shoulder treatments to the family. My daughter felt very relaxed and almost fell asleep (she fought it). My husband fell asleep almost immediately. I treated my son after an emotional upset. He said he felt much calmer and better afterwards.

I experienced one evening where my hands were tingling like crazy. I ended up putting my hands on our cats for about an hour, not petting them, just resting my hands on them. The cats were in heaven and my hands finally settled down. The one cat had had an ongoing problem with her eye (all sore and runny) that I assumed was from a scratch. The next morning her eye was completely fine again. A very abrupt healing that I can't help but attribute to Reiki."
Karen Small from America

"Full" Reiki treatments

When you visit a Reiki practitioner you are likely to receive a Reiki treatment lasting for about 50-70 minutes. Such hour-long sessions are usually referred to as 'full' treatments, and the sessions will usually involve the practitioner treating the whole body: the head and shoulders, the torso and the legs. For best results, the recipient should receive a number of treatment sessions, for example 4-6 sessions at weekly intervals. One Reiki treatment will probably do something for the recipient, but any effect is less likely to be long-lived when compared with the sort of results that can be obtained by building momentum over a course of treatments, where each further session builds on the work that has already been done. There is no reason why you shouldn't treat someone every day of you wish, but for most people weekly sessions work well. Leave too long an interval between treatments and you are likely to lose the 'momentum', so seeing someone at monthly intervals is not recommended, unless they are 'top-up' treatments following an earlier course of weekly sessions.

Probably the 'ideal' way to carry out a Reiki treatment is for the recipient to be lying on a treatment couch. They can relax totally and drift in and out of consciousness without falling out of a chair, for example, and the practitioner can get themselves comfortable standing up or in the seated position. If you don't have a treatment table, then you can improvise by using a bed or a sofa, but that is not likely to be so comfortable for you as a practitioner. Perhaps the best compromise of all would be to use a dining table with blankets on it to make it less uncomfortable for the recipient. I know a few people for whom this is quite acceptable. You could also try treating someone on a reclining garden chair, with you seated on a stool. If you are intending to deal with the general public then a proper treatment table is indispensable, and I include details of suppliers in the Second Degree manual and on our web site.

In this section there is a great deal of detail and we are going to consider a whole range of things to with the giving of full Reiki treatments. At the end of this section you can find a series of 'standard' hand positions that you can use to treat someone who is supine, but first I would like to outline a general treatment scheme, which I will then expand upon, and after that I will make some further general comments about treating people.

Starting the treatment

We can follow a very simple ritual to start the treatment and to get the energy flowing. Here is my suggestion:

1. Close your eyes and bring your hands into the prayer position
2. Take a few long deep breaths to still your mind
3. Remind your self that you are neutral in the process – **Affirm** that the treatment is for the 'highest good' of the recipient.
4. Imagine energy/light passing down to you from above, flowing through your crown down to your Tanden: **Connect**
5. Imagine/feel the energy building up in your Tanden; we work from the Tanden: **Build**
6. Spend some time feeling the recipient's energy field – see below
7. Spend some time 'scanning' the body – see below
8. Rest your hands on the recipient's shoulders
9. Feel yourself merging with the energy and with the recipient: **Merge**
10. Allow the energy to flow, and move on to other hand positions when ready: **Flow**

Merging with the energy

Once the energy is building in your Tanden you can feel yourself merging with the energy that is flowing down to you. You can do this by imagining yourself disappearing into the energy, blending with it, becoming one with it. You can 'bliss out' on the energy. Still your mind and be neutral and empty.

Merging with the recipient

When you feel yourself or imagine yourself merging with the recipient, what I mean is that you can imagine a 'closeness' or a 'connection' between yourself and the person sitting on the chair. Imagine or feel your energy field and that of your client beginning to merge, coming together. Feel yourself becoming 'one' with the recipient. There is no you and no them, just the energy. Still your mind and be neutral and empty.

Finishing the treatment

To bring the treatment to a close, there are couple of things that you can do. Firstly you can smooth down the person's energy field, a way of boosting and energising and settling their energy field at the end of the treatment. Make a number of sweeps above the recipient's body, moving from crown to feet (not the other direction). Intend that you are smoothing the energy field all round the client's body, front and back. Imagine that you are moving an invisible hula-hoop along the length of the person's body, smoothing the energy down

360 degrees around their body, as you move your hands from the crown to the feet. Do this a few times, but you need not go overboard.

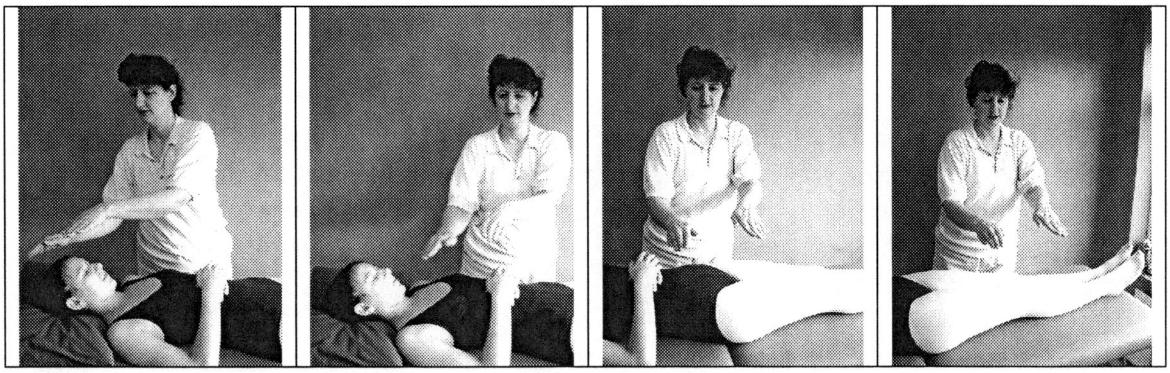

Now you need to 'disconnect'. You felt yourself merging with the recipient at the start of the treatment, and during the treatment; now you need to take a ritual 'step back' from them, so you might rub your hands together, or blow through your hands held in a loose prayer position in front of your face, or shake your hands by your sides a few times, or even carry out Kenyoku. Find something that says "I have disconnected" to you and do it at the end of every treatment. Your intention here is the important thing. Some people recommend that you need to wash your hands after a treatment to fully disconnect from someone, but I think that this is unnecessary for the purposes of 'disconnection'.

It is said that you should ritually 'disconnect' because you do not want to 'pick up' the recipient's problems and carry them away with you, and indeed this does seem to be a problem for hands-on therapists in general. But it is not a problem for people who practise Reiki: Reiki seems to have in-built protections. In fact many hands-on therapists learn Reiki specifically because doing so will protect them when they treat others and because Reiki helps to prevent the feeling of depletion that afflicts many hands-on therapists. Reiki boosts and invigorates you when you treat others and you are not giving of your own energy.

Working from the Tanden

The Tanden point is seen as the centre of our selves from the Oriental point of view, a seat of power, the centre of our intuitive faculties, the centre of life. Drawing energy into your Tanden is drawing energy into the centre of your life and soul. This area acts as a power centre that allows the amazing feats of martial artists to be performed, but also acts as the source of inspiration in Oriental flower arranging and calligraphy. Meditation, exercise techniques like Tai Chi and QiGong, martial arts and Usui Reiki can all develop the Tanden.

Using the power of the Tanden allows the Reiki practitioner to increase their intuition and the sensitivity in their hands. It allows us to empathise with the recipient but allows distance so we do not take on another's problems. Because of this, it is recommended that when you prepare to give Reiki you should first become aware of the Tanden and the centred feeling that this gives, and 'work from the Tanden' when you treat.

'Connecting' to the energy

The way that we have already described is the simplest way of 'connecting' to the energy, where you imagine or feel energy or light passing down to you from above, to build in your Tanden. Of course you are never not connected to the energy, so really what you are doing is to focus your attention strongly on your connection to the energy.

There are other ways that you can use to connect to the energy though. For example, you can use the hand position that you learned when carrying out Hatsurei ho, by raising your hands palms uppermost to the skies, and feel energy cascading through your hands, through your arms, into your body, down to your Tanden (see left). As you feel that strong connection, you can proceed to lower your arms.

An alternative would be to stand with your elbows bent, hands out to the sides with your palms uppermost, level with your waist, and imagine that energy is flooding down into your palms and into your crown, building in the Tanden.

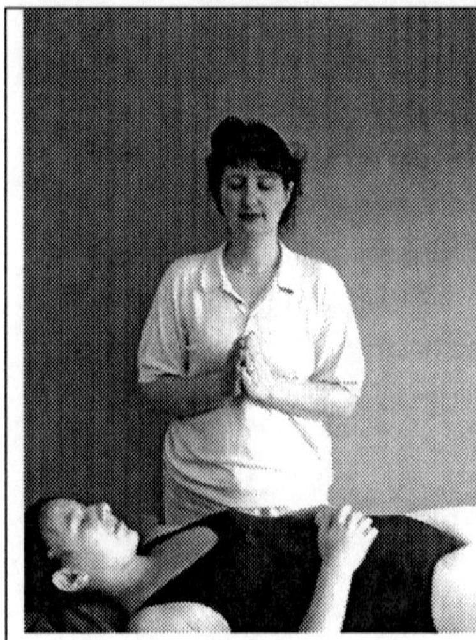

Connecting with hands in 'gassho' position

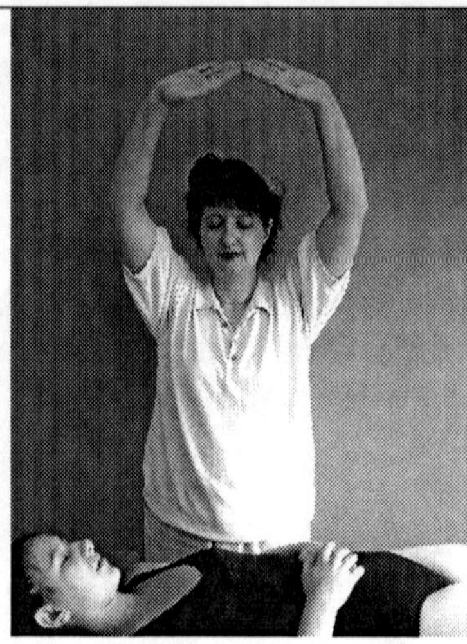

Connecting with palms towards the sky

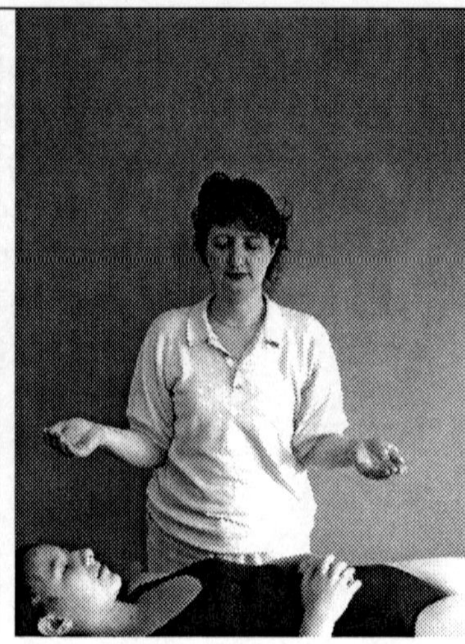

Connecting with hands held out to the sides

"Reiki On"

It is common within the world of Reiki for practitioners to say "Reiki On" silently to themselves when they first rest their hands on the recipient. Of course saying "Reiki On" does not switch the Reiki on, but having a little ritual like this can be useful; it can be a way of saying to yourself "OK, I'm doing Reiki now... let me be in the best frame of mind for doing Reiki".

Try this, and use this ritual if you feel better using it.

No-one seems to say "Reiki Off" to themselves at the end of a treatment session. Reiki is always with you, and what varies is the attention that you focus on your connection, you awareness of your connection.

How to hold your hands as you treat

Many people recommend that as you go through the hand positions you should keep your fingers together. You don't have to strain to do this, but just gently rest them together. Spreading your fingers apart is said by some to send a more gentle, diffuse stream of Reiki. Don't worry too much about this, because Reiki is not sensitive to your technique.

Reiki is basically a hands-on therapy, so you will be resting your hands on the recipient's body in a variety of positions. You need to make sure that you are not pressing down or bearing down on the recipient as you treat them. You should have a gentle and light touch, a 'feather touch', and when moving from one hand position to another you should move your hands off the body gently and slowly and allow your hands to come to rest gently in the next hand position. Abrupt and forceful movements should not be a part of Reiki.

Though some people within the world of Reiki are taught that you always need to have at least one hand resting on the recipient, for fear of losing your 'connection' to them (which then has to be regained in some way, by carrying out some sort of ritual), we need take no notice of these rules. 'Connection' to the recipient is down to your intent, not your hand positions, and you are connected to the recipient no matter whether your hands are. If you can connect to someone the other side of the planet by way of distant healing, then you can certainly connect to someone a couple of feet in front of you on a treatment table, no matter whether your hands are resting on them or not.

Your state of mind when you treat

The best results are obtained when you are calm and relaxed, becoming at one with the energy. You are aiming to be in a meditative state when treating someone, in the same way that you are in a meditative state when carrying out hatsurei, when self-treating and indeed when carrying out distant healing. If you are not used to meditating then you will probably find that your mind wanders at times, though you might be surprised by how easy it can be to have an empty mind sometimes when giving a Reiki treatment. Particularly if there is a lot of energy coming through, your mind can empty of its own accord and the treatment turns into a lovely meditation.

It will not always be like this, of course. Your mind will wander, more in some treatments than others, and you do not need to worry about this because you do not need to be in a perfectly meditative state all the time when you treat. This is an ideal to aim towards and you may never attain it, and that is no problem.

If you do notice that your mind is wandering when you treat, pay the errant thoughts no attention. Gently bring your attention back to what you were doing, imagine or feel yourself disappearing into the energy and merge with it, and allow the energy to flow. If your mind wanders again, do not worry about this – this is normal, this is human; gently bring your attention back to what you were doing, and merge with the energy and the recipient.

Though some teachers will say that it does not matter what you are thinking about, or what else you are doing when giving a Reiki treatment, you should realise that you will be a better channel for the energy if you can minimise distractions. So if you are giving a treatment while having an animated conversation with someone, you will not produce the best results because the energy will not flow so strongly. Do not chat to the recipient and do not chat with anyone else while you treat.

Letting your hands tell you how long to treat

When carrying out your full treatment you will start with the shoulders – treating these for about 10 minutes - and then spend about 4-5 minutes in each of the hand positions. If you can feel a lot of energy passing through your hands in a particular position then you can hold that position for longer, perhaps a lot longer if you feel it is necessary. You will usually find that after a while the intensity of the sensations in your hands will decrease, when the area has taken as much Reiki as it can for that session.

So what you are feeling in your hands can guide you in terms of how long you will spend in each hand position, with the general proviso that you should spend at least 2-3 minutes in each position.

Feeling the Energy Field

Before I have my students start their hand-on treatment, I recommend that they spend a little while developing the sensitivity of their hands to the energy field of their clients, and developing their sensitivity to the flow of Reiki. This can be achieved by practising feeling the recipient's energy field, and by practising 'scanning' (see below). Here are some instructions that tell you how to approach feeling the recipient's energy field:

Start with your arms raised to shoulder level, with your palms down, facing the recipient. If you have decided to use the 'connecting' hand position that we learned in Hatsurei ho, you can simply move your hands forwards and downwards towards the recipient. As you lower your arms from the 'connecting' position, hover your hands above the client's body and slowly 'bounce' your hands nearer and nearer the body until you can feel the person's energy field. You are looking to experience a feeling of pressure, density, a layer, some feeling of resistance or 'bounciness', a squashy marshmallow of energy. Move your hands up, and bring them down again to reconfirm that the layer is in the same place. Now move along a little and repeat the process, lifting the hands up and allowing them to bounce gently towards the body.

Is the energy field that you can feel the same distance away from the body all the way along the length of the body? Are there areas where the 'layer' is closer to the body than in other places? Does the 'layer' feel different in different places? How does it feel different? What conclusions can you draw from this information?

The level of the person's energy field can give you some indication of their energy needs. For example, in the case of a nurse who had done two long shifts and was very tired, but who had a good strong constitution, we found that the energy field was a good distance away from the body over the head and torso, but the energy field was depleted over the legs. In a lady with depression, the energy field plummeted very close to the body in the head area. In a lady with chronic fatigue, the energy field was very difficult to detect at all, and this has been noticed on a few occasions.

Can you feel smaller undulations in the energy field, and what might they mean?

The significance of these 'depleted' areas is simply that you will probably end up spending a bit more time than normal during the treatment working on those areas. They will probably be drawing more energy.

You can actually 'boost' or 'energise' the client's energy field at this stage if you want to: hover your hands over the person and imagine that Reiki is flooding through your hands and 'filling up' the energy field. Feel your hands move slowly away from the body as the energy field floods with Reiki. Move your hands to hover over another part of their body, and flood that section of the energy field too. Once you have done this a few times, try to feel the energy field again. What do you notice? Is the energy field now further away from the body compared to what it was like to begin with?

Please note that not everyone can feel the energy field the first few times they try this exercise. This not a cause for concern, since your sensitivity to such things usually builds over time, with practice. In fact a few people find that they cannot feel the energy field, though most people can feel variations in the flow of energy as they treat someone (heat and/or fizzing or tingling in their hands as they 'scan' or treat).

Not everyone in the world of Reiki practises feeling the recipient's energy field – this is not standard practice – so there will be thousands and thousands of Reiki people out there who have never tried feeling the energy field, and who give treatments happily and successfully. So this stage is not essential. But for people who can feel something, experiencing the recipient's energy field is a nice way of focusing your attention on the recipient, a way of helping to 'merge' with them; it is a practice that can provide you with some useful information about the energetic state of the person on the treatment couch too.

Scanning

Scanning is a standard part of a lot of Western Reiki courses, sometimes taught at First Degree and certainly taught at Second Degree level. People 'scan' at the start of a treatment to 'get the lie of the land', to discover areas of need, so that they have an idea of where they will need to spend more time during the treatment. People can also scan at the end of a treatment to see what effect Reiki has had on the energy being drawn by areas of the body that were prominent at the start. Some people scan to find the best places to put their hands, rather than following standard hand positions. Some people use a combination of standard hand positions, and hand positions discovered through scanning, different for each person treated.

To practice scanning, you should hover your hand or hands over the person's body. You do not need to find and rest your hand on the layer of energy: simply find a hovering distance that feels comfortable for you and will allow you to scan without making contact with any of the contours of the recipient's body. Perhaps it would be better to start by using one hand only, since your attention will not need to be shared between two hands. Now drift your hand(s) slowly over the body - not deathly slow, but equally not too quickly either because you may not be able to notice the changes in the sensations you have in your hands. Focus your attention on the sensations that you are experiencing in your palm and fingers and notice if there are any changes or intensification in what you are feeling as you drift from one area to another.

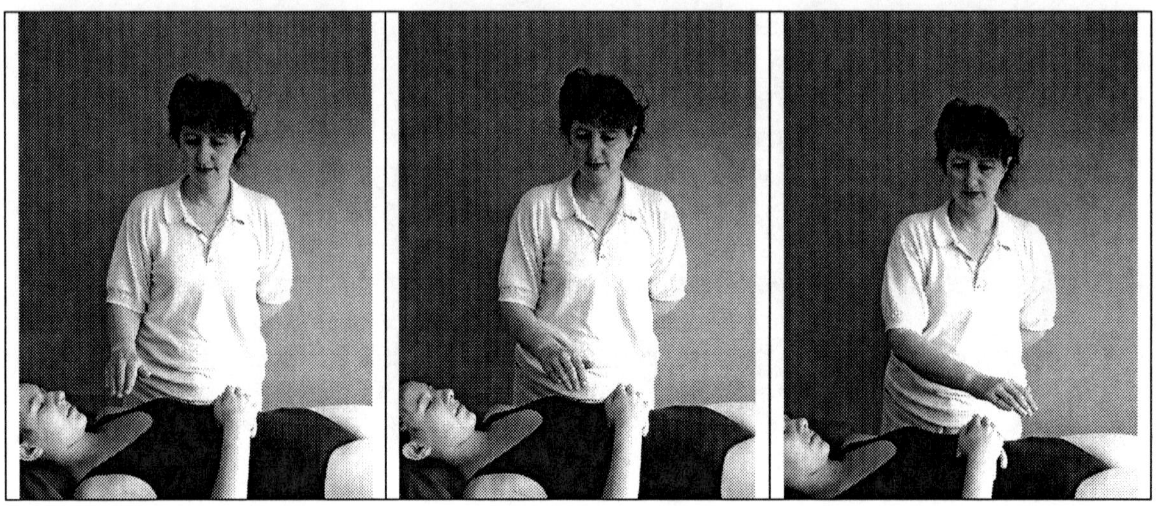

If you feel an area where there is more energy flowing - you may feel more fizzing or tingling, more heat, pulsing, magnetic effects, heaviness etc. - then move your hand away and then allow your hand to drift back to that area from different angles. Do you get the same feeling again and again? How large is the area that is drawing more energy? Is it the size of a 50p coin, or is it a broad band across the body?

Try comparing symmetrical areas of the body: the shoulders, hips, knees, and ankles. Hover your hands for a little while over one knee and notice how that feels; then do the same on the other side. What differences are there? Is one knee drawing more energy than the other is? Does this tie in with any problems that the client is experiencing: a current problem, or a past injury?

Joints in the legs – particularly the knees and ankles – can be good areas to use to practise scanning, since it is common for their to be a little ‘spike’ of energy, a little ‘dzzzt’ of energy that you can feel in your hand or fingers as you drift over the joint. This does not mean that there is necessarily a problem in the joint: we use our legs each day, putting pressure on and taxing the joints, and Reiki rushes in to support natural healing.

With repetition, your hands should become progressively more sensitive to the flow of energy, and this is useful information. Through scanning you can find out where you are going to spend more time during the treatment, and you can check to see what effect your treatment has had on the amount of energy being drawn by those areas of the body. Scanning can suggest additional hand positions that are not part of the 'standard' sequence that you will see below. While you may start treating people by resting your hands in each position for a certain number of minutes according to the clock, you can let your hands tell you when it is right to move on, as the flow of energy subsides in each treatment position.

Practice scanning whenever you treat someone and your sensitivity should develop.

When scanning, you should not get yourself into the frame of mind where you are thinking continually 'what is wrong here?', 'what have you got wrong here?'. Reiki can rush in to deal with perfectly normal and ordinary physiological processes: if you have had a big lunch then Reiki will rush into the stomach area to support digestion; they haven't got a stomach ulcer, Reiki is just supporting a normal physiological function. If you feel lots of energy rushing into the client's head, you are probably picking up on a busy mind or a tendency to headaches maybe. You can quite often detect menstruation or pick up which side is ovulating through the sensations you are getting your hands; there is no problem, it just a normal physiological process that Reiki is supporting, and which you are experiencing through your hands. People who exercise are continually damaging their muscles and joints and the body repairs that damage as a matter of routine, Reiki will rush in to support this natural process.

Reiki will also deal with things that seem to have been dealt with a long time ago. So although a person may have twisted their ankle months ago and everything is now fine, there seems to be some trace of the problem at some level that still needs to be dealt with, and Reiki will deal with it.

Reiki can deal with things have not happened yet. Many people believe that problems begin on the mental and emotional planes, and that it is only if these imbalances are not dealt with that they will condense or manifest as a physical symptom. On this basis, you may be resolving things that were 'on the boil' and might have materialised at some stage in the future.

Reiki works on all levels, so it is not just the physical body part under your hands that is being dealt with: it deals with mental and emotional correspondences of the various organs, it deals with spiritual aspects of a person, and it deals with chakras and meridians too. Sometimes it is simple: a person has a kidney stone, so there's a lot going on in the kidney area, but it isn't always that straightforward. Quite often you will be able to tell which knee is giving the person a problem, or you will pick up things happening on an emotional level in the solar plexus, for example, but don't worry about it. Simply trust that it is going to the right place, even if you don't know what is being dealt with. You don't need to know.

Someone can come for a Reiki treatment and not tell you what the problem is, and that will not have any effect on the quality of the treatment you give because you simply follow the flow of energy, spending longer treating the areas that are drawing the most energy.

Students' experiences: Scanning

"Scanning

Felt hot and spongy over head. Increased energy field distance around temples, hands felt pulled towards temples when close and then at a certain point whilst moving then away they felt like they were being pushed. Strongest sensation on the temples.

Shoulders, field was a lot closer than the head. Hands felt fizzy in places. Had to really concentrate and shut eyes at points to tune into the feelings but at all times hands felt warm getting hotter in certain positions.

Scanning my cat

Moved hand slowly down above the cat whilst he was asleep. As I reached his energy field he responded as though I was stroking him without opening his eyes. Did same thing again twice and he responded the same way. Scanned whole body and energy field felt the same distance along whole body. He purred and suddenly looked at me as if he had just enjoyed a big fuss!

Scanning my dog

Came down towards him whilst he lay asleep. As I came in touch with his energy he immediately raised his head, looked at me as though I had touched him and raised his leg. I moved away and then moved closer and again he repeated the same behaviour. I repeated this 6 times and 6 times he responded in the same manor. The only difference with him was my hands felt cooler not hotter!!!"

Sarah Quinn from Kent

"I have been working on the scanning with 3 people a few different times. Definitely felt some energy flow. Moved my hands away and brought them back to where the activity was. i scanned over my sister-in-laws knee, felt something going on, stayed there but left and scanned the rest of her body. After the scanning she asked me why i didn't stay there. Apparently that is her bad knee (which i did not know) and i felt some more warmth there but didn't feel confident to ask her if that was a area of her body while i was scanning."

Eloise Sicora from America

"The energy play varied day to day and with who I did it with. I thought I could feel something when I felt it with just my hands. My critical side kept questioning it though, which made it harder. Doing exercises with a partner's hand was more interesting to me. I could usually feel a lot of tingling in my hand. When I moved the hand side to side and up and down, I felt the energy moving around my hand. I frequently felt aware of the energy "field" before they did, but felt it stronger by the time they said they felt it. I guess I jumped ahead a bit and tried some of the other exercises in the manual (feeling energy around a partner's head and the balancing exercise). I could really feel energy around my husband and son's heads and they both said they felt it, particularly heat from my hands. When I tried pushing my husband off balance he felt the push and pull."

Karen Small from America

"For the energy exercises, the scanning varied greatly with subjects. I always felt the energy field, but there were much stronger sensations when I did my husband and son (more heat and tingling), versus my daughter. I came into this feeling my husband and son were most in need of Reiki, so perhaps the scanning is showing their greater need for energy? My son felt heat very strongly (I don't think he's "putting on"). He also was very aware of a "cushiony" feeling, corresponding to when I felt I was touching his energy field. Question: I notice two "layers" of energy. Is that possible? It seemed like I encounter something about 12 inches out (cushiony resistance), then feel a stronger field (tingling and heat) about 6 inches from the subject (the distances are very rough estimates, and vary).

I tried scanning our cats. I had much the same sensations as with people. Couldn't tell if they noticed anything. I sort of felt something with plants. Trees give a more distinct sense of energy for me."

Karen Small from America

Intuitive working

When you have had some regular practice in treating other people, Reiki may begin to guide you to the right areas of the body to treat, if you are open to the possibility of working intuitively. This is not essential though. Don't worry if you end up doing most treatments following the 'standard' hand positions, because it will still work! We talk about working intuitively on the Second Degree course, and learn a specific technique from Japan that opens you up to intuitive working, so your hands are drawn by what seem to be 'invisible magnets' to the right places to treat.

However, if you have in your mind an impression that your hands ought to be in a particular position then don't think about it, don't analyse it: just move your hands there to treat. If you have a word come into your head that gives you a position to work on, then follow that message. If you feel like your hands are 'drifting' on their own, just let them and be guided by them, while keeping in mind the need for propriety when treating others, particularly ladies.

Focusing on results

It is important that you do not become too attached to results, and to trust that the client is receiving what they need. Remember that you cannot mess up a Reiki treatment; you cannot leave a person worse off than they were to begin with, and you are not responsible for the results. Reiki First Degree works very simply: when you touch, the energy flows and produces a healing effect; when you take your hands away, the energy stops flowing into the person: 'hands on, Reiki on – hands off, Reiki off'!

The recipient is drawing the energy to areas of need, you are not responsible for the results of a treatment; the outcome is out of your hands.

Approach treatments with a neutral state of mind and do not try to 'force it' or impose your preferred solution on the situation. Simply let the energy flow and trust that it is going to the right place, that it is doing whatever is appropriate for the recipient.

Creating a Conducive Atmosphere

Treatments should usually be conducted in a relaxing area where both practitioner and recipient feel comfortable and have minimal outside noise and distractions. Make sure that the room is warm, turn the lights down and have some relaxing music playing. Maybe light some candles and burn some incense. If the client wishes to talk with the practitioner, the treatment will still work, but it is best if conversation is kept to a minimum because Reiki will flow better if you are calm and not distracted. Usually the Reiki energy relaxes the client so well that this ceases to be an issue after a very short while!

It is possible for some practitioners to access intuitive information about the client when they are giving the treatment. You should be very wary of passing this information on during the treatment because this could cause the client to become less relaxed, or even anxious. Some people would see such feedback as an intrusion, so discretion should be used. You may not be helping by passing such information on, and particularly in the early stages it is not easy to tell the difference between intuition and imagination! So just notice what is coming to you, and say nothing.

Treating 'both sides'

Some people are taught that you should always treat both sides – front and back – when you give a full treatment; recipients have to wake themselves up half way through the treatment and turn themselves over. This is very disruptive and is not necessary. Reiki is drawn to areas of need no matter what angle you fire the energy from, so you do not need to rest your hands on every square inch of the body for the treatment to be successful. If someone has a back problem then the energy will be drawn there even if you are treating the shoulders. The standard hand positions give good coverage over the length of the body and you do not need to turn someone over routinely; supine is fine.

In fact I have come across many Reiki people who were taught to 'cook both sides' and who now no longer do this because it is so disruptive and is unnecessary.

However, I would treat someone's back if they had a specific back problem. I would treat them prone for a while, working directly on the back, and then I would continue the treatment with a shorter version of the normal 'supine' treatment. Suggested hand positions for treating backs – and fronts - can be found below.

A few other suggestions about treatments

Here are a dozen guidelines and suggestions that were given to me when I took my Reiki First Degree course:

> Check your body hygiene - do you need to use deodorant or brush your teeth?
>
> Wash your hands before and after giving a Reiki treatment if you can.
>
> Suggest your client takes off their shoes, glasses, and loosen their clothes if needed
>
> Your client's legs should be uncrossed. It is said that crossing the legs inhibits the proper flow of energy through the body's meridian system.

As I understand it, Acupuncturists insist that their clients do not cross their legs for this reason.

Make sure your client is warm and comfortable on the treatment table. You might consider keeping a blanket handy, and you can place pillows under the person's knees to help support their lower back; it is best to do this routinely.

Place your hands on your client slowly and gently and remove them in the same way. Keep your hands still when holding each position. Otherwise it would be distracting to your client.

Keep your fingers together as much as you can, but don't make your hands ache in the process and don't worry too much about it, or about errant thumbs!

When your hands are over your client's face, be careful not to press on their eyelids or against their nostrils. I always carry out the head positions with my hands about an inch away from the skin because I think it is a more pleasant experience for the recipient - better than having someone's hands plastered all over their face.

When working on your client's head, be careful not to breathe on their face. Turn your head away slightly to breathe, as a matter of course.

When working on the client's neck, take care not to let the weight of your hands rest on their throat. Again, I have my hands about an inch or so off the skin, resting on the collarbones, or place my hands along the collarbones.

Do not lean on your client or apply undue pressure. This is Reiki, not massage!

Do not try to force the outcome; just let the energy flow.

Hand Positions: Supine Treatments

Here is a basic scheme. I have not included arms and hands in this, but treat them if that seems appropriate. You could rest one hand on the shoulder/elbow, and the other on the wrist/hold their hand. This can feel really comforting. You could also treat the Liver and Spleen areas when you are working on the torso.

You do not have to always treat symmetrical parts of the body. If you need to keep a straight back then you could treat the navel/hip, or liver/hip, and the upper leg/knee on one side of the body, and then do the same on the other side of the body. If a lot more energy is flowing into one knee, then rest both hands on that knee for a while to intensify the healing effect.

Here are some hand positions you can use, which illustrated Below:

Shoulders	Heart & Solar Plexus
Temples	Navel
Crown	Hips
Back of Head	Upper Leg
Front of Face	Knees
Throat	Ankles

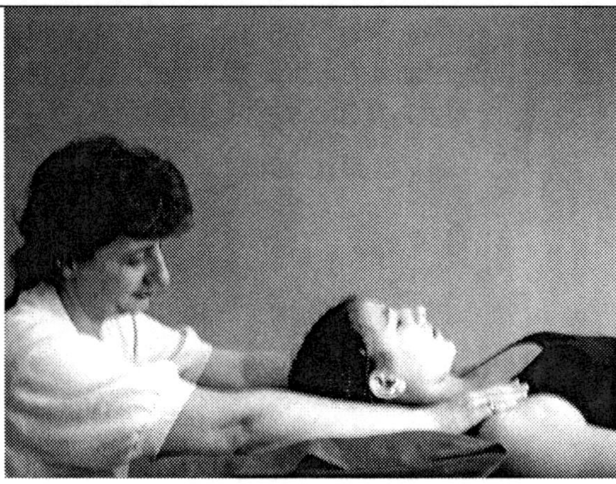

Shoulders

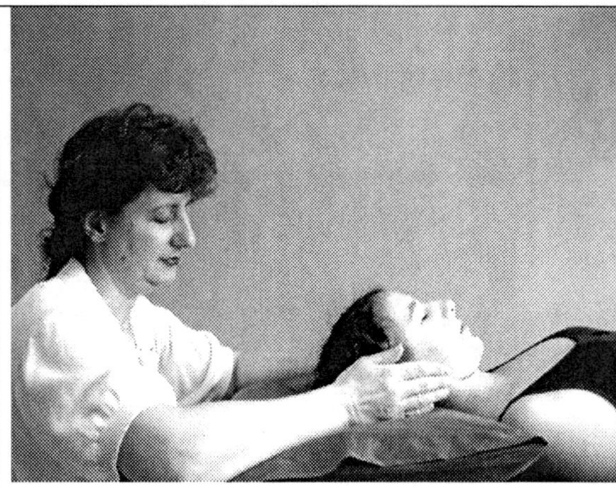

Temples

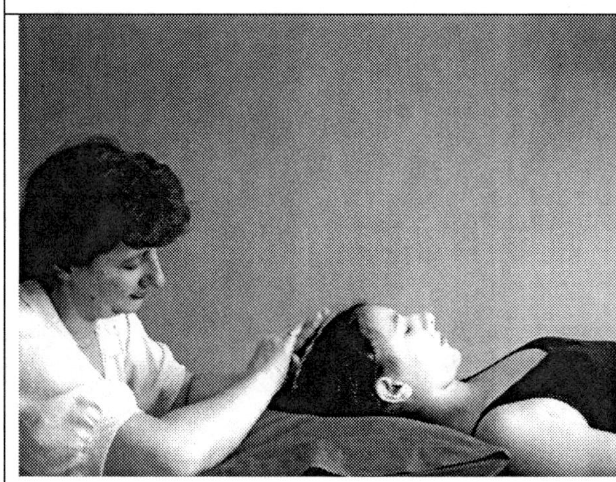

Crown

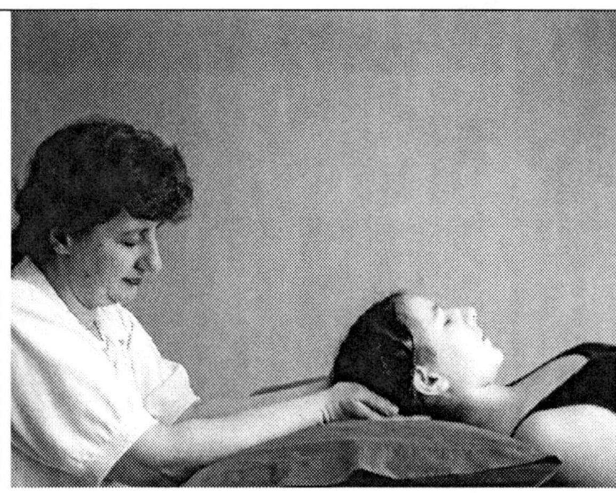

Back of Head

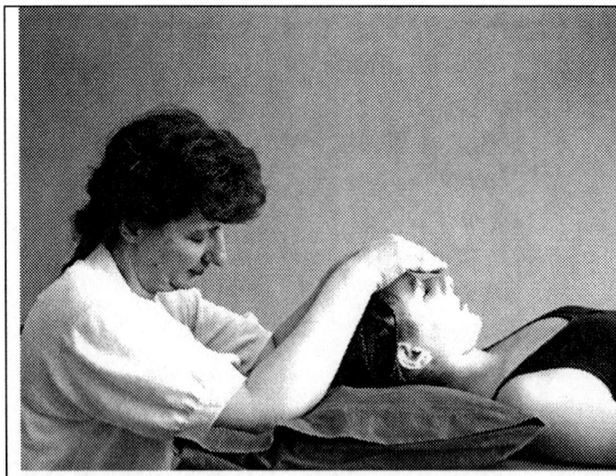

Front of Face

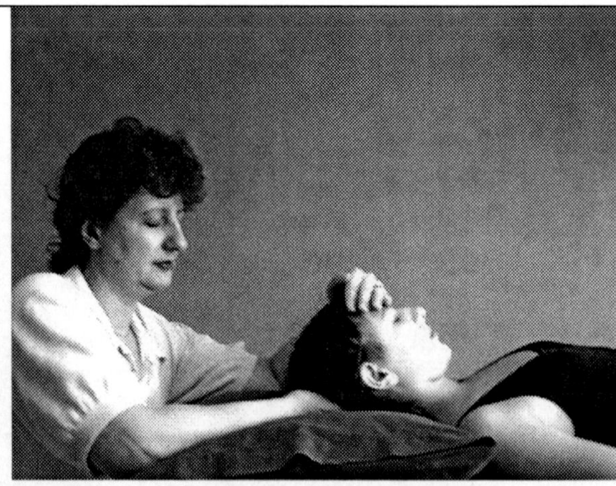

Alternative: back of head, and face, treated at the same time.

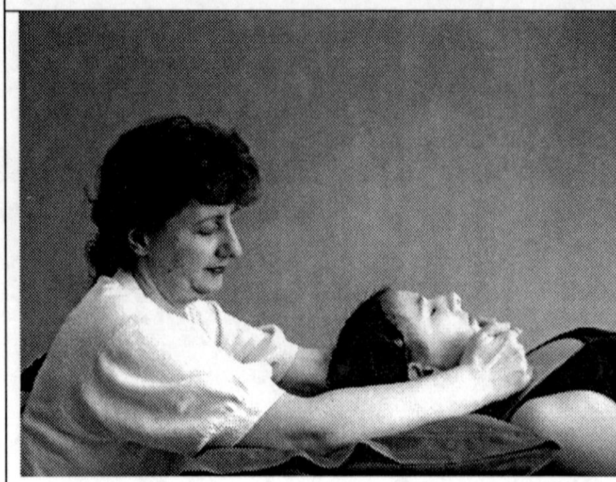

Throat

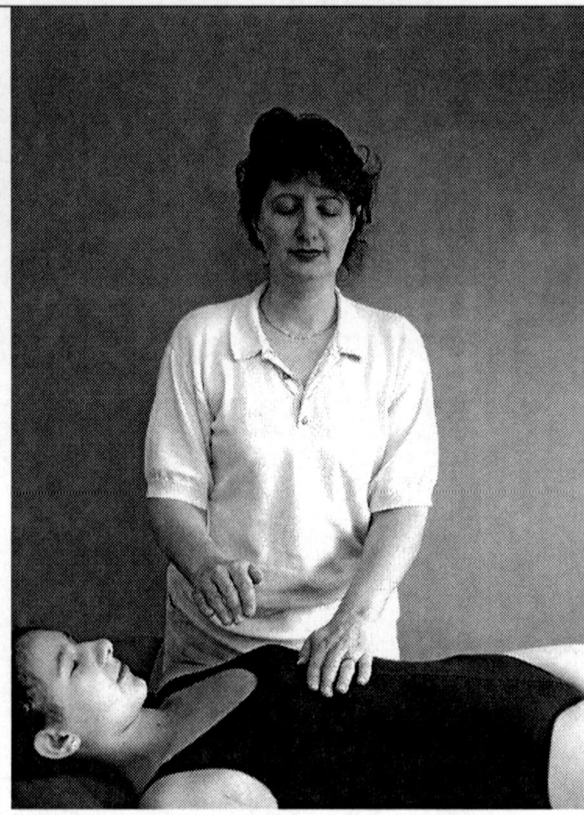

Heart & Solar Plexus

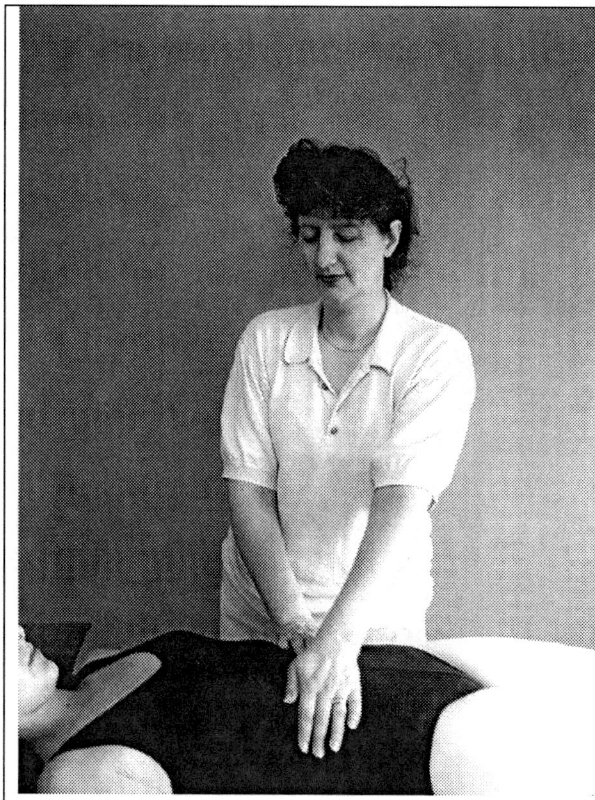

Navel

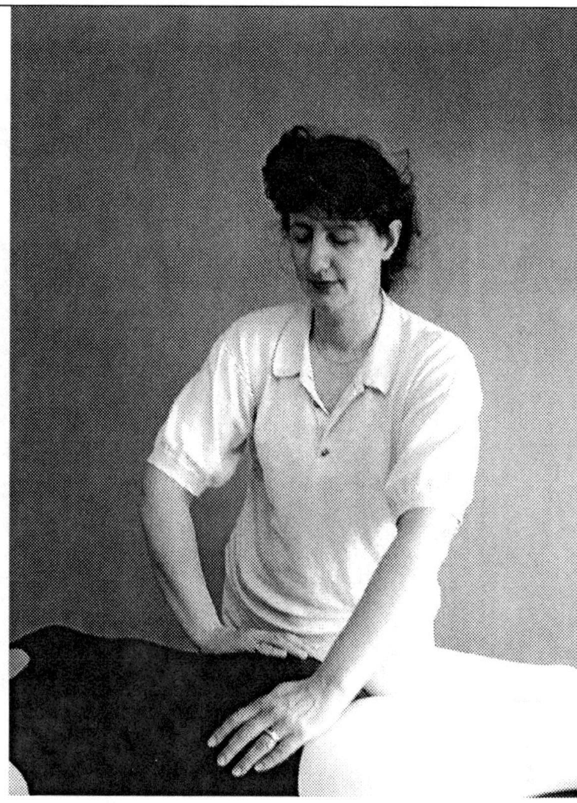

Hips

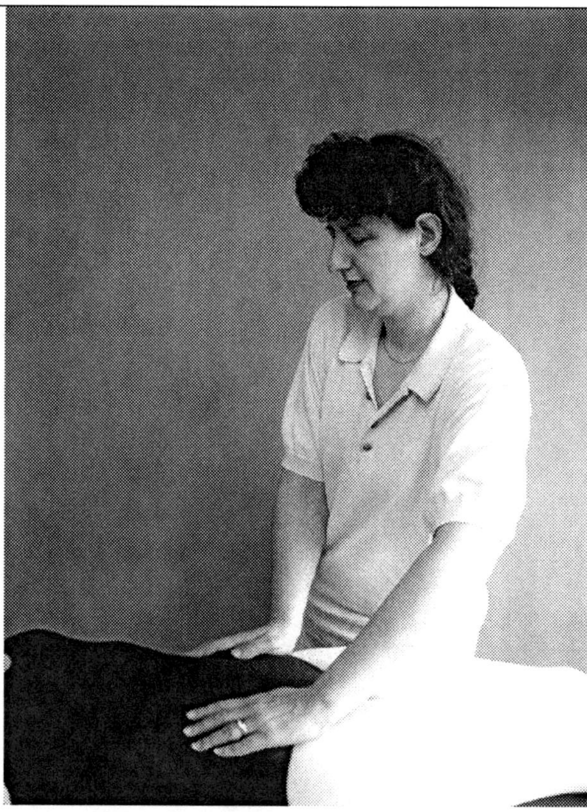

Hips (alternative)

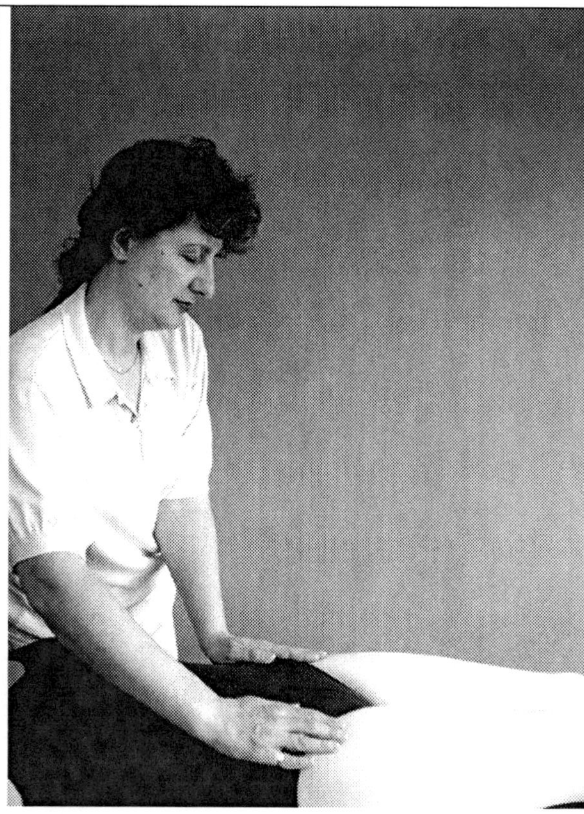

Hips (alternative)

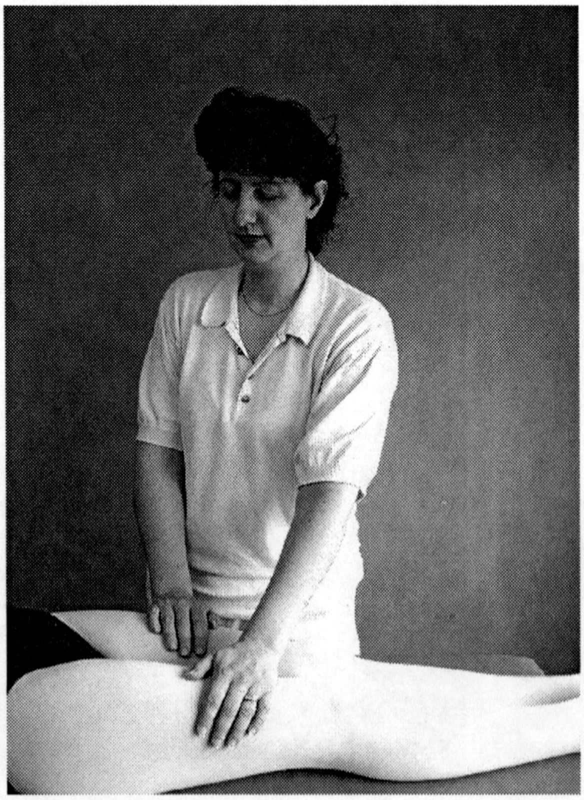

Upper Leg

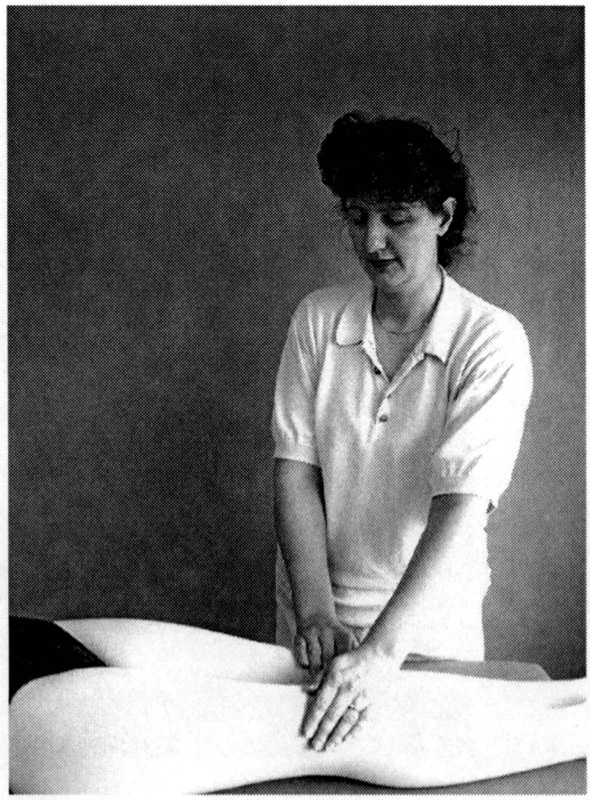

Knees

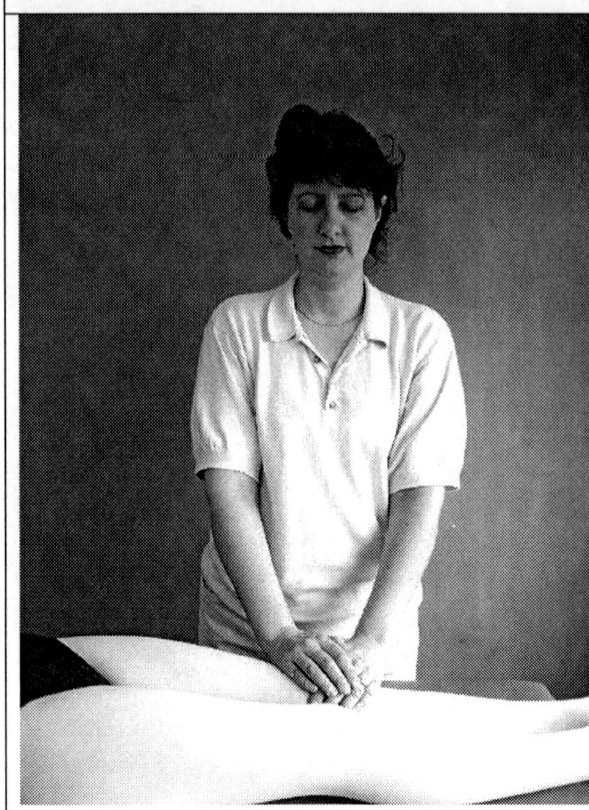

You can treat one knee with two hands if you like, if a lot of energy is flowing there

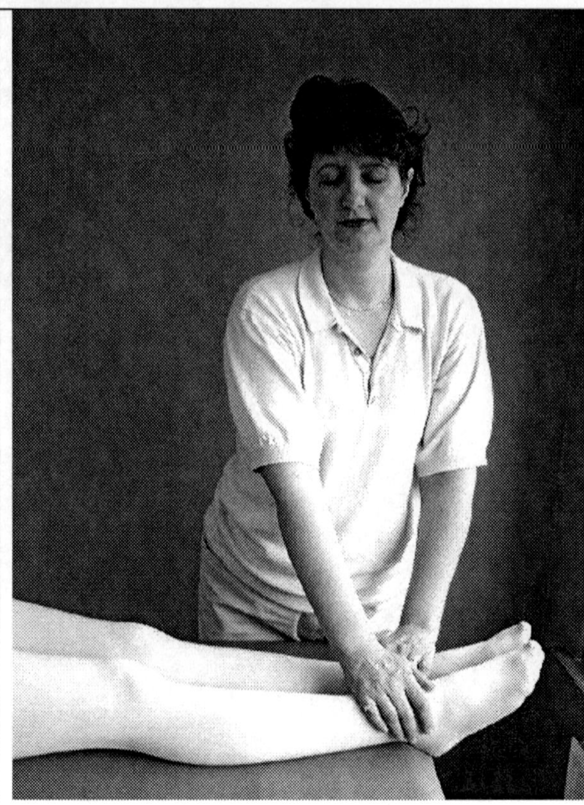

Ankles – or you can treat them by standing at the foot of the table

Just to make the hand positions on the head and shoulders completely clear to you, here are a series of shots taken from a different angle:

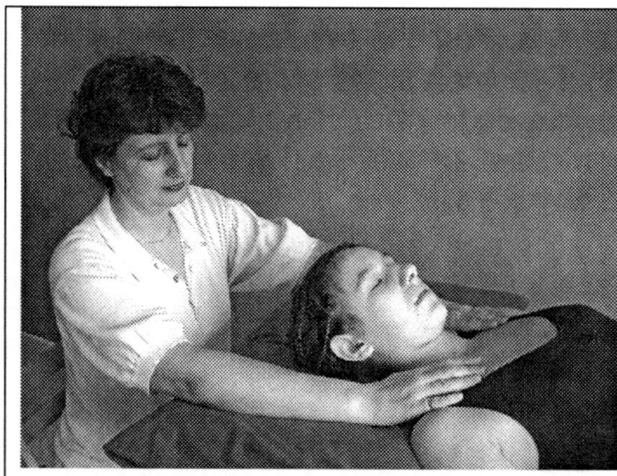

Shoulders

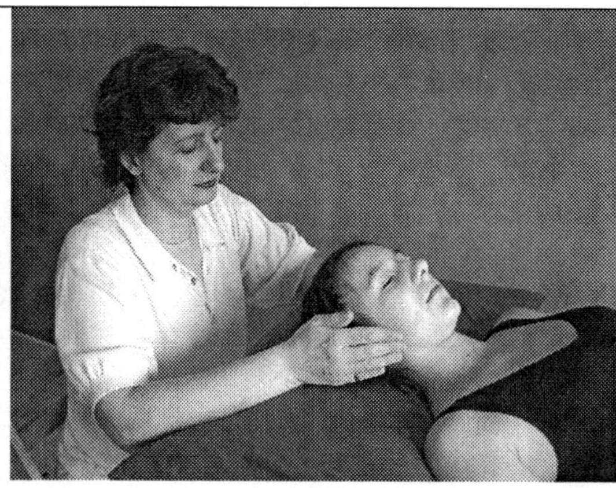

Temples

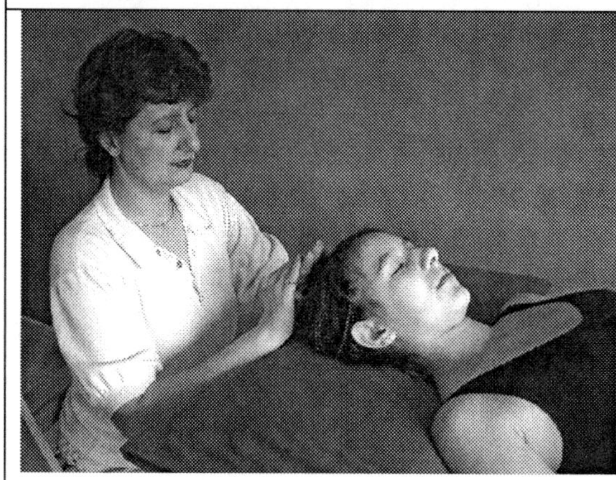

Crown

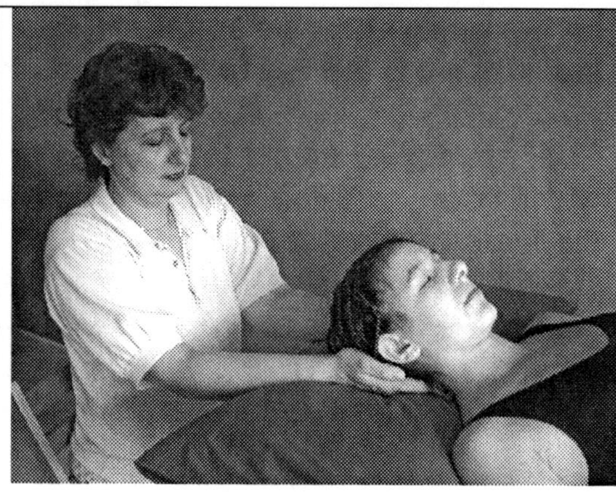

Back of Head

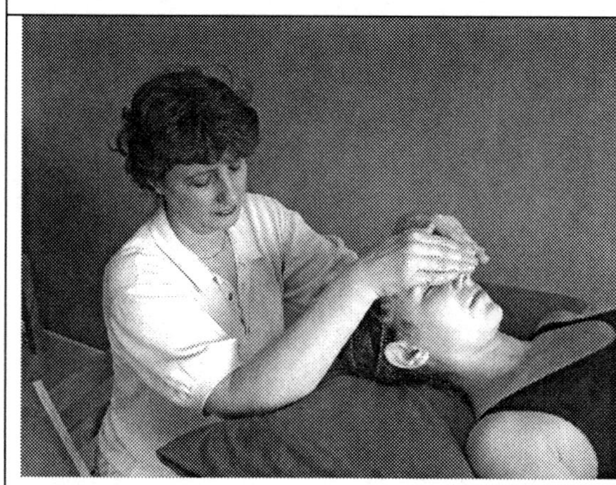

Front of Face

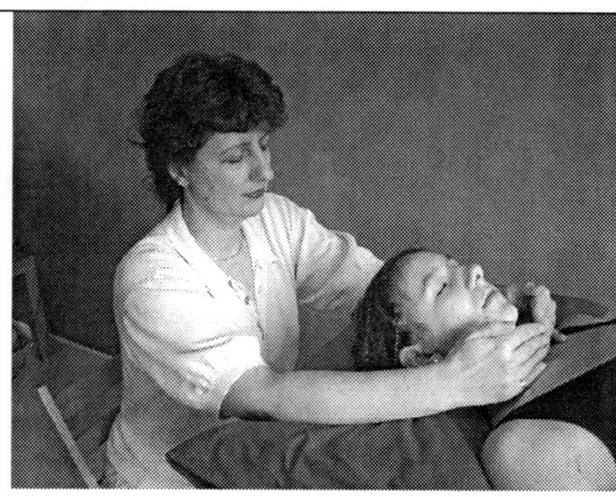

Throat

Dealing with Physical Discomfort when you treat

Sometimes you might find that it is uncomfortable for your back when standing by the treatment table treating both sides of the body at the same time, for example both hips or both upper legs. You can experiment with your body positioning and you may discover that you can stand more comfortably by turning your body so that you are facing more towards the recipient's head or feet, twisting your torso slightly, or even standing with your side rather than your chest facing the table when treating these positions.

Often such discomfort is likely to be caused by a treatment table that is too low for you. A table height that is suitable for giving massage is actually too low for Reiki practitioners. Massage therapists need the recipient to be lower down so they can lean over them and apply some downward pressure onto them, using the weight of their bodies, whereas Reiki people need to be able to stand with a straight back, not leaning forwards, gently resting their hands on the recipient. To judge the right height for you, as a rough guide, make your hand into a fist and dangle your hand by your side. Your fist should rest on the treatment table surface. If there is daylight between your fist and the table then it is too low for you.

But I mentioned earlier that you do not have to always treat symmetrical parts of the body, so if you need to keep a straight back in order to be comfortable then you could treat the navel/hip (or liver/hip) and the upper leg/knee on one side of the body, and then move round the table to do the same on the other side of the body, then finishing with the ankles in whatever way is comfortable for you. If a lot more energy is flowing into one knee, then rest both hands on that knee for a while to intensify the healing effect.

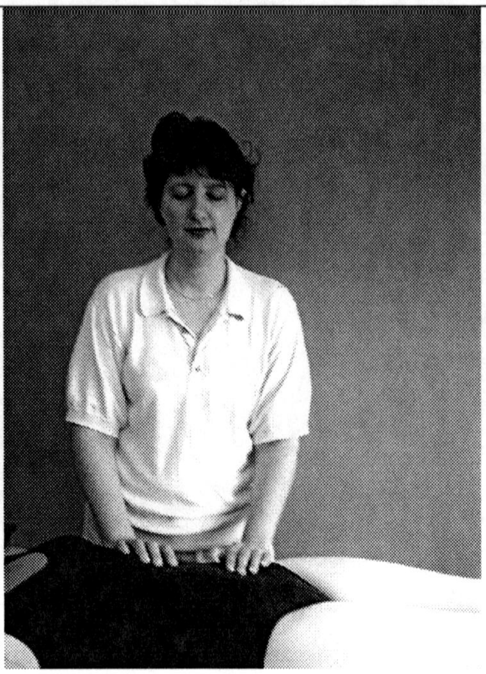

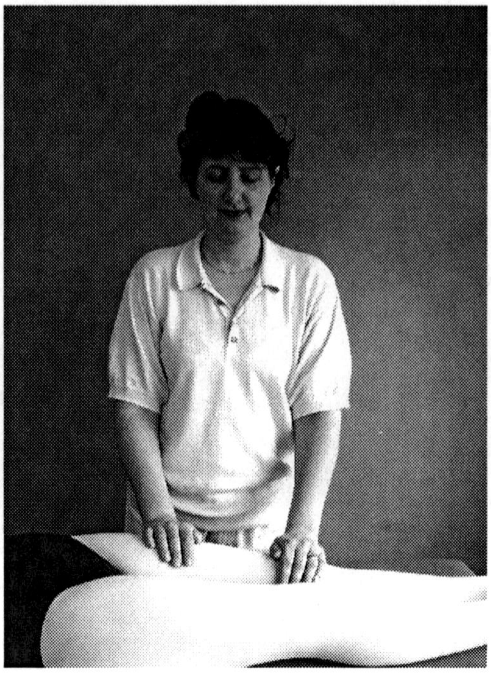

If you find that standing for any amount of time is still difficult for you when treating someone, then you can still give full treatments. You just need to be a little creative. Try sitting on a 'bar stool' as you treat the torso. Try lowering an adjustable treatment couch and sit on a stool or chair with castors on the bottom when you treat the torso. Then you can move from one position to another smoothly and easily, without having to drag or slide an ordinary chair.

Occasionally people will find that it is not the standing but the sitting that is the problem. In that case you can experiment with 'half-standing' using a bar stool, or you can stand to treat the head and shoulders, though you do need to make sure that the treatment table is high enough to make sure you are not leaving forwards, because that will hurt your back.

You do need to take care of yourself and make sure that you are comfortable when you treat someone. Physical discomfort will distract you, it will lessen your enjoyment of the treatment, and will prevent you from drifting into a gentle meditative state which you allows you to be the best channel you can be.

In the early stages you may find that your arms ache sometimes when you treat someone. With practice you will find the best way to arrange your limbs so that you are comfortable no matter what hand position you are holding.

Students' experiences: treating people supine

"My two treatments have gone well, although the second was quite different from the first. WIth the first I used the 'standard' hand positions as in the guide, but then on the second one I tried not to do this and just went with where I felt they needed to be. This is something that I have also done on the head and shoulder treatments, and kind of used a combination of the ones in the guide, and then also added in the one from the self treatment of holding my hands near the hairline, as this feels right in a lot of cases.

My volunteers said they felt mostly really relaxed, and some areas they felt more than others, but mostly that these were sensations in their head such as a 'busy-ness' of whizzing and colours. I felt the same sensations that I have previously, which are heat in my hands particularly and the fizzing in my hands. I still also feel sometimes that my hand is very heavy, which I am taking to mean that more treatment is needed in the area where I feel this. "
"T.B." from Norfolk

"I have done a full reiki treatment on 3 different people, once more scanning was not always positive but I did feel like electricity over the knees of one of the person treated who do have pain in this area.

The 3 of them could feel warmth (medium to very hot), also tingling sensation. One of them told me that she felt like her arms were lifting by themselves. They felt very relaxed during the treatment and one of them fell asleep. Only one of them saw a deep purple colour. Also one felt a slight crushing pain when my hand position was on the solar plexus.

The feedback was very positive, I performed the treatment during 3 consecutive days and one of the girls said that her sleeping pattern improved as she was having problems and they all were very relaxed and not tired."
Bruno Cassani from Essex

"I have practised reiki on my partner regularly and have been noting what happens. I normally start with scanning and can feel differences in the energy over certain areas, depending on how hes feeling and what kind of day he has had. If he has had a stressful day i can feel the inbalance as a swooshy feeling over an area of his head and then when i treat it i may have my hands there for 20minutes or so, whereas the areas that dont i do not treat for as long. I can feel tingling in my whole hands when i am treating, and he says he feels warmth in the area and extreme relaxation all over. I use both this tingling feeling and my intuition to decide when to stop treating the area, as the tingling seems to fade gradually and then it feels right to move on. I have also treated him without scanning first to see what happens and have found that the area that i first place my hands tends to be the most inbalanced area, and i feel that this is my intuition guiding me.

I have also practised reiki on my mother and she felt the same feelings as my partner, warmth in the area and relaxation, although she felt tingling too. She is quite a balanced person and i could feel this during scanning and treatment. I did not need to do a long treatment because of this but she said she felt really good after it.

I also practised on a freind. It took a long time to feel anything as i could not connect straight away. Again, she felt mainly warmth and relaxation but during scanning over her shoulders i could feel a cold sensation, not freezing cold but more like a breeze under my hand and the area was cool when i treated it, but did warm up fairly quickly. It has been interesting practising on different people and benificial, because when i am treating someone that i am especially close to it is very easy to connect, whereas it takes a bit longer on people that i am not so close to, but this is the practice that i need."
Emily Cook from Oxfordshire

"My main 'guinea pig' is my boyfriend and this is where i have made a lot of progress. He has been suffering from headaches and feels that Reiki is benefiting him more so than tablets. The sensations that i feel is like a disturbance over the head, a swooshing hot feeling. this does subside after a while of treating this area, and while the headache may not disappear completely, it helps him to deal with it a whole lot better. Another interesting thing that has happened was one day last week, I was giving him a full treatment but had not scanned him. Normally i will start from the head going downwards but on this occasion I went straight to his feet. I could feel a very cold spot over his right foot, the coldest that i have felt so far. I asked him if he

was aware of this and he told me that he had actually hurt that foot earlier whilst at work, but had not mentioned it as he wanted to see if i picked up on it!

Another friend i have practised on had a terrible tummy ache, but again had not told me this before the treatment, although this was more to do with embarrassment than anything else! During scanning I picked up on this, a hot almost prickly feeling, along with a strong swooshing sensations. I kept my hands in this area for about 30minutes before it began to feel more balanced. Once i had completely finished the treatment my friend then told me she had been having some personal problems and that for the first time she actually felt comfortable talking about it, as she had been bottling it up inside of her. When she left she was feeling a lot happier and able to deal with things.

I have also been giving my mother regular treatments. She has had a lot of health problems in the past and has a lot of experience with both conventional and complementary treatments. She feels that the Reiki treatments benefit her a lot and that she feels 'boosted' after every session. She does not need a long session when i treat her as she is a very balanced and happy person and this reflects during the treatment."
Emily Cook from Oxfordshire

"I've completed two full treatments with a resounding sucess, i could feel heat and tingling in my hands and both of my willing friends have felt significant changes within the treatments. I've also continued to treat head and shoulders where friends have busy lifestyles and cannot fit full treatments in. word seems to be spreading too as other frineds and neighbours are coming to me to have treatments! While i'm treating my mother in law i tend to hear what she is going to say before she says it whilst connected and this happens too with another close friend, when i see a colour in front of my eyes she will say that she can see that colour too.Most peaolpe i have treated have felt relaxed and more alert when i have finished and have nodded off not long after i have left too."
Niki Leach from Tyne and Wear

"Did 2 full Reiki treatments. The first was on my husband. He lay on the garden reclining chair but unfortunately fell through it just before I started the treatment, so had to use the bed. I think he needs to lose some weight!!) I sat on a chair at the foot of the bed. I played relaxing music and just had a lamp on. I reminded myself that the treatment was for his highest good and tried to blend with his energy. I did Kenyoko? (the dry bathing) and connected to Reiki. I scanned his body but didn't feel heat in any particular place. I placed my hands on his shoulders and started Reiki, I kept my hands there for about 3 mins. as I did with the rest of the handpositions down his body. I felt a thickness at his temples and a coolness when I was doing his crown. I had no particular feeling in my hands - no fuzziness etc. I asked my husband what he had felt, and he said that he heard a sound like whooshing water inside his head when I was doing his temples, and felt slight chest pain when I had my hand on his heart. Afterwards he said he still felt the heat around his face and head.

The second treatment was on my sister-in-law. I did the same as above and felt heat and thickness around her neck and shoulders where she had been having pain. At one point her shoulders were very hot, and afterwards she said she had felt heat in her shoulders traveling down to her chest. The next day she said her neck and shoulders felt much better.

While doing the treatments I sometimes found it hard to keep my hand in the positions too long - 3 mins maximum, otherwise my arms felt heavy I couldn't concentrate properly.

During the week I had a bad headache and reikied my head for about 10 mins. It surprised me how quickly the headache subsided."
Lindsay Long from Surrey

"I have carried out two full Reiki treatments this week on two different people one lasted for 45 mins the other 55 mins. I started both by scanning the body to detect any changes in the energy. On the first person I found an increase in energy around the right shoulder, both hips and right knee, the increase in energy was felt as an increased heat and pulsation in my hands around the shoulder and hips but the knee felt colder and I felt a very slight breeze which could be nothing, so I concentrated on these areas until the energy felt smoother.

The person I was practicing on said they felt increased heat around these area's especially intense around the knee.

I started the treatment by mentally dedicating the treatment to the greater good of that individual, then raising my arms and saying Reiki On it seems to work for me. When carrying out the treatment I felt very peaceful and relaxed, it's as if a space is made inside me for the energy to flow through and I felt connected and light. I finished by silently asking that the peron may continue to feel whatever benefits they received long after the treatment had finished, raised my arms silently said Reiki Off then lowered them and shook my hands. I felt very serene.

With the second person I didn't get comfortable initially which seemed to impede the flow of energy so I had to start again. I started as previously stated and proceeded to scan the body the areas I found with increased energy flow were around the persons heart which caused me some concern has this person had a stent inserted to a blocked artery a few months ago, the Solar Plexus and lower back also showed an increase in energy experienced by increased heat, tingling and pulsation in my hands and lower arms, the most affected area appeared to be The Solar Plexus. Again I waited for the energy flow to become smoother and then moved on. This person felt slightly nauseous during the treatment and felt increased heat around the lower back. I did a final body scan and then closed the treatment as before.

When I first started carrying out this treatment I could not become a channel as I had before because I kept getting distracted as I was not physically comfortable, once I had adjusted the environment so I was comfortable the energy could flow unblocked. It feels like being connected to the Divine energy an amazing experience.

I would like to say how much I have enjoyed the course and what a difference it has made to me, I am much calmer. I will definately be enrolling for the second level."
Susan Naylor from West Yorkshire

"The full body treatments have been very interesting. I have been scanning my volunteers before and after treatment and am generally finding that their energy field has grown bigger by the end of the treatment. I have found them to be a very relaxing experience for myself and 95% of the time my volunteers have nodded of to sleep. They have generally complained after treatment that it only felt like 5 minutes but have said that the next day they have felt wonderful and full of life.

I started by doing 45 minute treatments gradually increasing to 1 hour and have found that an hour is actually very easy to do and passes by very quickly even for myself. I am using relaxing music and incense during my treatments and this seems to add to the relaxing atmosphere.

I have experienced different sensations whilst treating. One person I treated one day and they felt very cold in most areas except for the neck, solar plexus and knees. It turned out he had been on a 12 mile bike ride that day and was exhausted but felt marvellously for his treatment. His energy field was very small down his legs. The next day I treated the same man and experienced something very different. He was in fact very hot all over and his energy field was the same size all over his body.

Another lady gave me a real dragging sensation from my hands in one knee and my hands also increased in heat here.

I have really enjoyed giving these full body treatments and have found them to be a lovely experience. It has been nice to finally get to that stage in my reiki course and really feel like I am helping someone."
Sarah Quinn from Kent

"Hi,have been treating a few people this week and the results have been great but a bit scarey!!!! They have said they felt relaxed and floaty and there bodys were very light.. One lady said she was left with her fingertips tingling and they felt rough, they all said that ailments had improved nearly 100 %.. A lady was brought to me by a friend and she had problems with her knees for yrs, not knowing this ,was drawn to that area, she has just informed me that when she awoke this morn the pains in her knees had GONE, she was so thankful as she has never been free from pain for 40yrs..I am getting a bit scared with these results is all this normal, I feel great too that I am helping people but is this the way it works so dramatically.. Some of them are friends and some are strangers ,at first I thought it was my friends helping me out saying they felt great etc but now I know they where telling me the truth.."
Christine Weston from Spain

Back treatments

I only treat backs if a person has a specific back problem, treating the person face down to begin with, and then continuing with a shortened version of the standard treatment in the supine position.

To treat backs, start with your hands resting on the back of the neck and the base of the spine for a while, and let Reiki flow up and down their back. Most back problems tend to be lower back problems, and you can find the problem area by scanning (or intuitively) if you like.

Assuming the problem is in the lower back, keep the lower hand in place, and every few minutes move the upper hand closer and closer to the lower hand, until it's resting on the problem area.

Then you can spend quite a while with both hands on or near the problem area, in various positions. For example, above/below, or at either side. When treating the back, you can also rest your hands on the Kidneys and Shoulders if you like.

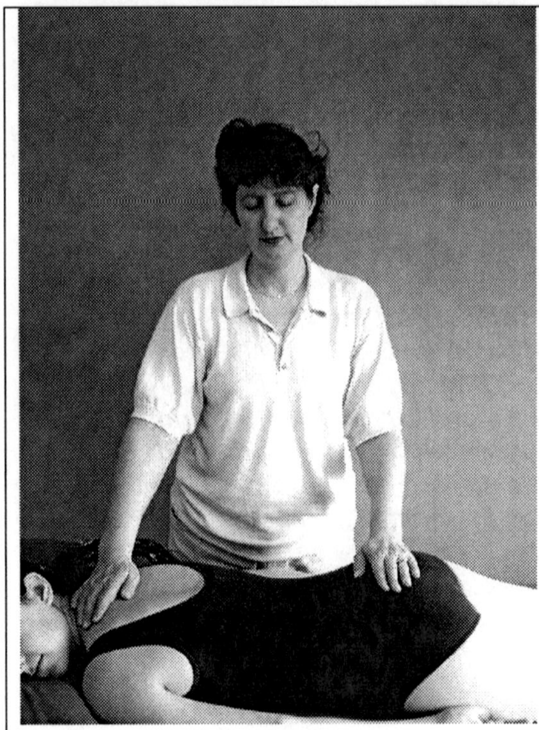	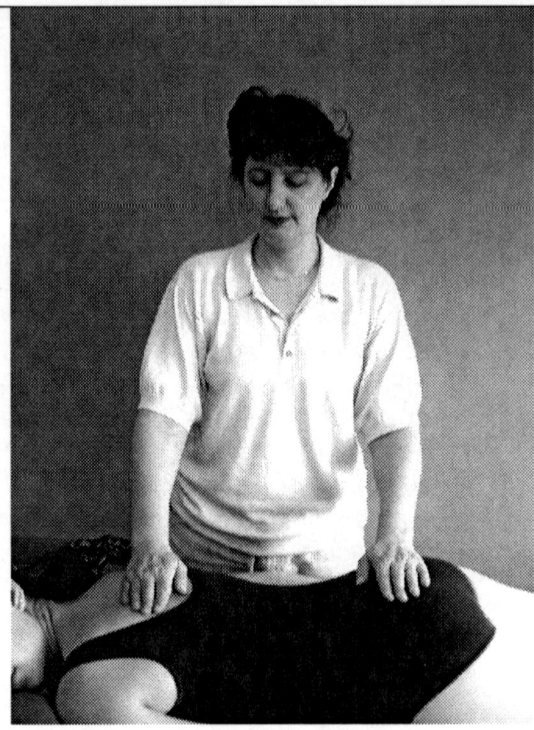
Back of Neck & Base of Spine	Move upper hand closer to the lower hand

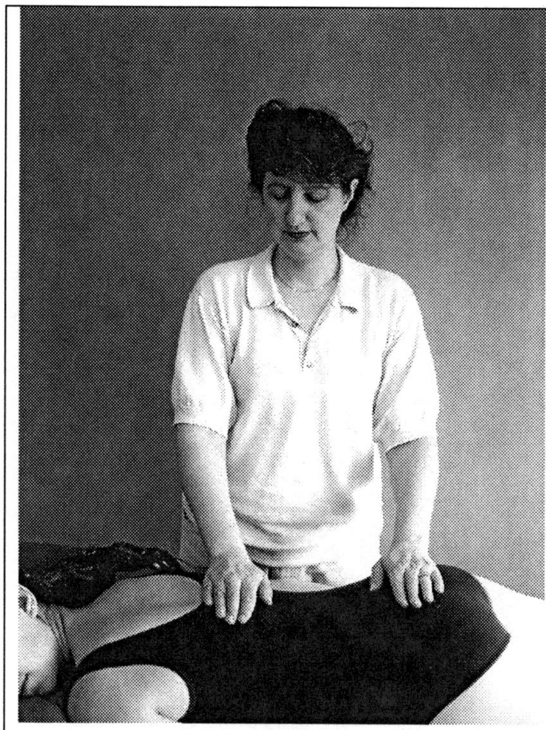

… and closer

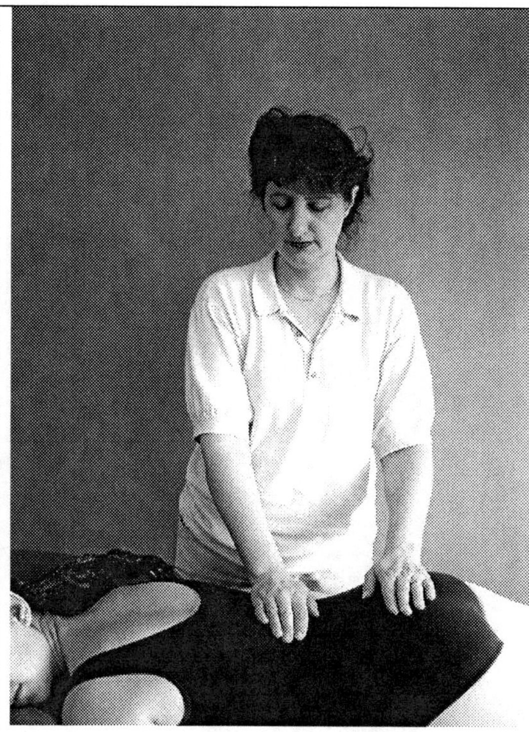

…and closer

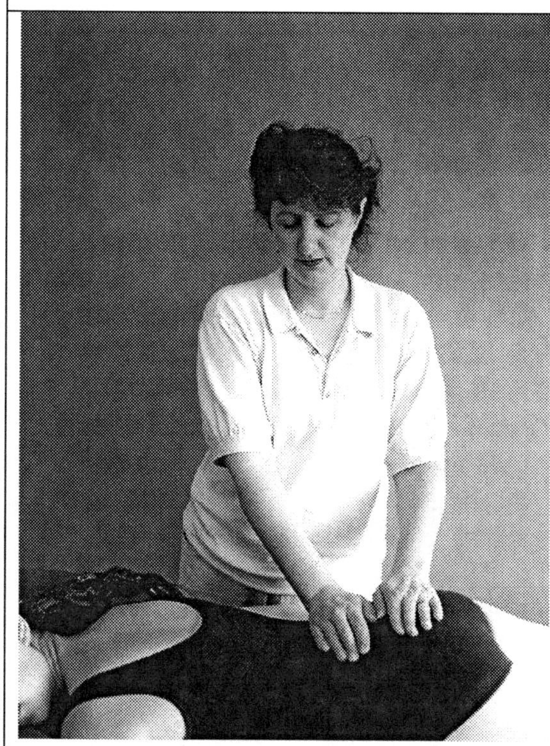

Hands adjacent to each other on lower back

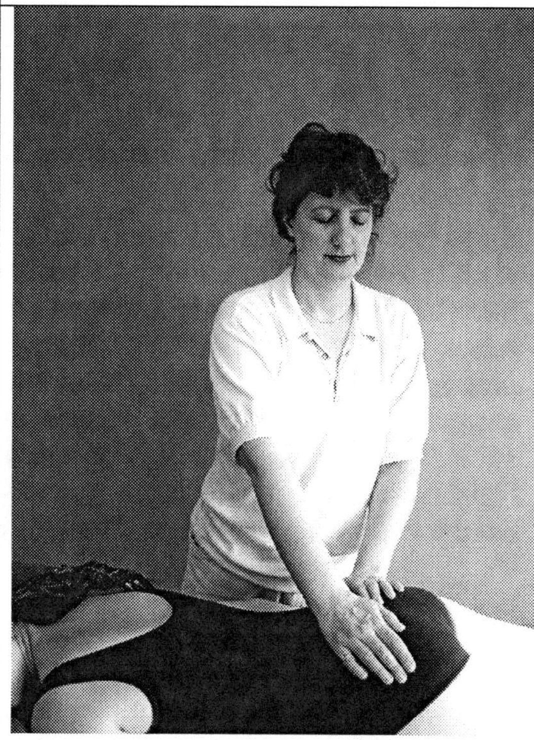

Alternative: lower back

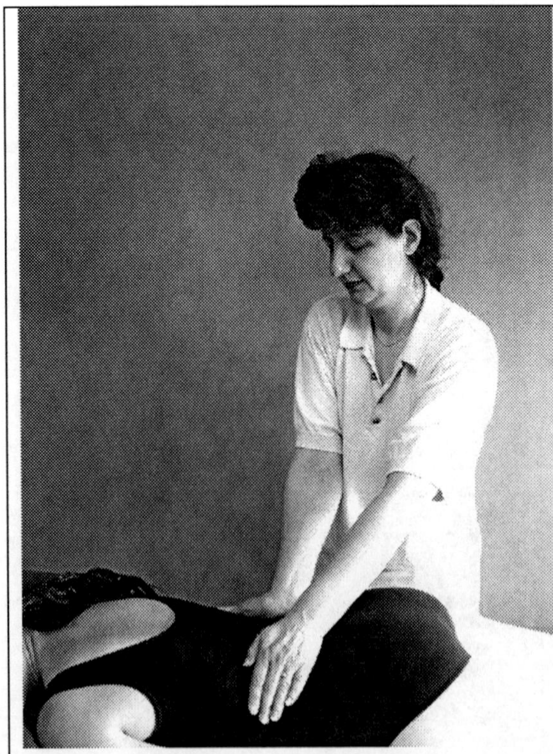

Suggestion: treating kidneys

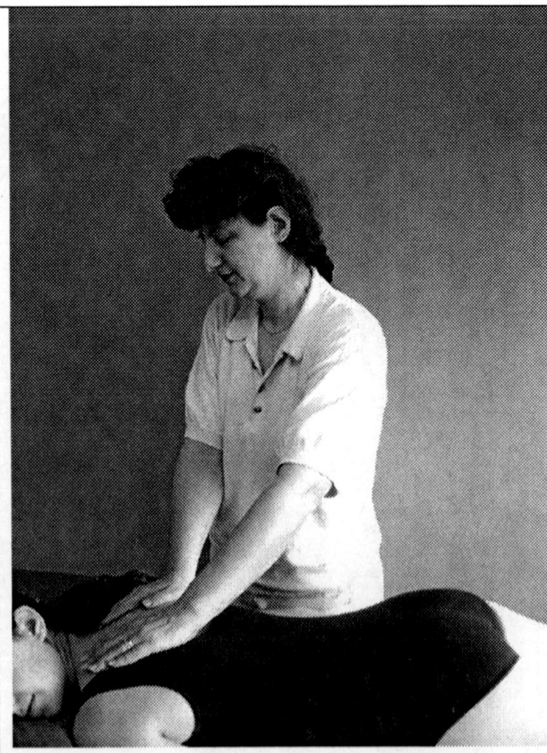

Suggestion: treating shoulders

The Hand Positions, Thoughts & Emotions

If you feel a lot of Reiki flowing into a particular area of the body, you may want to know why the energy is flowing there, and what this means. You may have to resign yourself to accepting that you do not know and do not need to know, because Reiki works on many levels, dealing with normal physiological processes, physical conditions, mental states, emotional states, spiritual aspects, stuff from the past (maybe even stuff from past lives, if you believe in such things), and stuff that is on the boil, waiting to manifest in the future. Reiki is not a diagnostic therapy and we should not try to tell recipients what we think is wrong with them. Doctors diagnose, Reiki practitioners do not.

But if you want to mull over such things, there are traditions that assign particular states of mind or emotions to particular areas of the body, or particular organs. For example, Chinese medicine attaches states of mind and emotions to meridians and their corresponding organs. Indian tradition thinks in terms of seven main energy centres running from the crown to the base of the spine. These energy centres are called 'chakras' and have their own sets of correspondences in terms of body systems, states of mind and emotions. Reiki will work on the organs/meridians of Traditional Chinese Medicine (TCM) as well as the Indian system of Chakras, and you do not need to know anything at all about meridians and chakras in order to practise Reiki safely and effectively. Chakra work is taught on some Reiki courses because Reiki was affected greatly by the New Age movement, but Usui and his students would not have considered this system. Their focus was the Tanden.

Here are some correspondences that I have noticed myself. If there is a lot of energy flowing into these positions, it seems to tie in (though not always) with the characteristics given…

Crown	Headaches, maybe depression/low spirits.
Temples	Busy mind, endless thinking about things, can't shut the mind up. Can't get to sleep properly because the mind won't keep quiet.
Throat	Inability to express themselves properly, holding back and not saying what they need/ought to say to people close to them.
Heart	Current emotional feelings being held back. If there seems to be no energy going into the heart, then this may be an emotional block, where someone has shut off emotionally to protect themselves.
Solar Plexus	More long-term emotional turmoil or unresolved issues being kept firmly under control. It easier to put a lid on these feelings, but they're still there, grinding away. Reiki will take the lid off them so they can be released.

Emotions are associated with various organs according to Traditional Chinese Medicine, and I have mentioned them below. You do not need to learn them, you do not need to pay attention to them, and you do not need to talk about them to people that you treat, speculating out loud about what might be going on with the recipient! They are included to demonstrate that your emotions do not just reside in your heart, but are all over your body.

In TCM, each of the five 'elements' is represented by a couple of organs (and their meridians). An imbalance in your Wood element might mean that you are angry all the time, or that you are suppressing anger, and anger is seen as residing in the Liver, an organ of 'Wood'…

Element	Organ	Emotion
Wood	Liver	Anger
Fire	Heart	Joy
Earth	Spleen	Sympathy
Metal	Lungs	Grief
Water	Kidneys	Fear

Finally, if you read books like “You Can Heal Your Life” by Louise Hay, you will discover a Western-based system that allocates particular states of mind and emotions to particular medical conditions that a person might suffer from, so we see a recurring theme in different cultures at different times.

Using Reiki with other Therapies

'Hands-On' Therapies

Reiki not only complements other therapies and disciplines, but can also increases their effectiveness. Even at First Degree level, Reiki will add a great deal to any hands-on therapy, for example Massage, Aromatherapy, Reflexology, and Indian Head Massage. Second Degree is seen as 'practitioner' level in the world of Reiki, though; there is a lot more to Reiki than you can learn on just one course!

Reflexologists that I have taught report being able to feel Reiki flowing through the palms of their hands, as Reiki flows into the client during the Reflexology treatment, and some have said that their treatments seem more effective now. My first Reiki teacher started out as a Reflexologist, and told me that she believed Reiki was more powerful.

Aromatherapists that I have taught have reported that their treatments seem more effective, and that their style has changed, becoming more slow and gentle.

One of my team of teachers now wonders why she learned all the therapies that she is qualified in, since in her opinion Reiki seems to do more for people.

Finally, Reiki seems to compensate for that feeling of being 'drained' that affects many complementary therapists involved in hands-on therapies. Reiki boosts and invigorates you as you treat others, and helps to protect you from 'picking up' symptoms from the people that you are working on - an occasional complication for hands-on therapists.

Spiritual Healing

Spiritual healers that I have taught have found that Reiki has made a definite difference to them in terms of the strength and consistency of the energy that they are channelling. They like the focus on self-healing, and the self-healing methods, which seem to be missing from most spiritual healing systems.

Crystal Healing

Crystal Healers too will find that crystals store the Reiki energy and this can then be used to enhance the quality of the crystal's power for healing. Crystals should be 'charged' by being held in both hands and allowing the Reiki to flow through for about 5-10 minutes. Further infusions of Reiki energy are necessary to maintain the crystal as a Reiki 'conductor'.

Treating Plants and Animals

Once you are 'connected' to Reiki, you can channel the energy into any living thing. Some Reiki people spend much of their time treating animals, with amazing results, and plants seem to respond well, too. We do not need to tie ourselves up with complicated rules and 'techniques' when treating other people, or animals or plants, because Reiki is simple. All we need to do is to rest our hands on – or near – the recipient and they will draw energy according to their need. We are just necessary bystanders in the process.

So if you want you can treat your pets and your houseplants, and use Reiki in the garden.

Treating Plants

Plants seem to respond well to Reiki. If you are growing something from seed then hold the seeds in one hand and cup the other hand over the top to "Reiki" them. Cut flowers can be given Reiki by holding your hands above the flowers as if you were blessing them, which is of course what happens.

Potted plants seem to respond better by having their roots treated, so you treat them by holding the pot between your hands.

Trees seem to accept Reiki through their trunks and are said to respond well to Reiki hugs. They are said to be amazing reservoirs of Universal Energy and as such reciprocate by giving an energy back to the giver.

Why not do some experiments… grow some plants from seed, giving Reiki to one group and not to the other. See what happens. Try giving some Reiki to your salad: does it seem somehow brighter and more colourful? Cut an orange in half and place the two halves face down on plates in the kitchen; Reiki one half and not the other, and note their rate of decomposition.

I have an ever-increasing group of Reiki students who report that their ailing houseplants spruced up after receiving some Reiki, even after only a week or so. I also know a student who has tangible proof of the effectiveness of Reiki in his allotment. He planted two bushes, one of which he Reiki-ed regularly. The Reiki-de bush is huge when compared with the non-Reiki-ed one. That was all the proof he needed!

Treating Animals

Animals benefit from Reiki treatments as well as humans and plants, and some Reiki practitioners specialise in treating animals, for example horses. Do be wary of courses advertising 'animal Reiki' - which you are supposed not to be able to use on humans - because Reiki is Reiki, whether you treat a human, an animal or a plant. When treating animals, it is recommended that you start by giving Reiki behind the ears, at the base of the skull, because this is said to have the effect of calming the animal, rather like resting your hands on the shoulders in humans.

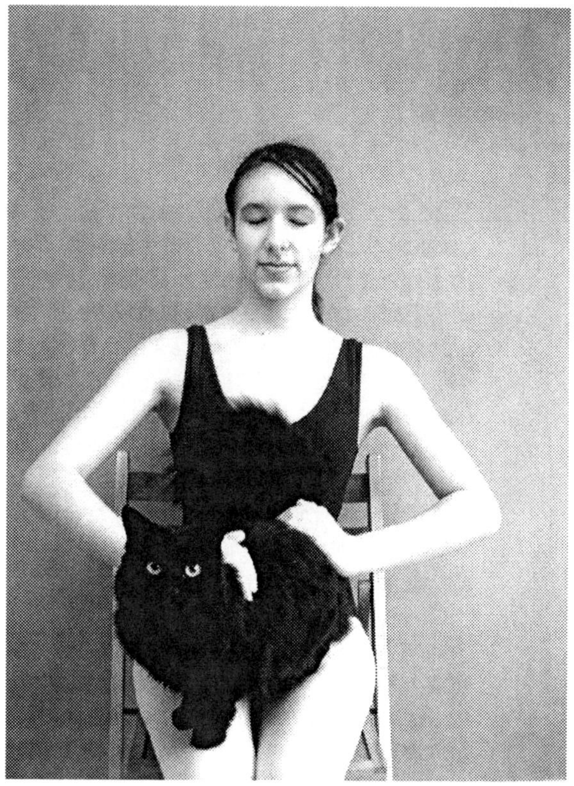

The size of the animal is unimportant, since each will receive the energy they need. Reiki will be as effective with a mouse as it will a horse, and don't worry about making small animals explode, because Reiki will only supply as much energy as an organism needs. Treat small creatures for small chunks of time, so a few minutes for a gerbil, 10 minutes for a cat, 20 minutes for a dog. Quite often they will get up and leave when they have had enough, so you can let them decide.

It seems that some cats and dogs really love Reiki, while others seem less keen. Perhaps they can see or sense energy more strongly than most people, and are startled by the sudden intensity of the energy coming from their owner. Maybe they are disturbed by the 'heat' that can be felt as the energy flows. Sometimes this can be intense and may put the animal off; you can get around this problem by treating with your hands hovering some distance from the animal rather than treating hands-on.

Sometimes Reiki can do some remarkable things: one man reported that his very unpleasant half-wild cat (which used to regularly attack him and his guests) started cuddling up on his lap and was very friendly with a guest that it always used to bite with no provocation. Another man was invited to treat a horse by a friend of his. He had never been near a horse before, and though was rather nervous, but ended up cradling the horse's head in his arms and hands. Unbeknownst to him, the horse had been mistreated in the past, was afraid of men, and would not allow anyone to touch its head. It behaved a lot better subsequently.

I have had only one experience of treating animals: a dog with a developmental disorder in a hind knee joint, leading to wasting of the leg. The leg also crossed over the other hind leg and the dog would not put weight on it. After six 20-minute Reiki sessions the dog now stands on its hind legs with both hind legs parallel to each other, and uses both hind legs for walking and running. See the section 'The effect of Reiki treatments' for details.

Students' experiences: treating plants and animals

"The horses reactions tended to be ones of relaxation and sleepiness which is good. I did try to treat the base of the back on one horse also, as I knew her to have a problem here. When I first tried to touch this area or even hover my hand above it, she would not have any of it and moved away, and took three attempts before she would let me just hold my hand above it. She remained quite alert whilst I did it though, but did tolerate it for about 5 mins. I will go back in short bursts to this area."
"T.B." from Norfolk

"I notice the cats enjoy being reikied, but only for about 5 mins - then they get fidgety and a bit agitated."
Lindsay Long from Surrey

"Went for a long walk with partner and dog today. Walked through the middle of a field of corn with my hands at my side close to the plants. Suddenly, about half way across, I became aware that my hands were becoming extremely hot and were really tingling in the fingers. They even changed colour slightly. I laid my hands upon my partner and he couldn't believe how hot they were.

It was an amazing feeling. My hands and feet have always been so cold. The tingling was a very nice feeling and it continued to happen across 3 fields of corn until we reached the road when it rapidly disappeared again. It was so wonderful because it happened subconsciously. I had no intention of scanning the plants and it hadn't even entered my mind that I would feel energy from them."
Sarah Quinn from Kent

"My dog hurt his leg and couldn't walk. I tried Reiki and he went to sleep when he awoke he was jumping around as if nothing had been wrong with him. I was amazed and so was my husband"
Christine Weston from Spain

Distant Healing

While some people are taught that distant healing is not possible at First Degree level, and that distant healing is only possible once you have been attuned to the distant healing symbol on a Reiki Second Degree course, this is not the case. From the moment that you start practising Reiki at First Degree you can send Reiki at a distance. You can do it now.

We do focus more on distant healing on our Second Degree course, the level where distant healing is usually taught, but here are some suggestions for methods that you might want to experiment with:

Self-Treatment meditation approach

You are familiar with the self-treatment meditation, where you imagine that you are treating a carbon copy of yourself, sitting on the floor in front of you in your mind's eye. Well why not put someone else in front of you in your imagination, and have in mind that energy is flowing into those five areas of the other person's head? You can even use the guided meditation audio track on your CD to guide you through this.

Here is a suitable simple scheme:

1. Close your eyes and take a few long deep breaths
2. Focus your attention on your Tanden point
3. Say to yourself that "this is to be a distant healing for the highest good of ...."
4. Imagine the person sitting on the floor in front of you
5. In your mind's eye, imagine or have in mind that energy is flowing into the person's head, in the five positions that you are familiar with
6. When you are ready to bring things to a close, imagine the person disappearing, take a few long deep breaths again, and bring yourself back

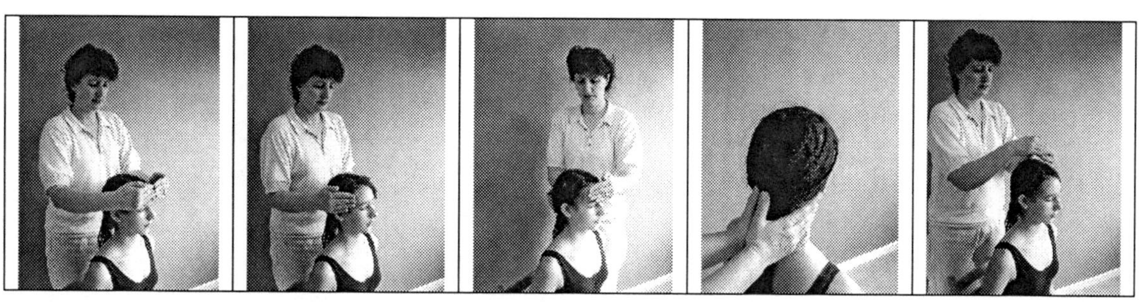

You do not have to be able to see the other person clearly in your mind's eye; you do not need to visualise well at all. It is sufficient to intend that the energy is flowing to particular areas of the head, or allow your attention to rest or to dwell on those areas, whether or not you can 'see' them. The energy will follow your focus and direct itself to where your attention is directed.

If you want receive some feedback from the recipient you will need to agree with them a set time for them to sit down to receive, and for you to send, the distant healing.

We suggest sending distant healing for about 10 minutes. The recipient may well be aware of things happening, but this will not always be the case.

An even simpler approach

The details of any ritual used in distant healing are optional, so we can take an even simpler approach. The bare bones of distant healing are to know where you are sending the energy – to set a definite intent – and to allow the energy to flow, so you could try this:

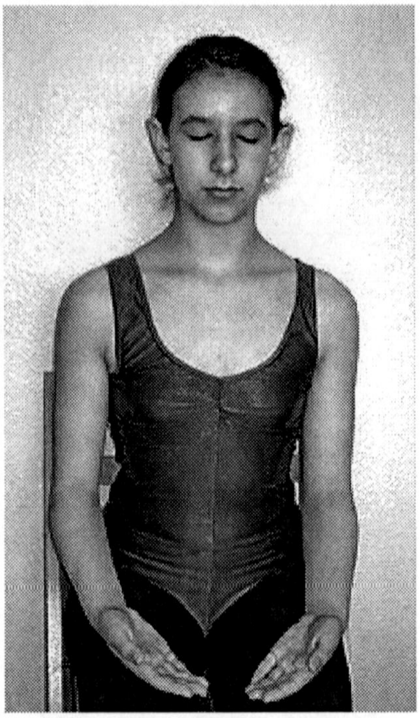

1. Close your eyes and take a few long deep breaths
2. Focus your attention on your Tanden point
3. Say to yourself that "this is to be a distant healing for the highest good of …."
4. Focus your attention on the recipient in your mind's eye
5. Feel yourself merging with the recipient, becoming one with them
6. Allow the energy to flow from you to them for as long as feels appropriate
7. When you are ready to bring things to a close, feel your attention withdrawing from the recipient, take a few long deep breaths again, and bring yourself back

FIRST DEGREE 'HOMEWORK'

After your Reiki course you will have received the traditional Japanese empowerments necessary to give you a permanent 'connection' to an unlimited source of healing energy. You have the Reiki ability for life now, and the energy is available to you at all times. I do hope that you enjoyed the course, and now you have the exciting task of trying Reiki out on yourself and other people. Good luck with that, and make sure that you get lots of practice!

You should re-read this manual and listen to the audio CD again. This will help to reinforce what you learned on the course, and focus you on the main points. The guided meditation tracks on your audio CD will help you to get in the habit of carrying out energy exercises each day and performing self-treatments each week.

If you are going to get the greatest benefit out of your Reiki then you are going to have to put by some time regularly to work with the energy. Just going on a course and then doing very little with your Reiki is not going to lead to the many positive changes that Reiki has to offer you. So below you can find my prescription for success at First Degree level. This is what you need to do:

1. Work on yourself regularly
2. Receive Reiju on Mondays
3. Live the Precepts
4. Practise on others

Work on Yourself

The system that Mikao Usui taught was all about working on yourself, and at First Degree level you have learned two methods for focusing the energy on yourself:

1. Hatsurei ho
2. Self-treatments – we recommend the self-treatment meditation

Both of these should be carried out daily.

'Hatsurei Ho' will help make you a progressively stronger and clearer channel for Reiki. The sequence takes about 12-15 minutes to carry out, though you can take longer of course. If you do Hatsurei ho at the same sort of time each day, it will become as normal and routine for you as brushing your teeth.

You have learned various approaches to self-treatment, including the Usui self-treatment meditation and the Western 'hands on' method. The Usui method (visualising that you are treating your self, using five hand positions on the head) is ideal to do when you are sitting in a train, on a bus or a coach, as a passenger in a car, or seated at your desk with your eyes closed during a lunch break. The hands-on method is ideal to do in bed, when you wake up in the morning or, more likely, when you get to bed at night. You don't have to always do a 30-minute self-treatment; if you only have 10 minutes, then do it for 10 minutes. Why not rest your hands on your heart and solar plexus as you watch television or listen to music; even this will produce some benefit for you.

Make these exercises a regular part of what you do, and you will intensify the beneficial effect that Reiki has on you. Your audio CD talks you through both Hatsurei ho and the Usui self-treatment meditation.

Receive Reiju on Mondays

The system that Mikao Usui established involved receiving empowerments from him again and again. Although it is impractical for you to travel each week to receive an empowerment from your teacher in person, we can echo this regular empowerment practice by you 'tuning in' to distant empowerments that Taggart sends out each week and which you can tune into any time on a Monday.

Perform Hatsurei (or just sit with your hands in the prayer position) and say to yourself "I'm ready to receive my empowerment from Taggart now"... and see what happens! Stay with your hands in the prayer position until you feel that the empowerment is over, or until a few minutes have elapsed.

Live the Precepts

Mikao Usui's precepts were one of the most important parts of his system, and as much spiritual development was said to come through following these as was possible through carrying out energy work. Focus on the precepts each day, remind yourself of them regularly and consider how they apply in your life.

Try to enjoy being in the moment, whatever you might be doing. Try not to dwell on the past and feel bad about things that you cannot change, and try not to dwell too much on the future, either, worrying about things that may never happen! All you have is this moment.

Be compassionate towards yourself, too, which means not beating yourself up for not being perfect, forgiving yourself as you forgive others, being light-hearted and trying not to take yourself too seriously. Be easy-going.

Practise on others

The wonderful thing about Reiki is that you can make a positive difference in people's lives, so get out there and plonk your hands on as many people as possible!

If you have your family around you, then practice on them. Rope in your friends and neighbours to be guinea pigs, and see what happens. Tell them that you have learned a Japanese relaxation technique, and that if they have a treatment session with you they will feel so calm, so relaxed, and so stress-free at the end of it. Not many people would say 'No' to that!

You don't necessarily have to carry out hour-long treatments on everybody. Go with what time you have available. Do 15-20 minute treatments on people's heads/shoulders while they are sitting in a straight-backed chair. Do short blasts on a painful knee. Treat your cat, your goldfish and your houseplants. Reiki your salad, and your glass of water, and see what happens!

The important thing is to use the energy regularly.

Moving on to Second Degree

Although you can stay at First Degree indefinitely if you like, and never move on from this level, most people do move on to Second Degree, and we recommend that you wait for a couple of months or so before doing this. The interval is there to give you a chance to get used to working with energy, to have any 'clear-out' settle down, to allow you to develop your ability as a channel, and to give you an opportunity to become comfortable with working on other people.

The benefits to you of Second Degree are in terms of both your self healing and your work on other people:

1. You will learn symbols and meditations that will deepen your self-healing
2. You will learn the use of symbols to enhance your treatments and distant healing
3. Your ability as a channel will develop further
4. You will learn how to move beyond standard hand positions to embrace intuitive working, making your treatments more of a blissful meditative experience.

APPENDIX

Sources of information about Japanese Reiki

Frank Arjava Petter

Frank Arjava Petter is a Western Reiki Master who has lived and worked in Japan since 1996. He is the author of several books about Reiki in Japan, including two books about the history of Reiki. The books are as follows:

'Reiki Fire'	Lotus Light, Shangri-La	Pub 1997
'Reiki – the Legacy of Dr Usui'	Lotus Light, Shangri-La	Pub 1998

Petter has spent time gaining the trust of Reiki practitioners in Japan, and has built up contacts with members of the Usui Reiki Ryoho Gakkai ('Usui's Reiki Healing System Association' - the Japanese association that carries Usui's name and was set up after his death by some of his students). He has also made contact with some traditional Japanese Reiki practitioners from other Reiki 'streams' in Japan, people who are carrying on Reiki traditions that seem to derive from Usui, but are separate from the Gakkai.

I was lucky enough to have spent two days training with Frank Arjava Petter and his wife Chetna Koyabashi in the Autumn of 1999; they are lovely people. Their researches and contacts with traditional Usui Reiki practitioners in Japan revealed a lot of the background to the 'real' story of Usui Reiki. It has to be said though that Petter is very much an observer looking in on something that he will never be a part of, and most of the information that he is passing on does not represent Reiki in its original form. Much of what the Gakkai do is not original Reiki, though it is being presented as such.

Hiroshi Doi

Hiroshi Doi is a member of the Usui Reiki Ryoho Gakkai in Japan, but he is not at Shinpiden (Master) level. He was taught by Mrs Kimiko Koyama, 5th President of the Gakkai, so his lineage would be: Mikao Usui, Kanichi Taketomi, Kimiko Koyama, Hiroshi Doi, and he has been through the Gakkai's training to at least Second Degree level. Thus Doi has detailed knowledge of the way that Reiki is taught by the Gakkai to this level. It is said that he may have been trained informally in Master techniques by Mrs Koyama, but it also seems that he received Master training via a Gakkai Master who split from what is now the Gakkai, after their headquarters was bombed in World War II. The lineage is said to be: Mikao Usui, Kanichi Taketomi, Ayako Sasaki, Hiroshi Ohta, Hiroshi Doi.

In addition to his studies within the Gakkai, whatever form they have taken, Mr Doi has trained as a Reiki Master in the Western tradition. Doi runs his own school of Reiki in Japan ('Gendai' Reiki, which means modern/contemporary Reiki). His school teaches a form of Reiki that is rooted in the practices of the Gakkai, but developed and modified by Doi, and he uses Western Reiki techniques and other healing techniques when he thinks that they work well. He is the first Japanese person trained in Gakkai techniques to come to the West to share his knowledge. I was taught the information that Doi presented to the West in Autumn 1999, though I have not trained with him directly. Again, much of what he has passed onto us is Gakkai Reiki, not original Usui Reiki, and that is where my interest lies.

Chris Marsh

Chris Marsh is a Reiki Master from the North East of England who has spent long periods in Japan over the last 30 years. He is the only Western Master (Shihan) of a Japanese fighting art (Samurai swordsmanship), he is a Tendai Buddhist, and he can speak and read Japanese. Because of his status within Japan - which has come through his involvement in a traditional martial art at the highest level - and through a family connection between his elderly martial arts teacher and people that were very close to Usui, doors have opened to him that have remained closed to other Westerners. He has made contact with traditional Usui Reiki practitioners who have not spoken to anyone else in the Western world. These are people who trained with Usui, made Reiki part of their lives, and passed what they had learned on to their children in an unchanged form. His is in contact with a group of surviving students of Mikao Usui: a group of people, the youngest of whom is over 100 years old, who are prepared to share some of Usui's practices. These contacts take us way beyond the 'Gakkai', to Usui's original method. I was in ongoing contact with Chris for several years from January 2000 and have trained one-to-one with him on a number of occasions; he is happy for me to pass on what he taught me.

Chris does not wish to become a world figure within Reiki, and his contacts do not want to be identified. They want to be left alone, and we should respect their wishes.

So through a strange series of coincidences I find myself in the position of being one of the few people in the UK able to teach the basic principles of Usui Sensei's original form. That will hopefully change over time, since I have been running 'update' courses for the benefit of other practitioners and Masters from all over the country since February 2000. Other people are running a few courses on these lines as well. I think that the more people who can be put in touch with traditional, fundamental techniques of Usui Reiki, the better, but change is slow.

The Usui Memorial

Below you can read a literal translation of the inscription on Mikao Usui's memorial stone. I have obtained the translation from Rick Rivard, a Reiki Master from Canada, whose generosity allows me to share this information with you without having to worry about copyright infringement!

We should remember that just because something is written on a stone obelisk does not make what is written there historically accurate in every respect, and the individuals who commissioned the memorial will have had a particular view that they wished to present to the world which may have led them to present or describe events in a way that could be interpreted differently.

We should also remember that the individuals who commissioned the memorial were taught something quite different from what Usui had been passing on to the majority of his students and had different priorities.

Having said that, it is has an interesting story to tell, and here are Rick's notes...

> ***Translation of the Usui Memorial at Saihoji Temple, Tokyo Japan***
> ***© Universal Copyright 1998, 1999, 2000 Emiko Arai and Richard Rivard***
>
> *This is a fairly literal translation of the Usui memorial, as we wanted you, the reader, to get as close a rendition to plain English as possible, without any paraphrasing. This allows you to decide how you would rephrase sentences and paragraphs. There are a few phrases that we haven't translated yet.*
>
> *All comments in (brackets) are either our translations of previous kanji or our explanation of previous words. Please note: there are no full stops or paragraphs on the original, so we have added these in to make it easier to read. Also, as in all translations, we had several choices of words for each kanji, and tried to pick what we felt best. Our thanks to Melissa Riggall, Miyuki Arasawa, Yukio Miura and Mr. Hiroshi Doi for their corrections offered.*

"Reihou Chouso Usui Sensei Kudoko No Hi"

Memorial of Reiki Founder Usui Sensei's Benevolence

It is called 'toku' that people experience by culture and training, and 'koh' that people practice teaching and the way to save people. ('koh' + 'toku'= 'kudoku; Kou = distinguished service, honour, credit, achievement; Toku = a virtue, morality)

Only the person who has high virtue and does good deeds can be called a great founder and leader. From ancient times, among wise men, philosophers, geniuses and (a phrase that means 'very straight and having the right kind of integrity'), the founders of a new teaching or new religion are like that... We could say that Usui Sensei was one of them.

Usui "Sensei" (literally "he who comes before", thus teacher, or respected person) newly started the method that would change mind and body for better by using universal power. People hearing of his reputation and wanting to learn the method, or who wanted to have the therapy, gathered around from all over. It was truly prosperous.

Sensei's common name is Mikao and other name was Gyoho (perhaps his spiritual name). He was born in the Taniai-mura (village) in the Yamagata district of Gifu prefecture (Taniai is now part of Miyama Village). His ancestor's name is Tsunetane Chiba (a very famous Samurai who had played an active part as a military commander between the end of Heian Period and the beginning of Kamakura Period: 1180-1230). His father's name was Uzaemon (it was his popular name; his given name was Taneuji). His mother's maiden name was Kawai.

Sensei was born in the first year of the Keio period, called Keio Gunnen (1865), on August 15th. From what is known, he was a talented and hard working student. His ability was far superior. After he grew up, he travelled to Europe, America and China to study. He wanted to be a success in life, but couldn't achieve it; often he was unlucky and in need. But he didn't give up and he disciplined himself to study more and more. One day he went to Kuramayama to start an asceticism (it says "shyu gyo" - a very strict process of spiritual training using meditation and fasting. (Another Japanese translation says "penance while fasting"). On the beginning of the 21st day, suddenly he felt one large Reiki over his head and he comprehended the truth. At that moment he got Reiki "Ryoho" (healing method).

When he first tried this on himself, then tried this on his family, good results manifested instantly. Sensei said that it is much better to share this pleasure with the public at large than to keep this knowledge to our family (it was customary to keep such knowledge in the family to increase their power). So he moved his residence to Harajuku, Aoyama, Tokyo. There he founded "Gakkai" (a learning society) to teach and practice Reiki Ryoho in April of the 11th year of the Taisho period (1922). Many people came from far and wide and asked for the guidance and therapy, and even lined up outside of the building.

September of the twelfth year of the Taisho period (1923), there were many injured and sick people all over Tokyo because of the Kanto earthquake and fire. Sensei felt deep anxiety. Everyday he went around in the city to treat them. We could not count how many people were treated and saved by him. During this emergency situation, his relief activity was that of reaching out his hands of love to suffering people. His relief activity was generally like that.

After that, his learning place became too small. In February of the 14th year of the Taisho period (1925), he built and moved to a new one outside Tokyo in

Nakano. (Nakano is now part of Tokyo, and is also the location of the Saihoji temple, his resting place). Because his fame had risen still more, he was invited to many places in Japan, often. In answering those requests, he went to Kure, then to Hiroshima, to Saga and reached Fukuyama. It was during his stay in Fukuyama that he unexpectedly got sick and died. He was 62 years old. (In Western terms, Sensei was 60 - born August 15, 1865; died March 9, 1926 according to his grave marker; however, in old Japan, you are "1" when born and turn another year older at the start of the new year).

His wife was from Suzuki family; her name was Sadako. They had a son and a daughter. The son's name was Fuji who carried on the Usui family (meaning the property, business, family name, etc. Born in 1908 or 1909, at the time of his father's death Fuji was 19 in Japanese years. We do know now that Fuji also taught Reiki in Taniai village).

Sensei was very mild, gentle and humble by nature. He was physically big and strong yet he kept smiling all the time. However, when something happened, he prepared towards a solution with firmness and patience. He had many talents. He liked to read, and his knowledge was very deep of history, biographies, medicine, theological books like Buddhism Kyoten (Buddhist bible) and bibles (scriptures), psychology, jinsen no jitsu (god hermit technique), the science of direction, ju jitsu, incantations (the "spiritual way of removing sickness and evil from the body"), the science of divination, physiognomy (face reading) and the I Ching. I think that Sensei's training in these, and the culture which was based on this knowledge and experience, led to the key to perceiving Reiho (short for "Reiki Ryoho"). Everybody would agree with me.

Looking back, the main purpose of Reiho was not only to heal diseases, but also to have right mind and healthy body so that people would enjoy and experience happiness in life. Therefore when it comes to teaching, first let the student understand well the Meiji Emperor's admonitory, then in the morning and in the evening let them chant and have in mind the five precepts which are:

First we say, today don't get angry.
Secondly we say, don't worry.
Third we say, be thankful.
Fourth we say, endeavour your work.
Fifth we say, be kind to people.

This is truly a very important admonitory. This is the same way wise men and saints disciplined themselves since ancient times. Sensei named these the "secret methods of inviting happiness", "the spiritual medicine of many diseases" to clarify his purpose to teach. Moreover, his intention was that a teaching method should be as simple as possible and not difficult to understand.

Every morning and every evening, sit still in silence with your hands in prayer and chant the precepts, then a pure and healthy mind would be nurtured. It was the true meaning of this to practice this in daily life, using it. (i.e. put it into practical use) This is the reason why Reiho became so popular.

Recently the world condition has been in transition. There is not little change in people's thought. (i.e. it's changing a lot) Fortunately, if Reiho can be spread throughout the world, it must not be a little help (i.e. it's a big help) for people who have a confused mind or who do not have morality. Surely Reiho is not only for healing chronic diseases and bad habits.

The number of the students of Sensei's teaching reaches over 2,000 people already. Among them senior students who remained in Tokyo are carrying on Sensei's learning place (Dr. Hayashi took title to the school in November, 1926 and together with Mr. Taketomi and Mr. Ushida, re-located it to Shinano Machi in 1926, and ran it as a hospice) and the others in different provinces also are trying to spread Reiki as much as possible. Although Sensei died, Reiho has to be spread and to be known by many people in the long future. Aha! What a great thing that Sensei has done to have shared this Reiho, which he perceived himself, to the people unsparingly.

Now many students converged at this time and decided to build this memorial at Saihoji Temple in the Toyotama district (boundaries have changed and the Saihoji temple has been in Nakano district (1986) and is now in Suginami district) to make clear his benevolence and to spread Reiho to the people in the future. I was asked to write these words. Because I deeply appreciate his work and also I was moved by those thinking to be honoured to be a student of Sensei, I accepted this work instead of refusing to do so. I would sincerely hope that people would not forget looking up to Usui Sensei with respect.

Edited by "ju-san-i" ("subordinate third rank, the Junior Third Court (Rank) -- an honorary title), Doctor of Literature, Masayuki Okada. Written (brush strokes) by Navy Rear Admiral, "ju-san-i kun-san-tou ko-yon-kyu"("subordinate third rank, the Junior Third Court (Rank), 3rd order of merit, 4th class of service" -- again, an honorary title) Juzaburo Gyuda (also pronounced Ushida).

Second Year of Showa (1927), February

Mikao Usui Talks about his System

Below you can read something that Mikao Usui is claimed to have said about his healing system. It comes from something called the Usui Reiki Hikkei, which is a 'manual' given to all students of the Usui Reiki Ryoho Gakkai. I have obtained this translation from Rick Rivard, a Reiki Master from Canada, whose generosity allows me to share this information with you without having to worry about copyright infringement.

The majority of the contents of Usui's 'manual' are not actually original Usui techniques: they are later additions, despite what is claimed in a few prominent books on the subject. However, the following sections do appear to have come from the man himself, but it is important to point out that there does seem to have been some 'editing' carried out (this is a polite way of saying that things have been distorted to present a version that may not completely represent the truth) and we shouldn't necessarily accept what is presented here as gospel.

Students were originally expected to prepare their own manuals, and they would write questions in the back, hand the manual to Usui, and Usui would write the answers. What you can read below would appear to be a compilation of questions and answers from a number of students' manuals, and the text that we have in the West comes from Mrs Kimiko Koyama (Hiroshi Doi's teacher), the 5th President of the 'Gakkai. Here are Rick's notes...

Explanation of Instruction for the Public
By Founder of Usui Reiki Ryoho, Mikao Usui

Richard R. Rivard, B.Sc.   Reiki Master / Teacher -- www.threshold.ca

"It is an old custom to teach the method to only my descendant for keeping a wealth within a family. Especially the modern societies we live in, wish to share happiness of coexistence and co-prosperity. So I don't allow my family to keep the method to ourselves.

"My Usui Reiki Ryoho is an original, it's nothing like this in the world. So I would like to release this method to the public for everyone's benefit and hope for everyone's happiness. My Reiki Ryoho is an original method based on intuitive power in the universe. By this power, body gets healthy and enhances happiness of life and peaceful mind.

"Nowadays people need improvement and reconstruction inside and outside of life, so the reason for releasing my method to the public is to help people with illness of body and mind."

Q. What is Usui Reiki Ryoho?
A. Graciously I have received Meiji Emperor's last injunctions. For achieving my teachings, training and improving physically and spiritually and walking in a right path as a human being, first we have to heal our spirit. Secondly we have to keep our body healthy. If our spirit is healthy and conformed to the truth, body will get healthy naturally. Usui Reiki Ryoho's missions are to lead peaceful and happy life, heal others and improve happiness of others and ourselves.

Q. Is there any similarity to hypnotism, Kiai method, religious method or any other methods?
A. No, there is no similarity to any of those methods. This method is to help body and spirit with intuitive power, which I've received after long and hard training.

Q. Then, is it psychic method of treatment?
A. Yes, you could say that. But you could also say it is physical method of treatment. The reason why is Ki and light are emanated from healer's body, especially from eyes, mouth and hands. So if healer stares or breathes on or strokes with hands at the affected area such as toothache, colic pain, stomach-ache, neuralgia, bruises, cuts, burns and other swellings with pain will be gone. However a chronic disease is not easy, it's needed some time. But a patient will feel improvement at the first treatment. There is a fact more than a novel how to explain this phenomenon with modern medicine. If you see the fact you would understand. Even people who use sophistry can not ignore the fact.

Q. Do I have to believe in Usui Reiki Ryoho to get better result?
A. No. It's not like a psychological method of treatment or hypnosis or other kind of mental method. There is no need to have a consent or admiration. It doesn't matter if you doubt, reject or deny it. For example, it is effective to children and very ill people who are not aware of any consciousness, such as a doubt, rejection or denying. There may be one out of ten who believes in my method before a treatment. Most of them learn the benefit after first treatment then they believe in the method.

Q. Can any illness be cured by Usui Reiki Ryoho?
A. Any illness such as psychological or an organic disease can be cured by this method.

Q. Does Usui Reiki Ryoho only heal illness?
A. No. Usui Reiki Ryoho does not only heal illness. Mental illness such as agony, weakness, timidity, irresolution, nervousness and other bad habit can be corrected. Then you are able to lead happy life and heal others with mind of God or Buddha. That becomes principle object.

Q. How does Usui Reiki Ryoho work?
A. I've never been given this method by anybody nor studied to get psychic power to heal. I accidentally realised that I have received healing power when

I felt the air in mysterious way during fasting. So I have a hard time explaining exactly even I am the founder. Scholars and men of intelligence have been studying this phenomenon but modern science can't solve it. But I believe that day will come naturally.

Q. Does Usui Reiki Ryoho use any medicine and are there any side effects?
A. Never uses medical equipment. Staring at affected area, breathing onto it, stroking with hands, laying on of hands and patting lightly with hands are the way of treatment.

Q. Do I need to have knowledge of medicine?
A. My method is beyond a modern science so you do not need knowledge of medicine. If brain disease occurs, I treat a head. If it's a stomach-ache, I treat a stomach. If it's an eye disease, I treat eyes. You don't have to take bitter medicine or stand for hot moxa treatment. It takes short time for a treatment with staring at affected area or breathing onto it or laying on of hands or stroking with hands. These are the reason why my method is very original.

Q. What do famous medical scientists think of this method?
A. The famous medical scientists seem very reasonable. European medical scientists have severe criticism towards medicine.
To return to the subject, Dr. Nagai of Teikoku Medical University says, "we as doctors do diagnose, record and comprehend illnesses but we don't know how to treat them."

Dr. Kondo says, "it is not true that medical science made a great progress. It is the biggest fault in the modern medical science that we don't take notice of psychological affect.

Dr. Kuga says, "it is a fact that psychological therapy and other kind of healing treatment done by healers without doctor's training works better than doctors, depending on type of illnesses or patient's personality or application of treatment. Also the doctors who try to repel and exclude psychological healers without doctor's training are narrow-minded."

From Nihon Iji Shinpo
It is obvious fact that doctors, medical scientists and pharmacists recognise the effect of my method and become a pupil.

Q. What is the government's reaction?
A. On February 6th, 1922, at the Standing Committee on Budget of House of Representatives, a member of the Diet Dr. Matsushita asked for government's view about the fact that people who do not have doctor's training have been treating many patients with psychological or spiritual method of treatment. Mr. Ushio, a government delegate says, "a little over 10 years ago people thought hypnosis is a work of long-nosed goblin but nowadays study has been done and it's applied to mentally ill patients. It is very difficult to solve human intellect with just science. Doctors follow the instruction how to treat patients by medical science, but it's not a medical treatment such as electric therapy or

just touching with hands to all illnesses." So my Usui Reiki Ryoho does not violate the Medical Practitioners Law or Shin-Kyu (acupuncture and moxa treatment) Management Regulation.

Q. People would think that this kind of healing power is gifted to the selected people, not by training.
A. No, that isn't true. Every existence has healing power. Plants, trees, animals, fish and insects, but especially a human as the lord of creation has remarkable power. Usui Reiki Ryoho is materialised the healing power that human has.

Q. Then, can anybody receive Denju of Usui Reiki Ryoho?
A. Of course, a man, woman, young or old, people with knowledge or without knowledge, anybody who has a common sense can receive the power accurately in a short time and can heal selves and others. I have taught to more than one thousand people but no one is failed. Everyone is able to heal illness with just Shoden. You may think it is inscrutable to get the healing power in a short time but it is reasonable. It's the feature of my method that heals difficult illnesses easily.

Q. If I can heal others, can I heal myself?
A. If you can't heal yourself, how can you heal others.

Q. How can I receive Okuden?
A. Okuden includes Hatsureiho, patting with hands method, stroking with hands method, pressing with hands method, telesthetic method and propensity method. I will teach it to people who have learned Shoden and who are good students, good conduct and enthusiasts.

Q. Is there higher level more than Okuden?
A. Yes, there is a level called Shinpiden.

Poems of the Meiji Emperor

Meiji Renno Gyosei

What follows in this section are a small sample of the 125 special poems that are used in the Usui Reiki Ryoho Gakkai (Usui memorial society) for students to study and meditate upon as part of their Reiki training. The form of poetry is called 'waka' poetry and the Meiji emperor, who was the 122nd Emperor of Japan, wrote these poems. The following information comes partly from Hiroshi Doi, a man who is a member of Usui's Reiki Association in Japan (the 'Gakkai), and the person who brought some of the Gakkai teachings to the West.

I have obtained the translated poems from Rick Rivard, a Reiki Master from Canada, whose generosity allows me to share this information with you without having to worry about copyright infringement. Here are Rick's notes, which begin with Hiroshi Doi's explanation. Some of the poems are a little difficult to understand. Translation of such things does not seem easy...

> *"It is said that Emperor Meiji was a great psychic. His goodness was generated to all over the country like sun, his feeling was broad-minded and plentiful like the ocean, his will was strong, his belief was full of love and as broad as the land. In Meiji era, most politicians were so called great people who experienced much difficulties in the changing era from Edo SAMURAI period to Meiji democratic period, but they got strained and sweat when they were meeting Emperor Meiji, not by Emperor's authority but by Reiki power.*
>
> *"USA president F. Roosevelt said, "Japanese people must be happy to have such a great Emperor. Japan will progress and develop with the Emperor Meiji." Emperor Meiji did not talk a lot but wrote a lot of WAKA poetry to express himself. These are recognised as great poetry in Japanese literature. Usui-sensei respected the Emperor Meiji, and selected 125 WAKA poetry as GYOSEI to use in Reiki lesson."*

Here are some of the Poems:

You have a right pure soul if you have nothing to be ashamed of in front of God, whom you cannot see, who knows you all. I wish everyone had such soul.

I have consecutive unhappiness and pain that I cannot control. Easy to think that there is no God, I tend to think that the other person is to blame for it. Is this really blamed on other person? Am I always right without any fault? No, I can remember that I also have many faults. This is blamed on me, I know that this is the result I bring, and now I am free from ill feeling.

I stand at the spring green field, looking up at the clear blue sky, and I wish I could get the broad sky in my mind.

If you get a beautiful, bright and scratch-less jewel, without constant polishing and cleaning, it will lose its brightness by a little dust. So human heart also, beautiful and pure heart cannot be kept without constant polishing.

Human, that is manifestation of a God, should always have hope, bright and broad-minded heart as God has, whatever may happen.

Water does not oppose any vessels and it is stayed as the vessel form. Water seems to be obedient, flexible, and not self-assertive. However, water can break rocks with its consecutive concentrated drops. So people should also have flexibility for any situation such as thought and human relationship, and have consecutive concentration to do something important.

People have been liked pine tree because it is said that pine tree bring good luck. And people evaluate the shape and balance of pine tree, but the real worth is different. When the coldest winter came after the lapse of many years, pine trees could survive deep snow and storm though other trees died all. Pine trees showed their toughness and people evaluated the great pine trees.

Today I had nothing to do and I find that now is evening. I felt sorry for that at first, but I changed my mind that this is not so bad, is it? Yes, it is BAD because any moment is very precious for people and I waste my precious time today. Well, however, I should not regret my passed day for so long. Now I try to live my new day without regret.

A person's feeling is flowing out through a looking glass or mirror.

In this world all, from the sea to the plain, and the rest, the waves and nature have their own noise, sound.

At night when the waves get free and the flowers bloom, these silenced the disciples of the earth.

Printed in the United Kingdom
by Lightning Source UK Ltd.
132927UK00001BA/5-16/A

9 787774 595369